John Clare

Simon Kövesi

John Clare

Nature, Criticism and History

Simon Kövesi
Oxford Brookes University
Oxford, UK

ISBN 978-1-349-59185-5   ISBN 978-1-349-59183-1 (eBook)
DOI 10.1057/978-1-349-59183-1

Library of Congress Control Number: 2017935570

© The Editor(s) (if applicable) and The Author(s) 2017
The author(s) has/have asserted their right(s) to be identified as the author(s) of this work in accordance with the Copyright, Designs and Patents Act 1988.
This work is subject to copyright. All rights are solely and exclusively licensed by the Publisher, whether the whole or part of the material is concerned, specifically the rights of translation, reprinting, reuse of illustrations, recitation, broadcasting, reproduction on microfilms or in any other physical way, and transmission or information storage and retrieval, electronic adaptation, computer software, or by similar or dissimilar methodology now known or hereafter developed.
The use of general descriptive names, registered names, trademarks, service marks, etc. in this publication does not imply, even in the absence of a specific statement, that such names are exempt from the relevant protective laws and regulations and therefore free for general use.
The publisher, the authors and the editors are safe to assume that the advice and information in this book are believed to be true and accurate at the date of publication. Neither the publisher nor the authors or the editors give a warranty, express or implied, with respect to the material contained herein or for any errors or omissions that may have been made. The publisher remains neutral with regard to jurisdictional claims in published maps and institutional affiliations.

Cover illustration: Toby Jones as John Clare, standing outside a residential home that was once an asylum, in High Beach, Epping Forest, from Andrew Kötting's feature film *By Our Selves* (Soda Pictures, 2015).

Printed on acid-free paper

This Palgrave Macmillan imprint is published by Springer Nature
The registered company is Macmillan Publishers Ltd.
The registered company address is: The Campus, 4 Crinan Street, London, N1 9XW, United Kingdom

For Wilfred, Cassius and Vanessa

Acknowledgements

I am grateful for the generous assistance of librarians at the Oxford Brookes University Library, Northamptonshire Central Library, Peterborough Central Library, the Bodleian Library, Oxford, and the British Library, London. At Oxford Brookes, my especial thanks go to Emma Barwell, Joanne Cooksey, Brian Rivers, Jayne Stuart and Jackie Tagg for their administrative and technical support.

I have been lucky to have been variously motivated, advised, stimulated, informed or steered aright in the understanding upon which this book is built by each of the following: Ben Ackland, Christopher Armitage, Richard Astle, Jonathan Bate, Ronald Blythe, Kasia Boddy, Nick Campbell, Jon-Paul Carr, Gerry Carruthers, Tim Chilcott, Paul Chirico, Claire Cox, Peter Cox, Katharine Craik, Richard Cronin, Greg Crossan, Bob Cummings, Benjamin Doyle, David Dykes, Paul Farley, Eóin Flannery, Tim Fulford, John Gardner, Mina Gorji, Huw Griffiths, Nick Groom, Jon Herring, Scott Hess, Robert Heyes, Jane Hodson, Richard Hunt, Caroline Jackson-Houlston, Freddie Jones, Toby Jones, Bridget Keegan, Paula Kennedy, Anne-Marie Kilday, Robert Kirkpatrick, Peter Kitson, Andrew Kötting, Erin Lafford, Daniel Lea, Rodney Lines, Josie Long, Kirsteen McCue, Scott McEathron, James McKusick, Dorothy McMillan, Emma Mason, Nigel Messenger, David Morley, Mary and Peter Moyse, Valerie Pedlar, Nicole Pohl, Rob Pope, Caroline Pung, Mark L. Reed, Jon Roberts, Johnny Rodger, Roger Sales, Simon Sanada, Robin Schofield, Brian Shields, Iain Sim, Iain Sinclair, Jane Stabler, Fiona Stafford, Ron Steggall, Stephen Sullivan (and his students at Dame Alice Harpur School in Bedford), Kelsey Thornton, Sam Ward, Eric White, Simon J. White and Peter Wordsworth.

My understanding of John Clare is indebted to all I have met or corresponded with through the John Clare Society. For me, this welcoming body is at the heart of the communal, shared enthusiasm for the poet and his world. I also owe a deep debt of thanks for all the insights my students have given me across the years.

Two people stand out across my time working on Clare. My PhD supervisor at Nottingham Trent University, John Goodridge, remains a fount of knowledge, motivation and friendship. And the maverick newspaper man who published my two prefatory Clare selections in 1999 and 2001, the late Mike Gorman, was an inspiration in troubled times.

For permission to reproduce the image on the front cover from the feature film *By Our Selves* (Soda Pictures, 2015), I am grateful to the actor playing Clare, Toby Jones, and the filmmaker, director and straw bear, Andrew Kötting. For permission to quote lines from his *Edge of the Orison: In the Traces of John Clare's 'Journey out of Essex'* (London: Penguin Books, 2005) as the epigraph to the final chapter, I am grateful to Iain Sinclair. Some of the work here derived in part from the following articles and chapters: 'John Clare's "I" and "eye": Egotism and Ecologism' in Amanda Gilroy (ed.), *Green and Pleasant Land: English Culture and the Romantic Countryside* (Leuven and Paris: Peeters, 2004), pp. 73–88; '"If I knew that any other use was made of my desires I should be mad": Competing Narratives of the Politics of John Clare's Language', *The Drouth*, 19 (Spring 2006), 35–41; 'Beyond the Language Wars: Towards a Green Edition of John Clare', *John Clare Society Journal*, 26 (2007), 61–75; 'Finding Poems, Making Text: John Clare and the Greening of Textual Criticism', *Romanticism*, 17.2 (2011), 135–47; 'John Clare &...&...&... Deleuze and Guattari's Rhizome' in John Rignall, H. Gustav Klaus and Valentine Cunningham (eds), *Ecology and the Literature of the British Left: The Red and the Green* (Aldershot: Ashgate, 2012), pp. 75–88; 'John Clare's Horizons', *Essays in Criticism*, LXIII.4 (October 2013), 375–92. My thanks go to the editors and publishers of these pieces.

For their love, tolerance and patience, I dedicate this book to my once-in-a-lifers: my sons Wilfred and Cassius, and my partner Vanessa.

Contents

1 John Clare and Place   1

2 Clare and Ecocentrism   79

3 Clare Making Text; Making Text of Clare   127

4 Looking, Painting, Listing, Noting: Clare, Women and Nature   161

5 Conclusion: Clare as Our Contemporary; Clare as History   215

Bibliography   239

Index   255

ABBREVIATIONS

Barrell	John Barrell, *The Idea of Landscape and the Sense of Place, 1730–1840: An Approach to the Poetry of John Clare* (Cambridge: Cambridge University Press, 1972)
Bate, *Biography*	Jonathan Bate, *John Clare: A Biography* (London: Picador, 2003)
By Himself	*John Clare By Himself*, ed. Eric Robinson and David Powell (Ashington and Manchester: MidNAG/Carcanet, 1996)
Critical Heritage	*Clare: The Critical Heritage*, ed. Mark Storey (London: Routledge & Kegan Paul, 1973)
Deacon	George Deacon, *John Clare and the Folk Tradition* (London: Francis Boutle, 2002. First pub. 1983)
EPI and EPII	*The Early Poems of John Clare 1804–1822*, ed. Eric Robinson and David Powell, assoc. ed. Margaret Grainger, 2 vols (Oxford: Clarendon Press, 1989)
JCSJ	*The John Clare Society Journal*, vols 1–35 (2016), continuing series
John Clare in Context	*John Clare in Context*, ed. Hugh Haughton, Adam Phillips and Geoffrey Summerfield (Cambridge: Cambridge University Press, 1994)
Letters	*The Letters of John Clare*, ed. Mark Storey (Oxford: Clarendon Press, 1985)
Living Year, 1841	*John Clare: The Living Year 1841*, ed. Tim Chilcott (Nottingham: Trent Editions, 1999)

LPI and LPII	*The Later Poems of John Clare 1837–1864*, ed. Eric Robinson and David Powell, assoc. ed. Margaret Grainger, 2 vols (Oxford: Clarendon Press, 1984)
MPI, MPII, MPIII, MPIV, MPV	*John Clare, Poems of the Middle Period 1822–1837*, ed. Eric Robinson, David Powell and P. M. S. Dawson (Oxford: Clarendon Press. vols I-II: 1996; vols III-IV: 1998; vol. V: 2003)
Natural History	*The Natural History Prose Writings of John Clare*, ed. Margaret Grainger (Oxford: Clarendon Press, 1983)
New Essays on John Clare	*New Essays on John Clare: Poetry, Culture and Community*, ed. Simon Kövesi and Scott McEathron (Cambridge: Cambridge University Press, 2015)
Nor.	Northampton Manuscript, John Clare Collection, Northamptonshire Libraries and Information Service, as listed in [David Powell], *Catalogue of the John Clare Collection in the Northampton Public Library* (Northampton: County Borough of Northampton Public Libraries, Museums and Art Gallery Committee, 1964)
ODNB	*Oxford Dictionary of National Biography* (Oxford: Oxford University Press, 2004; online edn, 2015), www.oxforddnb.com
OED	*Oxford English Dictionary Online* (Oxford: Oxford University Press, 2004; online edn, 2016), www.oed.com
PD	*Poems Descriptive of Rural Life and Scenery* (London: Taylor and Hessey, 1820. First edition.)
Pet.	Peterborough Manuscript, Central Library, Peterborough, as listed in Margaret Grainger, *A Descriptive Catalogue of the John Clare Collection in Peterborough Museum and Art Gallery* ([Peterborough]: [Peterborough Museum Society], 1973)
VM	*The Village Minstrel and other Poems*, 2 vols (London: Taylor and Hessey, 1821)

CHAPTER 1

John Clare and Place

INTRODUCTION: PLANTING CLARE IN PLACE

John Clare has always been a poet known for his commitment to a particular place. The following words of Ronald Blythe are characteristic of celebratory appreciations of the qualities of Clare's uniquely placed work:

> No other rural poet possesses his authenticity. None was more insulted in his lifetime for displaying it... And what a glory of place and native words has been shown to us... He is of all our poets the most intensely indigenous, a few fields and woods and wastes providing everything he needed for his exact response to their message.[1]

Underpinning a great deal of modern critical discourse about Clare, serving as a prop to many creative works responding to the poet and framing his overall position in contemporary and popular culture, is the widely accepted idea that he is *the* 'poet of place', *sui generis*. Justifiably, Clare's commitment to specific locales is praised as evidence of his acute 'sense of place' – whether it be to cottage, village, natural feature, field or region. In truth there are many poets regarded similarly, some of them far more prominent than Clare (William Wordsworth and Henry David Thoreau probably chief among them[2]). Yet place has been peculiarly prevalent in readings of Clare because he is, like so many labouring-class poets, a writer whose situatedness – whose geographical place and socio-economic positioning – is the mainstay of the frame through which he is regarded from the outset of his public career. This was how he was presented, and it is the predominant manner in which he is still read. Clare follows hundreds of poets marketed in a similar fashion: Ann Yearsley ('Lactilla'), the 'Bristol milkwoman'; Robert Bloomfield, the Suffolk 'farmer's boy' and shoemaker; Allan Cunningham, the Nithsdale stonemason; James Hogg, the Ettrick shepherd. These are just a few of the better-known impoverished poets of the period whom Clare certainly read,[3] though Cunningham he met through the *London Magazine*, and Bloomfield he corresponded with. The list of poor poets situated in the literary market in this manner across the eighteenth and nineteenth centuries is far longer.[4] For such poets, 'place' is both topographically located and socio-economically determined. I will argue that these are not discrete or separable facets or meanings of 'place': they are always both present in the critical and cultural 'placing' of the poet and the poetry. Clare was to be the peasant poet of Helpston; and more widely (but not too much) the Northamptonshire poet. Village, county and the odd town such as Stamford are mentioned in early prefatory commentary, so that a national audience might get its bearings to read a poet who was to be decidedly local. These were the circumscribed bounds of Clare's emplacement for his readership, as Elizabeth Helsinger writes:

> Clare – like Burns or Bloomfield before him – was identified with the social as well as the geographical place that was his subject. For readers both then and now, he is the 'Northamptonshire peasant,' whose mobility, social or geographical, would deny the stability his rural scenes are understood to recall.[5]

In the first public pronouncement about Clare's poetry in 1818, the Market Deeping-based publisher J. B. Henson sought excuse for the poems that were to follow in the 'humble situation which distinguishes their author'. At the same time Clare himself thought he might be 'building "Castles in the Air"'[6] in aspiring to be a published poet, while in his 1820 *London Magazine* piece on Clare, Octavius Gilchrist tentatively suggested that 'Clare's genius is not framed for sustained or lofty flights'. Gilchrist set out the grounded co-ordinates of Clare's poetry, in the month the latter's first collection was to be published: 'minute observation of nature, delicacy of feeling, and fidelity of description'.[7] Nature, feeling, fidelity: Clare's poetic tripod, centred on Helpston, somewhere near

Stamford, stood simply on the soil, taking pictures from the ground – unsuited for 'lofty flights' or 'Castles in the Air'.

While criticism of Clare's work has of course become more sensitised to the ideological pressures of class, I will argue that the foundational reference points for assessments of his work have not changed much at all in two hundred years: nature, feeling, fidelity persist as limitations on readings of Clare, because of the often unsung and sometimes mythicised peculiarities of class and labour in his particular case. This is a general characteristic that continues even when (or especially when) critics consider Clare 'both the poet of place and displacement' – as Tom Paulin influentially put it in 1994, following Elizabeth Helsinger, who said much the same in 1987.[8] This is now the orthodox critical interpretation of Clare's edgy relationship with place. If it is forms of 'displacement' that more obviously are the critical focus of a lot of work on Clare, 'place' itself remains largely unconsidered – hidden in plain sight, as it were – or ignored, because Clare's supposed dislocation and alienation from place are the dominant concerns. This is a problem because, if not assessed, the 'placing' of Clare effects a restraint on what critics allow for his poetic ambition, especially if it is assumed that there can be no 'placing' of the poet precisely because processes of 'displacement' are the ostensible focus.

This chapter reflects upon the problems inherent in valuing Clare for being 'down to earth', considers what that might mean for his critical 'placing' and offers a critique of the ways ecocriticism uses Clare for its own contemporary ends; ecocriticism, I argue, necessitates a further deracination of Clare and his class, even as it ostensibly seeks to renew a valuation of the localism in writers like Clare. This chapter then considers how Clare himself forged a displaced (and purposefully *de*-placed) idea of supreme poetic success, through the supranational and exoticising model of Byron. Next, returning to the origins of his birthplace, the discussion considers Clare back in his cottage, now a museum, and reads him as a mapped, contemporary, placed place name. Finally, in order to liberate Clare's poetry from over-determining critical topophilia, the argument tracks the displacing, detaching journey of Clare's most successful nineteenth-century poem, which, severed from his name and his place, took flight like no other.

From the start of Clare's career, readers have had to cope with the manner in which his patrons sought to keep him rooted in social place, even while seeking to celebrate Clare's close and unique observations of that same locality, and that same social strata. Lord Milton, Wentworth

Fitzwilliam, offers a key case in point in February 1820. On being presented with a copy of the first edition of *Poems Descriptive*, he wrote to John Taylor:

> His talents are very extraordinary, his productions being consider'd, as they must be, the effusions of an uneducated Genius: but to make the most of the powers Nature has bestow'd on him, books must be furnish'd, not so much to enrich his mind as to give him the first rudiments of education, Grammer, & classical language – this must be done by degrees – in the meanwhile the proposal made by you, & the liberality with which you push it by example, I shall have the pleasure in seconding & in contributing £100 towards an annuity for him – bred up in habit of labor, I do not think that it would be usefull to him, to withdraw him altogether & at once from those habits – should he go on successfully & no doubt he will, in the exercise of his Genius, he will by degrees rise above his present rank in life & become a member of a much more elevated Society but for his own sake, in every point of consideration, this change had better not be brought about too rapidly.[9]

Clare might well change as a result of literary fame, he suggests, but this must be controlled, and in tandem his education must be polished. This kind of early delimitation and ossifying *placing* of Clare's talents – and the emphasis on management of linguistic and (by implication) moral wildness – form a foundational prejudice with which the criticism and editing of Clare have always felt they must contend and wrestle. Yet in a strange case of negating self-assertion, Clare criticism has itself formed in a situated reaction against this breed of social placing, by focusing too much – for many – on a combative and positivistic revaluation of the social contexts in which Clare's poems were produced.[10]

Mina Gorji's response to criticism's social 'placing' of Clare is to emphasise his literary sophistication: 'too much attention has been focussed on his social circumstances in ways that risk occluding his literary achievements', she writes. The locality of his poetry is still significant for Gorji, however, as '[q]uestions of place animate Clare's imagination'.[11] Richard Cronin identifies the critical place of Clare as awkwardly suspended between the twin poles of his village and of a literary world to which he aspired, and Clare ends up being estranged by both and comfortable in neither.[12] Cronin's modelling of estrangement is reproduced even in those areas where Clare is seemingly 'placed' comfortably: especially, that is, in his relation to – and relating of – the natural world.

As Nicholas Birns points out, even when criticism is valuing Clare highly for his representations of the natural world, there is an ever-present implication that is not so flattering:

> John Clare has long been seen as a poet of nature. The implicit suggestion in this view is that he was a poet of nature rather than of something else. That something else is usually a Wordsworthian or otherwise Romantic notion of the imagination. 'Nature' with respect to Clare's poetry has a sort of down-to-earth connotation. It suggests an empirical terrain whose brute factuality limits any metaphorical of philosophical dimension.[13]

Birns identifies as 'down to earth' the undermining limitation of Clare being presented as a 'nature poet' relative to his Romantic peers. The idiom Birns uses carries the weight of a common phrase that the middle classes cope with, categorise and sometimes praise, the seeming bluntness, or lack of learned politesse, of something or someone working class. Such an unsophisticated, 'direct' person, or cultural formation thereof, might be explained to others as being 'down to earth'. The *OED* does not provide the full range of meanings as I would understand them for 'down to earth'. It defines the phrase only as 'back to reality... interested in everyday affairs; not affectedly superior; realistic; ordinary'. However, 'earthy' is in part defined as 'grossly material; coarse, unrefined... down-to-earth, unpretentious'. So the phrase is slippery, malleable and its meaning inflected by context. But still, regardless of the explicit intention, location and delivery of its use, 'down to earth' must always carry with it an implicit assertion of naturalised, downwardly pointing class difference. The idiom appears enough to form a sort of symptomatic if hitherto latent trail, a trail we will now follow through some modern critical commentary on Clare.

In her introduction to the *Natural History Prose Writings*, Margaret Grainger writes that '[l]ike Cobbett, Clare's writing is down-to-earth', while she maintains that 'Elizabeth Kent's style of writing, a combination of down-to-earth common sense and sensibility, was in tune with [Clare's] own'.[14] In their introduction to the first volume of the *Early Poems* – and cross as ever with perceived snobbery and what they see as John Taylor's 'censorship' of Clare – David Powell and Eric Robinson write:

> Contemporary taste, especially Taylor's, suggested that poems in dialect, especially poems dealing with marriage and courtship in a down-to-earth

way, were not acceptable to the middling class but should be confined to the halfpenny sheets of itinerant ballad-vendors.[15]

Here, 'down-to-earth' is used to characterise the sexually direct, blunt, unsophisticated traits of Clare's tales that they claim Taylor could not stomach, yet it reinforces stereotypes about working-class life even as it seeks to defend it from editorial prejudice. Johanne Clare, interpreting Clare's statements on the essential role of poetry, uses the phrase idealistically as a positive interpretation of what Clare wants for poetry in resisting class-led predeterminations, while necessarily overlooking any class dimensions of the idiom:

> If poetry was to transcend the rule of historical change, it must reflect the truth of nature since only nature was constant, was capable of perennially renewing itself. Poetry must be brought down to earth, pared down to its universals, freed from the stigma of class.[16]

Her last sentence, it seems to me, is not 'freed from the stigma of class' precisely because she uses 'down to earth', which is an expression founded on, and redolent with, class distinctions: she redelivers the 'stigma of class' in her language even as she attempts to reject it. Theresa M. Kelley reveals some parenthetical nervousness in using the phrase when she describes the prose of Clare's 1841 'Journey out of Essex' as being couched 'in a voice and diction that are local, phonetically spelled, barely punctuated, down-to-earth (as they say)' – but uses it anyway, and blames others for its appearance.[17] Revealing that the phrase can be expressly about class position, landscape historian Ian D. Whyte claims that Clare's 'anti-enclosure sentiments ... indicate an opposition between elite views of landscape and more down-to-earth peasant viewpoints'.[18] For Michael O'Neill, the sonnet form's 'age-old, often courtly pentameter [is] given new energy by the down-to-earth dialect of "proged"' – a word in Clare's 'The Mouse's Nest'; while he seeks to praise Clare's innovation, the dialect use is characterised as a low-born intrusion of a high-brow space.[19] And finally, Clare's greatest biographer, Jonathan Bate, deploys the phrase with explicit intent when he wants to categorise the kind of social fun Clare experiences with local friends: 'Clare's health did indeed improve when he began spending time in the down-to-earth company of his fellow-villagers.'[20] When accounting for Clare's seeming obsession with writing about Mary,

Bate writes: 'Because Mary was always elusive, she served as a screen for more down-to-earth memories that would have been painful to articulate directly.'[21] And when contrasting Clare's 'Don Juan' with the biblical paraphrases the poet was writing simultaneously in 1841, Bate resorts to the phrase again: 'During the very same weeks that he was writing in this spiritual vein, Clare was also composing his most down-to-earth, angry, cynical, sexually charged poem: "Don Juan."'[22] Bate has written extensively and influentially about the fact that poetry can write, like no other cultural form, 'of the earth'. For him, poetry is therefore a necessity for human consciousness in sustaining the natural world and fostering its proper treatment.[23] But his uses of the phrase 'down to earth' in his biography do not carry that same sensitivity to the politics of language, or to the classism of deploying dead, naturalising metaphors that situate working-class forms at the 'base' socially and culturally, and – in the case of implied sexual behaviours – morally.

Tracking the fortunes of just one phrase in criticism of Clare might seem to be a narrow evidence base. I would argue that, though thin, the breadcrumb trail of this phrase does yet offer a sense of wider if still unacknowledged problems in the study of Clare that emerge because of class, and place. With its easy admixture of the 'naturalist' and the hierarchically classist, this phrase 'down to earth' reveals that critically, as often as not, Clare's art is only permitted to be 'down to earth' even by his most ardent of advocates. The idiom takes on the comedic, cartoonish weight of a heavy pair of working boots, keeping Clare grounded, earthy, homely, his walks circumscribed by the weight of a freighted class track. Or it would be clownishly comedic, were the effects not so deleterious. The environmentalist's valuation of the 'earth' can be a critical straightjacket if we do not pay attention to the placing, determining prejudices of class-inflected 'earthiness'. The 'placedness' that drives so much critical work predetermines ideologically that Clare's art can only be as stolidly and doggedly 'honest' and materialist because he should only be 'down to earth'.

In 1873, the well-meaning if limited J. L. Cherry wrote of some specific lines in Clare's poem 'Address to Plenty' that they 'have always been admired for their Doric strength and simplicity, and the vivid realism of the scene which they depict'.[24] Cherry's terminology here follows in a direct line from Gilchrist's earlier tripod (as I call it above) of 'nature, feeling, fidelity' in Clare's work, yet Cherry offers a more masculinised and Victorian inflection: 'strength', 'simplicity', 'realism'. As it was for Cherry, so it continues in some critical responses today. Angus Fletcher offers a version of this prevalent version of Clare's art in 2004:

> He wrote his sonnets, especially, in the form of poetic notes, often sitting on the ground to write his thoughts down – and his later *Northborough Sonnets* are an almost mesmerizing exercise in camera work. He registers sounds and sights as the modern lens catches the dispersed flux of city minutiae.[25]

Clare is frequently regarded as if he were a documentary photographer, pointing his eyes at a green thing, clicking his lids, imprinting a precise yet unthought and unmanaged scene, and then watching as poetic text pours out in faithful record of the place: perfect mimesis means there can be no 'lofty flights'. The Romantic myth of the passive artist playing sounds in a natural breeze[26] is conflated in Clare's case with rootedness, with an implied lack of artistry, with a lack of educationally derived sophistication, with an autodidactic 'honesty' and with a parochial naivety – all still assumed by some critics across all literary periods to be mainstays of the way working-class life makes art of itself. And the way we make critical sense of this now is not through the Aeolian harp, but through the clicking of the camera. And so the staple version of Clare's aesthetics is redelivered: rooted, artless; more natural heart than learned mind; an etiolated version even of Friedrich Schiller's 'naïve poet'.[27] He is a lens, or else a 'retraction/into pure eye', as the poet Wendy Mulford couches it.[28]

As we will see, Clare is himself responsible for the promulgation of an artistic process founded on the denial of his own agency in the making of his work, and on the denial of the work's artfulness too. As Paul Chirico has explored in depth, following initial composition 'in great haste' Clare expresses a lack of ability to rewrite or self-edit.[29] Some of Clare's models of artistic composition set out to erase any personal or identifiable responsibility for the work he produces. In fact it is not to be 'work' or 'art' at all, but 'nature' instead, as defence and as primary allegiance. Of course that tendency to deny control, to disavow identification through an abnegation of purposeful responsibility, is as much a trait of Clare's social position as it was a version of fashionable Romantic myth-making organicism. In Clare's case the naturalising model was adopted by way of a cap-doffing apologia for the poetry that follows: it was tactically installed in a variety of guises to secure acceptance in an audience that might not otherwise understand how an 'uneducated' man could 'do' poetry, other than to regard it as yet another mysterious process of fecund, organic nature; the work of God, not the thought of a man.[30] Nature poet writes poems about nature, naturally. The answer to the question 'how did he do it?' (and the question 'how *dare* he do it?' which lurks interrogatively beneath) was occasionally provided by Clare in the least unsettling manner possible, at least in class terms: it wasn't him, it just happened, he found the poetry in the fields, or he kicked it out of the clods and popped it on the brim of his hat. He knew his locality well, so he found the poems in that place; or else, even more organically, he was rooted in the soil, so the poems grew within and were exhaled into words.

These remain dominant ways of appreciating Clare's 'placed' creativity. Poet Kim Taplin typifies how this modelling of creativity is redelivered in popular ecocritical language when she writes:

> the vigour of his poetry and the power of his testimony is drawn very expressly and directly from actual, local trees... What did concern him was the sharing of his deepest feelings and paying the tribute of exact praise to the sights and sounds and manifold events of the natural world that aroused them... Clare was above all intent upon showing his feelings, because that seemed to him the proper human response to nature and to man's insensitivity to it. He participated in it: he was a denizen of nature. When it was damaged or destroyed, he suffered damage and destruction in his own psyche.[31]

To be fair, in Taplin's popularising critical anthology of tree writing the task is to offer a special place for Clare in relation to the trees he writes about, and she fully achieves that. But there is hazard in her romanticisation of intimacy between tree and poet, in that it removes any space for artistic thought: between the snapping of a branch and the dissolution of Clare's temperament there is nought but green feeling. It might be attractive to think that 'Clare feels like a tree'. But even the most inspired and unscientific ecocritic would have to admit that trees do not 'feel' in a manner we can understand. In Taplin's sentimental account, proximity to a natural body in a place is lauded, while mind is erased.

This book sets out to present a Clare who changed his mind and his models of creative conception, who theorised the writing of poetry and the forging of writerly identities, and who conceptualised formal issues in practice and on purpose. This book commits to the idea that Clare did this with a poet's intellectual deliberation, as he wrote socialised, class-informed and artfully poetic accounts of human and natural worlds in rich conjunction, in a variety of forms, from a variety of positions and in a diverse array of moods. A singular 'placing' of Clare often works against a critical emphasis on variation and experimentation, just as the naturalisation of him into a 'denizen of nature' might deny him an intellectual volition or a social situation. In its attempt to theorise Clare's green politics, this book will invest itself throughout in problems emanating from his manuscripts, and will consider how editing has constructed versions of his textual life, and how it might do so in the future. In its analysis of how Clare represents women – in love and lust poems, in lists and letters – this book will consider poems and attitudes that are not ostensibly ecocentric at all, partly to test out theorisations of Clare's ecocentric aesthetics. Finally, this book will consider the central problem of history when we try to consider Clare through contemporary creative responses to his life and work. In many ways, this book is as much about critical and theoretical practice as it is about Clare, and so the argument attempts to make clear why such a focus is necessary in the peculiar case of this unique poet.

Clare in Space

The watershed moment in Clare criticism of John Barrell's groundbreaking reading in 1972 is the starting point of the predominance of 'place' in the study of the poet.[32] Barrell's work has been reconfirmed recently by Franco Moretti's 2007 reconfiguration of the manner and mode of literary understanding in his *Graphs, Maps, Trees: Abstract Models for Literary History*.[33] Following Barrell and others, Moretti advocates a data-informed and illustratively mapped sense of the co-ordinates of a text, to develop fresh ways of interpretative historical reading. For Moretti and to some extent for Barrell's book, place becomes precise, material, empirical. Yet today in Clare studies, Barrell's finely mapped and historically aestheticised 'sense of place' has, I think, become something unquestioned, something passively accepted by all readers and teachers of Clare's poetry and prose. Because Barrell is assumed to be foundationally right (and I think he is too, I should add), his book's ideas have become detached from their original intentions. Clare just is a poet of a place; and a fraught poet of a place made fraught and changed by other agents – be it through enclosure, 'improvements', Clare's being moved to another home or Clare's being sent to an asylum. His poetry 'documents' particularities of place; and his 'best' poetry works iteratively over real tracks and across spaces that we might touristically locate today – even if only to bemoan modernity and its tarmac, housing developments, power lines and pylons.[34] As we are about to see, the historicised and aesthetic sensitivity of Barrell to place is lost, in the rush to deploy Clare's place to certain contemporary ends.

The extension of critical inquiry – and theory – into 'space' was already in train before Barrell's book appeared. Following Gaston Bachelard's lead, in 1967 Michel Foucault famously suggested that the 'present age may be the age of space ... an age when space is presented to us in the form of relations of emplacement'.[35] This was answered in rich fashion by Henri Lefebvre's influential *The Production of Space* in 1974, which claimed that space was a social product, determined by history, property and production.[36] Human geographer Yi-Fu Tuan assessed the co-dependency of space and place in an influential study of 1977: space is the more freely abstract term and is defined by movement, while place was more static and stable.[37] In 1980s *The Practice of Everyday Life*, Michel de Certeau makes a similar – and at the time increasingly typical – distinction:

> A place ... implies an indication of stability ... space is composed of intersections of mobile elements. It is in a sense actuated by the ensemble of movements deployed within it ... in relation to place, space is like the word when it is spoken, that is, when it is caught in the ambiguity of actualization ... In contradistinction to the place, it has none of the univocity or stability of a 'proper'.[38]

In 1991 Frederic Jameson charted in postmodernism a 'spatial turn', a '"great transformation" – the displacement of time, the spatialization of the temporal – [which] often registers its novelties by way of a sense of loss'.[39] Charting the dominance of place by the philosophy of space, in 1997 Edward S. Casey pointed to more recent correctives from thinkers who have followed Heidegger, and have made place dynamic, processual, socio-political, an event in itself rather than a container for events, and a phenomenon that is not necessarily locatable or stable; Casey concludes that 'place is beginning to escape from its entombment in the cultural and philosophical underworld of the modern West'.[40] Even with these broad tendencies for a revaluation of space and rich considerations of place, philosopher J. E. Malpas is unconvinced in his 1999 study: work on 'place' as a concept has been neglected, 'in a tendency for place to be viewed as secondary and derivative of spatiality and temporality'.[41] While it may be true that Malpas's assessment of the relative paucity of theorisations of place relative to space has been answered in part by the wide array of ecologically informed work published since on site, situation and bio-region, in Clare studies I would contend that the sidelining of place continues, in even the most recent decent criticism (and luckily there has been a lot of that since the 1990s[42]). Place remains something that Clare criticism needs to address and problematise more, if only because it is so dominant, so hegemonic and, oddly enough, so unspoken.

Alongside broad philosophical developments in the consideration of place, an emerging 'green' presence in critical thinking has also necessitated assessments of the concept of place. There has been a return to localism through developments in environmental criticism, in part as a resistance to the forces and injustices of global capitalism – and possibly as a counterweight to postmodernity's supposed rootless mobility too – and attention to Clare as an exemplar of someone with an acute 'sense of place' has grown since the 1990s. A widespread revaluation of the local has made Clare even more attractive as an object of study in recent years. Surveying twentieth-century American environmentalism, Ursula K. Heise has mapped a set of tensions in environmental criticism between the global and the national, the travelling migrant and the localised inhabitant. Her conclusions leave her concerned about localism:

> the environmentalist emphasis on restoring individuals' sense of place, while it might function as one useful tool among others for environmentally oriented arguments, becomes a visionary dead end if it is understood as a founding ideological principle or a principal didactic means of guiding individuals and communities back to nature.[43]

As Heise demonstrates, modern ecocriticism has always thought that 'place' should be central to its concerns and its ethics, but has struggled to make localism have a global rather than a parochial reach. The strategic problem here is that if green politics are too localist, or seen to be parochial, they might be dismissible in national and international arenas, and so will not lead to any sort of organised change in habits of consumption, industry and governmental policy. This is a problem of scale: what is the dimension of the local? What is the size of a 'place'? For Yi-Fu Tuan, place 'exists at different scales. At one extreme a favorite armchair is a place, at the other extreme the whole earth.'[44] A green agenda leads us further to ask through what taxonomies of space (room, garden, city, region, nation, bio-region, continent, planet) do people feel *responsibility* to their habitat? This is also a problem of natural science – in that global-scale environmental processes are constituted by countless tiny, localisable shifts, changes, accidents and human decisions.[45] Clare's localised environmental concerns – often though not always at the smaller end of the scalability of human interaction with the natural world – are treated with mobility in terms of their presentation of an ethical pronouncement on the sanctity of a natural place, and its 'abuses' by humans, and are deployed to support an agenda. Certainly this is a prop to educational inclusions of Clare in school curricula: that children might learn how better to treat 'the natural world' by reading Clare. And by a stretching process of scalable analogy, Clare can be 'made relevant' to any locality – large or small – where a feature or process of natural origin comes into close touch with humanity, and loses out.

Sometimes, critics 'deploy' Clare as a sort of proto-ecological weapon in a manner which *displaces* him both in terms of space and in terms of history. Kate Rigby offers a prime example. In *Topographies of the Sacred: The Poetics of Place in European Romanticism*, she moves from Clare to here and now, into a panicked future and back again, at a dizzying pace. She is worth quoting at length, not least because her travels take her to infinity and beyond. Starting with John Barrell, Rigby writes:

> one senses that Barrell's interest in Clare is not merely historical. Certainly, from a contemporary ecocritical perspective, it is Clare's untimeliness, his resistance to the forces of dislocation that were reshaping his world, which guarantees the significance of his work today, above all for those not reconciled to the condition of global tourist and who identify with others actively resisting the loss or despoliation of their own places of belonging. The present movement to reclaim a sense of place, as evidenced within the literature, philosophy, and practice of bioregionalism, as well as in the struggles of colonized people to regain their traditional lands, has nonetheless emerged at a point when the process of dislocation, or 'deplacialization,' to use Casey's term, has assumed a new order of magnitude. The forces of capitalist modernization that in Clare's day necessitated the creation of straight new roads linking the newly enclosed fields of Helpston with the expanding market town of Peterborough are now generating vast communication networks in cyberspace in the context of an increasingly integrated global economy. Meanwhile, the planned redesign of Northamptonshire and elsewhere through parliamentary enclosure might today be seen to find a hypertrophic counterpart in the ambition to terraform Mars. Where once, with the dissolution of feudalism, peasants were

emancipated to find work in another parish, and later, with the expansion of empire, the poor were encouraged to seek their fortune in the colonies, now we are told that technology will free us from planet Earth, ravaged as it is by industrialization and threatened on all sides by meteors and black holes.[46]

Rigby is at the extreme end of a general pattern in Clare studies of a kind of environmentally self-interested and deracinating rewriting of Clare's own accounts of enclosure and other forms of environmental harm (as he saw them). Rigby's written criticism here is a victim of her perfectly laudable attempt to re-inspirit places through a mixture of ecoscience and poetic disquisition, and rightly her method takes her all over the place(s). She models in chiaroscuro form a well-trodden path, a semi-holy rite of passage, that a conservationally minded Clare enthusiast takes on the hunt for the faint tracks laid down in Clare's poems. Rigby's agenda overrides history, actual landscape and any detail of Clare's supposed proto-environmentalism, and in its portentous, breathless insensitivity it becomes eco-pompous. The irony for a book putatively about 'sacred' places is that the places mentioned are treated on occasion with such telescopic tactlessness from a position of postmodern privilege. What Rigby risks in the urgency to make Clare relevant to a contemporary polemic is an oversimplification of the ways in which identification with and understanding of place are informed and delimited by issues of class.[47]

If Rigby ignores class, she ignores Barrell's conclusions too, overlooking his correction of a critical myth circulating in 1972 that persists to this day.[48] Through a careful mapping of land-tax assessments, population and the enclosure award, Barrell investigates two main critical assumptions about enclosure: that Helpston smallholders and the poor were destroyed by enclosure, and that Clare persistently built a causal link between enclosure and economic hardship. For Barrell there is little evidence for either; nor for the general story, in Helpston's particular case, that as a force of rampant capitalism (as it is widely regarded by ecocritics), enclosure ripped land away from small farmers and loaded it onto the large landowners; nor is he fully convinced that enclosure offered a panacea – or that the poorest were not affected by it. Barrell concludes that in trackable socio-economic terms, Helpston seems not to have been damaged or reordered much at all by enclosure – at least in terms of size of holding and tax paid (he spends a good deal of the book considering the aesthetic and relational impacts on Clare and his milieu of the loss of open field farming, of course). The greatest immediate benefit of enclosure, Barrell finds, would have been to the wage labourer who could work in the enclosure gangs. Barrell's conclusion is rarely considered by ecocritics today, because it is inconvenient to an ecocritically anti-capitalist positioning of Clare:

> had it not been for the enclosure, the demand for labour would have diminished considerably, and the problem of poverty would have been that much more severe. The enclosure... though conceived at a time of great agricultural prosperity, was carried into execution during an agricultural depression. But the actual work of enclosing – the making of new roads, the planting of hedges – could not be put off until better days; and in this way the enclosure must to some extent have protected the labourer of Helpston from the effects of the depression, in that it enabled him to tap his employer's capital for his wages, instead of waiting for them to come out of his employer's falling profits.[49]

Barrell admits the effects upon the poorest and the landless cannot be captured by the data to hand, and so 'we still cannot measure the effect of the loss suffered by the agricultural labourers of traditional ways of supplementing their wages'. It is in his critiques of the loss of 'common rights' that Clare is keenly and acerbically consistent in his verse. However, Barrell surmises that even there, 'the measurable effects of enclosure were far less important to Clare than those which the tradition of rural protest told him to expect and recognise'.[50] Rigby is not alone in ignoring these findings when discussing Barrell, Clare and enclosure.

Rigby inherits an ecocriticism that is in part an offspring of the positioning of Clare as a proto-ecologist. Ecocriticism starts, as Jonathan Bate and Edward Goldsmith point out, in 1964, with Robert Waller, editor of *Mother Earth* and author of what is widely regarded as the first ever ecological literary criticism – about enclosure, and Clare.[51] And so Rigby is not alone: her work is part of the systemic urgency in the humanities generally that green thinking has to make itself explicitly relevant to contemporary problems; that it has to try to be scientifically engaged in a present, material environment, the way natural sciences might more directly be. Clare as green protest poet and ecocriticism itself were formations born at the same time, seemingly conjoined, if 'untimely'. Clare as ecowarrior is part of the founding mythos of the ecocritical adventure.

To address this complex of issues, I will turn first to Clare himself and then to Michel de Certeau.

'WILD AND IRREGULAR': ENCLOSURE AND TACTICS

Perhaps the most common feature of ecocritical statements about Clare and enclosure is the elision of Clare's labour. It seems that when we focus on Clare as a poet, we sometimes have to forget his life as a labourer. The two were awkward bedfellows for Clare too:

> My fondness for study began to decline and on mixing more into company [of] young chaps of loose habits that began by force and growing into a custom it was continued by choice till [I] became wild and irregular and poetry was for a season thrown bye   these habits were gotten when the fields were inclosed mixing among a motly set of labourers that always follow after the News of such employments   I usd to work at setting down fencing and planting quick lines with partners whose whole study was continual cont[r]ivances to get beer[52]

This account does not sit at all well with Clare as a proto-ecologist – or as a happy labourer of the fields – or as someone who could combine real work and writing poetry. Clare's 'untimeliness' is the inconvenience Rigby names, and she is happy to name it but to ignore the jarring problems of Clare in an actual time and an actual place, of which his autobiography provides a version. Other than setting him up in play as a native ecowarrior fighting the anonymous forces of global capital, Rigby also ignores Clare's class; that is 'untimely' too, presumably. Clare's prose account is unashamed testament to the fact that he was himself an 'encloser': he was poor and the money for fencing and planting hedges was pretty good – good enough to buy drink, at any rate. Enclosure here is condemned by Clare, but not for 'reshaping his world', nor for 'loss or despoliation of...places of belonging', nor for loss of 'traditional lands', nor for 'deplacialization', 'capitalist modernization' or the 'planned redesign of Northamptonshire' or 'industrialization' – all Rigby's terms. In this pass at enclosure – one of many – the only thing Clare worries about, while he recalls digging the fences and lines of hedges into the straightening circumstances of a landscape that he himself was helping to transform, is the social pressure from other labouring men to drink. Enclosure labour loosens morals, but this is a social impact of being with new male companions and of having a little money – neither of which can be classed as 'environmental' concerns. The effect of enclosure Clare worries about at this specific moment of recollection is determined by class, alcohol and the pressures of socialising masculinity: his concerns are local, social and moral. Here he cannot be constructed as the ecological fantasy of a sin-free green messiah, but – by his own account – is instead a messy, complex, paradoxical, anxious, changeable and context-dependent person. This means that Clare can be one of those tools of enclosure in his labouring life, as much as he can give *in poetry* a voice to protest about the effects of enclosure: an enclosure in which he had a labouring hand; an enclosure which opened him up to new friends, experiences and social influences; an enclosure about which he would protest, once he had seen its effects on an entirely different scale, and from a different vantage point in his life. There is no ethical paradox here, if we consider class, money and context. Clare's concern is only about the 'wild and irregular' habits that working in an enclosure gang allows, for the adoption of which Clare blames his fellow itinerant male labourers (a pattern of blaming others for leading his behaviours astray that we can track across his autobiographical prose). The poet who is almost always characterised as someone who favours the 'wild and irregular' forms of unenclosed common lands and uncultivated meadows, heaths and woods is here seen to decry human behaviour which he himself characterises as such. Enclosure prevents reading and writing because it is hard work, and because hard work leads to even harder drinking: the culture of enclosure work is – jarringly enough – 'wild and irregular'. In the process of enclosing his parish, in which Clare has a literal hand, the social dimensions of labour and poetry are at odds. This was not a fleeting job across a couple of days: John Barrell implies that Clare worked on the enclosure of Helpston, in his early twenties, for four years from 1813–1817 (which might be true, but as he worked in other places during that period, it could only have been for sporadic stints).[53]

On a similar front, while Clare and many commentators mention his work at lime-kilns in the villages of Bridge Casterton, Pickworth and Ryhall in the late 1810s, they do not mention the main reason lime was in such demand at the time. In 1841 Clare was to write that 'Bricklayers want lime as I want ryhme'.[54] But as the poet would surely have known, a huge demand for this multi-purpose material came from agriculture. As historians attest, the proliferation of lime-kilns across England in the eighteenth century and into the nineteenth was informed by the emerging understanding of the benefits of lime, and was driven by enclosure. For improvement of soils, lime was used liberally as a fertiliser, as a regulator of soil acidity and to improve drainage.[55] Clare's work at lime-kilns coincided with his first efforts to make his writing public, the money enabling him to drag himself out of debt and save towards the printing of proposals for a collection of his verse. At a time when his family persistently faced penury, the money was crucial to his prospects as a writer, at least as far as he interpreted his circumstances and prospects at the time. When Clare writes of his life as a lime-burner, he never mentions the use of lime for improving newly enclosed land. He does mention, however, that the social stigma of yet another lowly job meant that Martha Turner's family were sniffy about her association with him.[56]

How might we account for Clare's responses to his various emplaced situations, when they appear paradoxical or inconsistent? Michel de Certeau delineates two categories of responses to – or 'ways of operating' within[57] – orders of power, which he also situates in relation to orders of space: strategy is for the powerful; tactics are the recourse of the weak. Those who can be strategic do so in their mobility across, and definitions of, space, and in their confident delineations of their 'proper' place; those who can only be tactical in the face of power do so in part because they struggle to find places of their own. De Certeau writes that 'strategies are able to produce, tabulate, and impose these spaces, when those operations take place, whereas tactics can only use, manipulate, and divert these spaces'.[58] Discussing a specific and localised case of 'a North African living in Paris', de Certeau describes what we might call a minoritarian position (following Gilles Deleuze and Félix Guattari[59]) that seems to me to describe the position of Clare in relation both to his place and to literary culture:

> He...creates for himself a space in which he can find *ways of using* the constraining order of the place of the language. Without leaving the place where he has no choice but to live and which lays down its law for him, he establishes within it a degree of *plurality* and creativity. By an art of being in between, he draws unexpected results from his situation.[60]

De Certeau has organisations in mind at this stage, though his modelling is clearly meant to be descriptive of the individual too. If the powerful, mobile subject is able to delineate ownership of place and demarcate spaces with the security of a long, strategic view, being confident in assertions over time and seeing 'far into the distance',[61] the weak have recourse to tactics and tricks, trespassing and theft:

> a *tactic* is a calculated action determined by the absence of a proper locus. No delimitation of an exteriority, then, provides it with the condition necessary for autonomy. The space of a tactic is the space of the other. Thus it must play on and with a terrain imposed on it and organized by the law of a foreign power... It operates in isolated actions, blow by blow. It takes advantages of 'opportunities' and depends on them, being without any base where it could stockpile its winnings, build up its own position, and plan raids... It must vigilantly make use of the cracks that particular conjunctions open in the surveillance of the proprietary powers. It poaches in them. It creates surprise in them. It can be where it is least expected. It is a guileful ruse... Lacking its own place, lacking a view of the whole... a tactic is determined by the *absence of power* just as a strategy is organized by the postulation of power. [The tactical exhibits] an intellectual creativity as persistent as it is subtle, tireless, ready for every opportunity, scattered over the terrain of the dominant order and foreign to the rules laid down and imposed by a rationality founded on established rights and property.[62]

John Goodridge and Kelsey Thornton's influential modelling of Clare as a 'trespasser' – as someone who enters the field of literature furtively, 'stealing' away from a working day to do so, taking a leap over the wall into the gentrified estate of literature to read and to write[63] – makes relevant de Certeau's account of the tactical adaptability and creative fertility of the disenfranchised and the dispossessed. De Certeau also helps us understand Clare's awkward relationship to places the ownership and control of which he was not socio-economically placed to understand, let alone aspire to – and these include his cottage and all the environs of his village described in his verse. Clare's work at enclosure – and the sort of threat of after-work drinking (itself a kind of rebellion against social and hierarchised strictures of 'sober' responsibility) – is a tactic of the disempowered. There was no economic space for Clare to consider *not* doing the paid work of enclosing his village, or of lime-burning; choice is a product of socio-economic power, and he had none. There was no front for resistance because poverty denied space for that activity, just as it denied him any say in the Westminster-driven national processes that were demarcating new territories and driving the need for lime. Clare's opportunity to make an intervention into the process of enclosure at this stage was as a labouring hand; his 'tactic' was to earn money from a new source. Poetic and polemic tactics Clare played with a long time afterwards, in both the prose above and – from an entirely different and distanced point of view – the 'enclosure elegies'. With both de Certeau and Clare's own account of his part in the enclosure process in mind, and with the ambivalent impacts of enclosure as Barrell finds them, these 'enclosure elegies' might be better characterised as the 'enclosure polemics'. They are adopted stances, poetic performances, tactical displays of a rebellious stance, rather than 'documentary' evidence – though they are often taken as such, as if they were witness statements to the great crime of enclosure. Taking his own determined line through this set of issues, Robert Heyes questions the prevalent idea of these poems even being based on a specifically Helpston experience of enclosure:

> Consider, for example, the group of poems which are usually referred to, somewhat pretentiously, as 'Clare's enclosure elegies'... These poems are always treated as Clare's response to the enclosure of his home village of Helpston. However, by the time Clare was writing there was a long tradition of anti-enclosure verse, something Clare would have been well aware of from his extensive reading. Being someone who was always prepared to experiment with any verse form or genre which he came across, it is entirely possible that these are poems in this tradition, with local place names merely thrown in to give an appearance of verisimilitude. My point is that no one has ever shown that these poems are, in any meaningful sense, about the enclosure of Helpston; indeed no one has ever made the attempt. It is simply assumed that it must be so, and the argument proceeds on the basis of guesswork and wishful thinking.[64]

Under Heyes's interrogation, even the enclosure poems appear shaky in terms of their grip on, commitment to and knowledge of the particularities and histories of place. Heyes is right to question the 'authenticity' of the poems in relation to enclosure, if for no other reason than that they are poems, and so they will follow (or move away from but still be influenced by) literary traditions and pre-existing cultural forms. Clare's anti-enclosure polemics offer a mode of *exhibiting* resistance to state power, through a local paradigm; this is not the same as saying that the enclosure poems offer secure documentary evidence of the ravages of the process. That Clare has other responses to this process of state power too – including exploiting it for hard cash – shows just how dynamic, even momentary, could be his representation of and relationship to enclosure.

By way of an extension of considerations of the tactics of the powerless in relation to place, we turn now to two early and quite distinct poems as case studies. The first places its protagonists in a context of such helplessness that even the opportunities of de Certeau's tactics seem unavailable; the second is about Clare's own house and is ostensibly about domestic, familial security. The first is a poem that denies any possibility of domestic security – and one in which work for pure survival in an exposed world is the only sense of 'environment' offered. In 'The Workhouse Orphan, A Tale' of 1821,[65] Clare has the story of Mary Lee delivered by '[o]ld shepherd robin' (l. 5) who, for the first twenty-five lines of the poem before he begins her story, seems as content in his exposed occupation – with his audience of enraptured children – as Wordsworth's 'Old Man Travelling' does. But just as in Wordsworth's poem, this seeming comfort lasts only until the poem allows him to speak, and then his tragedy unfolds.[66] If in Wordsworth's succinct poem there is a problem of understanding in that the speaker 'over-pastoralises' the old man before the latter speaks, in Clare's poem absolute trust is established between the speaker and his staged audience of children – because they have bonded through the levelling discourse of play. To the children, Robin the shepherd tells his tale yet again as he's told it '[t]imes out of number' (l. 38) like a benevolent Ancient Mariner, but with a far more willing audience, and in some ways with a far more horrific story. The horrors of Robin's story have such grounded and local proximity to the context in which the children live as to be remote from the fantastical, the sensationalist or the gothic. What the shepherd unravels to his audience of children is a tale of social horror: homelessness, rejection, displacement, isolation, alienation, betrayal, madness and death.

What Clare's concrete knowledge of workhouse life for children might have been is hard to discern, though the likelihood of his family ending up in one was present at times throughout his early years.[67] The threat of the workhouse was held up to a young poet by those villagers who sought to ridicule his habits:

> I began to wean off from my companions and sholl about the woods and fields on Sundays alone   conjectures filld the village about my future destinations on the stage of life, some fanc[y]ing it symtoms of lunacy and that my mothers prophecys woud be verified to her sorrow and that my

reading of books (they woud jeeringly say) was for no other improvement then quallyfiing an idiot for a workhouse, for at this time my taste and pasion for reading began to be furious and I never sholld out on a Sabbath day but some scrap or other was pocketed for my amusement.[68]

Alongside madness, the workhouse is the stock threat dished out to the person who is not conforming, not following commitments to ostensibly industrious and utile labour, or the social conventions of the church-going Sabbath. The workhouse is a bogey man for the labouring poor. Clare offers an extended account of the 'shatterd workhouse of the parish poor'[69] in the long satirical poem of village life *The Parish*, which is much more materially thorough about the design of the workhouse itself than is presented in this poem – suggesting there was one in Helpston, or close by at least, that Clare knew well. And the poem known as 'The Lament of Swordy Well' sees the land reach out to anthropomorphise itself as an immiserated 'workhouse for the fields' – a weird reversal of analogy that only prosopopoeia could offer.[70] As with the enclosure poems, to treat 'The Workhouse Orphan' as documentary evidence of historical fact – plain and simple – would be to ignore the sheer artistry on show here; this is not to deny Clare's artistic or historical integrity at all, just to remind this present reading that the text in hand is a narrative poem, a story told by a story-teller who himself might well be a fiction. Robin is certainly set up as a reliable narrator, however.

As a structural effort the poem is finely wrought, staggering its delivery of narrative layers with a novelist's precision and a dramatist's sense of building urgency. The proximity of Robin to his audience of children is secured by a scene of rich and dynamic summer play, followed by the setting for the tale of a 'moaning autumn in her oldest hours' (l. 21). Having 'sought a tree & sat us by his side' (l. 26), and thus settling the children to an attentive hush, Robin begins by asking them to think of their summer just gone, by way of a stepping-stone of melancholia towards the tale to come. The tale has further bystander-style proximity in that Robin himself was born a bastard child, 'despised' (l. 56) by his mother and cast into charity care, alongside the central subject of the poem, Mary Lee[71]:

> 'With Mary Lee the parish was my lot
> '& its cold bounty all the friends I got
> 'Dragd from our childhoods pleasures & its plays
> 'We pind in workhouse sorrows many days

'Were many wants recievd their scant supply
'Were pity never came to check the sigh
'Save what laws force tyrant overseers
'Whose bitter gifts was purchasd with our tears
'There ragd & starvd & workd beyond our powers
'We toild those hours you spend in gathering flowers
'Nor mothers smiles had we our toils to cheer
'But tyrants frowns & threatnings ever near
'Who beat enfeebld weakness many times (ll. 57–69)

In a few short lines the poem moves from the 'childish glee' (l. 7) of the shepherd playing with the children, through to its absolute denial in the life of the young shepherd and his orphan friend Mary Lee. The denial of anything akin to secure, loving or family life is repeatedly attested to; even other children despise these two because of their utter poverty. The 'place' of Robin and Mary Lee – the setting they occupy, the whole environment they know as children – has simple dimensions:

'Thus workhouse misery did we both abide
'Till our own strength its poverty supplyd
'& service freed us—freedom did we find
'In labour there to slavery left behind
'& Mary grew in spite of every harm (ll. 73–7)

They seem to work their way out of this workhouse world – but the style of the syntax in these lines does not cleanly liberate them from the inhabitations of 'workhouse', 'poverty', 'service' or 'slavery'. Still, it appears that all of these places are temporarily 'left behind' – and the two make it into adulthood. Yet Mary Lee is rendered so naive and unworldly by the crippling development afforded her by the workhouse that she is immediately deceived by the flattery of a 'big young coxcomb farmer Follys son' (l. 85). At this point the tale takes a familiar enough turn: pregnancy out of wedlock is lifted straight from folksong tradition, and was the core issue of the poem 'Dolly's Mistake' that roused such censorious activity in Clare's early patron, Lord Radstock.[72] Sure enough, Mary Lee has a child, and while the father appears to nominally support the child initially, she is reconfirmed as an outcast:

'Now pind & starvd despisd by all she knew
'Too weak for toil yet wishing to pursue
'Some means for life now linkd with tender tye

'Which but for that had been a joy to dye
'She made her matches & her burthen bore (ll. 121–5)

This work of match-making is not sufficient, so Mary Lee begs and seeks food in the fields, and is now doing so with her baby. The exposure of this young mother and her child to nature is absolute. The natural world is now her place, her 'environment' beyond the workhouse, but of course, given her abject socio-economic situation, there is no succour here. Clare constructs her destitution through Robin's deft storytelling skills with a despairing companionship with birds:

'She oft was seen to wander round the fields
'& sought the berrys which the autumn yields
'Feeding with birds that twitterd by her side
'Content to spare her what the proud denyd
'Thus oft half famishd she from town sojournd (ll. 133–7)

No tactics are available to her, other than the pathetic trespassing theft of foraging. The death of her child a few lines later, to which Robin himself is a witness, sends her into a delusional state, and she makes a 'cradle' for her child out of grass (l. 158). With nameless others, Robin takes her back to 'misfortunes den' (l. 163) – the workhouse – but by now 'she coud not live' (l. 165) and she dies. The tale then makes its final bitter mark – and secures for Mary Lee a home at last, sardonically, in the harsh particularities Robin provides of her position in the ground:

'In the cold grave from every ill she slept
'Nor felt the distance which distinction kept
'North side the church no choice will occupy
'Force finds the workhouse tenants room to lye
'Where cold winds frown & sunbeams never come
'There mary rested in a better home
'A lone cold corner by the charnell pent
'Were nettles spread her only monument (ll. 171–8)

'Down to earth' now, Mary Lee is exposed yet again by the stifling social 'distinction' that the church constructs in its apportioning of burial space, the quality and position of her final 'home' being based on her wealth and status. Clare makes it clear: there is no tactical 'choice' for people like Mary Lee, and the same 'force' which drives her to the workhouse as a child has driven her to the 'lone cold corner' of the churchyard. Interestingly, in the forty-three-line section on the workhouse in *The Parish*, Clare writes that the building 'was not contrived for want to live but dye/A forced consern to satisfy the law'.[73] Here the 'force' that constructs the place is never aimed at providing home or safe place for the poor at all: it is a legal necessity only – built by order of the state and with no social love, as far as Clare's hard-hitting satire sees it at any rate. And similarly in 'The Workhouse Orphan' there is no 'home' in the churchyard for Mary Lee – alive or dead. Nature bears a miserable face too for the body of this woman. This is a poem of 'environmental protest', because it is all about Mary Lee's constantly inhospitable environment. The qualities of her attachment to nature are exposure, isolation, destitution and death. Mary Lee's class position cuts out any form of sentiment for 'nature', or any hope of 'connectivity' or broody decadent simmerings of 'dark ecology'.[74] This is one of Clare's most controlled and important poems of social fury, and one of many that has been anthologised but critically ignored. It was not published in Clare's lifetime.

The next poem for consideration has been more widely studied and is a poem about cottage security, offering a domesticated, homely 'sense of place' that Mary Lee could never know.[75] The sonnet 'To My Cottage' appeared in 1821 in *The Village Minstrel*, Clare's second collection. Here is that published version:

> Thou lowly cot, where first my breath I drew,
>   Past joys endear thee, childhood's past delight;
> Where each young summer's pictur'd on my view;
>   And, dearer still, the happy winter-night,
> When the storm pelted down with all his might,
>   And roar'd and bellow'd in the chimney-top,
> And patter'd vehement 'gainst the window-light,
>   And on the threshold fell the quick eaves-drop.
> How blest I've listen'd on my corner stool,
>   Heard the storm rage, and hugg'd my happy spot,
> While the fond parent wound her whirring spool,
>   And spar'd a sigh for the poor wanderer's lot.
> In thee, sweet hut, this happiness was prov'd,
>   And these endear and make thee doubly lov'd.[76]

The oldest meaning of the word 'cot' is 'a small house, a little cottage; now chiefly poetical, and connoting smallness and humbleness, rather than the meanness and rudeness expressed by hut', according to the *OED*. 'Hut' is present in the poem in the penultimate line. The poeticisation of 'cot' is signalled in the translatory title, in the sense that 'cottage' is the dominant term that does not need explanation. It is in the Romantic period that 'cot' begins its shift to the current meaning of a small bed for a child (the *OED*'s earliest instance occurring in 1813). This meaning is implied in this poem too, because this is Clare's cottage imagined as it was when he was born. The cottage is a cradling place of enclosed, familial protection – replete with the cosiness of a baby's bedding. It is the epicentre of safety as the child first experienced it. In recollection, the 'cot' was at its best when the season brought awful, noisy weather – Clare's understanding being perfectly consistent with Gaston Bachelard's passionate valuation of this same experience:

> faced with the bestial hostility of the storm and the hurricane, the house's virtues of protection and resistance are transposed into human virtues. The house acquires the physical and moral energy of a human body... Such a house as this invites mankind to heroism of cosmic proportions. It is an instrument with which to confront the cosmos.[77]

While the influence of this building on Clare's mind as a child, and as a poet, should not be under-estimated, this is a home yet, as Valerie Pedlar notes, the word 'home' does not appear in this poem at all.[78] That naked absence is indicative of how this internal place is configured in the recollected child's mind – a child's mind which is itself recollecting its earliest times in the cottage. Is the poem really that sure of 'home'?

Though not featuring a traditional sonnet 'volta', the moment of counterpoint in this sonnet – a place where it *ever so slightly* turns – is subtle: the working 'fond parent' takes the sonnet externally in its considerations when this adult mind 'spar'd a sigh for the poor wanderer's lot'. The relatively secure, domesticated working woman considers someone who might be outside – a 'poor wanderer'. Notably, she is not called 'mother' here, but given the neutralising title 'parent'. A poem dedicated to a wombic place of security moves beyond it, in female consideration of a rootless, possibly homeless, nomadic 'wanderer'. This is much more than tokenistic. This adult act of thought for the 'wanderer' is an affection at the learned core of Clare's childish understanding of what a family home is: it is a place that offers love and protection, yet it is also always communitarian in opening itself up to the displaced, the transitory, the exposed.

The parental definition of how the child's environment is to be conceptualised is foundationally significant. As theorist of space and place Yi-Fu Tuan puts it, the 'first environment an infant explores is his parent... necessary not only for the child's biological survival, but also for developing his sense of an objective world'.[79] The place as defined by the sensations of the child is understood through the cottage's protective material qualities, but for all its ostensible defensiveness in relation to a wild outside world, it is not closed off from it. This place is social and open sympathetically to a wandering, mobile world, as defined by the parent.

It is crucial too that the world of hand-producing work is present here, inside what we might call the 'domestic sphere' – though it would be reductive to label it so. As John Goodridge has noted, Clare repeatedly appreciates 'a vital root of his art in the rhythms and patterns of women's domestic and agrarian work'.[80] And so here too, the cottage is a 'sphere' of familial domesticity and domestic work, but it is also one that houses a woman's cash work – labour for money. This is a place threatened by the 'vehement' energies of wild weather – so much so that 'mother' and 'home' are left to be implications rather than statements of determined facts. Valuation of the cot is established upon a persistently sensory and parentally ethical awareness of what it would be like to be without it: home is not assumed and it is not owned, so it is not named. The woman is never 'only' a 'mother' – she is a cash worker too, centred on her spinning rather than the child, and so she is called 'parent'. The working day might be long over in the outside world of barn and field, but in the home, for the woman, it persists. This is reminiscent of a distinction in a later Northborough-period sonnet, the first five lines of which read:

> Tis late the labouring men come dropping in
> The old cat licks herself before the fire
> The work is done the maid sits down to spin
> & the old cart horse free from muck & mire
> Stand in the stall & eats his whisp of hay[81]

Here, in this untitled sixteen-line sonnet, the speaker does not seem at all sensitive to the fact that while the men, the cat and the horses can relax, clean up and eat of an evening, 'the maid sits down to spin' immediately 'work is done' – meaning of course that for her, the work is not done at all. The evening retreat to the cottage marks just a shift in the nature of labour, not its end, for the women in this short poem. This is a community shifting gear, coming inside, at the end of a labouring day; but for women, the home is just another stage for a different mode of work. In 'To My Cottage' the speaker's sense of place is coherent, yet somewhat hesitant, because it is framed by thoughts of unliveable weather, exposed wandering and the house as a site of adult work. It is precisely this ethics of place, created in and by the cottage home, that leads to Clare's conceiving of poems like 'The Workhouse Orphan'. Place is never straightforward in Clare, and primarily because of issues of class.

Genius Loci: Tracking Clare

As we have seen, class and place can be ignored if the 'green' agenda of ecocritics is forceful, or if material histories are conflated too keenly with specifically contemporary concerns. Similarly, when a modern form of 'green' anger drives a reading of Clare and the tracking of his places, the conflation of his poetic tracings of environmental concern in (or out of) a specific historical situation are de-historicised and deployed to enhance and articulate versions of modernity's own environmental situation. Co-ordinating palimpsests of maps old and new might offer the same locations, and named places and place names in Clare's poems might be ticked off a list or marked with a grid reference, but much of the places' historical environmental distinctions can be lost and conflated. This conflation of time that the self-same process of locating poetic places seems to allow and inspirit can lead to awkward results, if predetermined by the polemics that brought the reader to value Clare in the first place. Commonly now, if historical attempts are made by a touristic green criticism seeking the spirit of Clare's place, the result is often a feeling of loss, perhaps because the landscape is so different to what it is understood to have been in Clare's day, or because – as Jameson says above – in our postmodern situation the 'spatialization of the temporal' always inscribes a 'sense of loss'. In some critics, it is I think assumed that the vivid evidence of loss – of time passing, landscapes shifting, and of our distance from Clare's environments – is felt to be the *same affect* as Clare's own critically reiterated sense of displacement and alienation. The next inevitable step it seems, to 'immerse' critically in Clare's place once that loss is felt, is to avoid the pylon-stalked horizon and to focus on the tiny, to get low down and eye level with flowers and grass and to muffle the noise disruptions of cars and trains, by diving into the midst of some of the remnants of copses and heaths that remain 'in place' as they might have been (maps tell us) in

Clare's time. The sentimental adoption of Clare's posture of hiding (a frequent tactic he uses to avoid the nose-pokey surveillance of the village[82]) is touristically to duck out of and to avoid the wider environmental facts of his locality now. The localised in miniature becomes Clare's ever-narrowing world. That Clare microcosm becomes – if we forego logic and pace and scale and history – a model for the blue planet. And for Rigby, beyond the blue planet, to a red one. Why not?

History is unmapped and displaced, *pace* Rigby, in the focus on the placing of Clare's place, on the 'foot-stepping' of the biographical critical inquiry, through the tracing of his poetic pathways on the clean lines of tarmac and concrete of modernity, because the tracks, inhabitations and tactics of the rural poverty Clare charts are ugly, temporary and always undergoing a process of erasure. When, in self-regarding panic about the fate of the globe, green criticism seeks out commonalities with the Clarean past, through a cod Romantic sense of spiritual eternities in a named place, it wilfully avoids the histories of environment altogether, and the intrusion of contradictory accounts – relativism, slippery meanings, fictions, historical facts and figures, paradoxical behaviours and the temporary tactics of the poor. In its keen weaving of an atemporal green thread, ecocriticism sometimes conflates places past with places present, to secure the rigging for its contemporary moral agendas. It is the position of this book that ecocritical work (or any other theory-driven approach) on Clare does not have to be ahistorical.[83] Equally, the historicising critical work that attempts to place Clare in a site and a socio-economic situation does not have to be anti-theoretical or anti-ecological. There might also be ways into reading Clare as a presence in our contemporary situation without entirely evacuating our sense of his place, and without diluting or oversimplifying his conflicting histories or ignoring our own historical prejudices. Clare can be our contemporary without our forgoing so much of his past, as we will explore in the final chapter.

Tracking Clare's various moves of place, and following uncritically his own Romanticisation of his located identity, the general story of Clare runs as follows: so elevated and acute were his senses, so attentive was he to the meaning of his material location, so accurate were his documentations of place and so dependent were his subjectivity and understanding on familiar locations, that to take the poet out of the place is to mean the poet is no more. Stabilised and grounded by the poetic tripod of 'nature, feeling, fidelity', such approaches value first and foremost poems such as the early 'Helpstone', which, as James C. McKusick writes in his influential book, works in 'establishing a frame of reference for the subsequent poems in the collection and bearing witness to the priority that he accorded to his sense of rootedness in the local environment'.[84] At the other end of this slice across Clare's 'rootedness' sits 'The Flitting', a poem written in response to his move from Helpston to Northborough in 1832,[85] which seems to offer autobiographical access to a defining moment of crisis in his 'personal journey' – and is either a poem 'of alienation in the immediate aftermath of the move', as Jonathan Bate[86] describes it, or else a response to the experience of the exchange of 'one experience of nonbelonging and homelessness for another', as Sara Guyer has written recently; Clare, Guyer writes, had 'an excessive attachment to place that reveals a scene of minor, unremarkable movements as the occasion of profound displacement'.[87] Shalon Noble reads 'The Flitting' as a destructive move: '[a]fter the move to Northborough, Clare's poetry takes a markedly dark turn'.[88] There is no certain evidence for this, beyond the odd lyrical poem if treated as autobiography, and a life story that unravelled some five years *after* his move to Northborough. But Noble is following a well-worn track. In his elegiac poem of 1967, James Reeves thought Clare an extreme case proving that 'Man is born homeless'.[89] Following Edward Storey's biographical line, Cecil Scrimgeour sees a self-defeating paradox of passions in Clare:

> On one side of himself he wanted to assert himself socially and raise himself to the esteem granted to a master-poet; on the other side his devotion to his native Helpston country scene was a haunting passion and to be separated from it was to undergo a kind of death.[90]

More recently, Theresa M. Kelley finds irony in his attachment to place, noting 'a paradoxical logic of Clare's poetic adhesiveness to place' – a place that enclosure meant was owned by others, so that his recourse to resolutely local and common language becomes an assertion of intent from an impossibly defeated social and environmental position.[91]

Yet in general, the story about the impossibility of Clare's situation supports both those critics who read Clare as a poet of place, like Barrell and McKusick, and those, like Guyer and Noble, who read him as a poet who was always 'homeless'. This is a problematic term, surely, with regard to the *actually* homeless people Clare knew and valued so much (gypsies especially – though of course the conception of home for them was antithetical to its normative constitution in fixity, or in ownership or residence), and to the homes that he made and worked on with his large family. To call Clare 'homeless' is to ignore what the word means – is to use it metaphorically – and, dangerously, to ignore class. Being 'homeless at home' – a key *poetic* phrase for recent Clare criticism – is not the same as being simply 'homeless'. Even at the end of 'Reccolections &c of journey from Essex' when the phrase appears most pointedly and bleakly, Clare writes:

> so here I am homeless at home & half gratified to feel that I can be happy any where[92]

The second half of this sentence is hardly ever regarded, because for contemporary critical stories it is necessary for Clare to be only alienated, and even 'half' gratification at his being 'happy any where' is too complex. Critics do not allow for Clare's own determination to be gratified, to work against his own alienation, if that is what his written account of experience persistently attests to. A completely alienated poetic subject offers easier and more dramatisable critical pickings, but overall this becomes a slipshod and damaging story, delimiting Clare and placing him artificially, with only partial commitment to the subtle and complex evidence Clare himself offers. Given its context, in the concluding lines of the famous prose account of Clare's escape from the Epping Forest asylum, 'happy' cannot convince us, of course, and is not meant to, but similarly its intended presence cannot be denied and should not be ignored. Do we just ignore the word 'happy' and the struggle to attain it in that excruciating attempt to see the cup half full – in that hesitant 'half gratified'? By way of conclusion to his most epic, daring and purposefully-intentioned and homeward-bound of adventures, Clare states that he could be 'happy any where'. This is a remarkable conclusion for someone at the end of a line he drew and followed, for someone so drawn to home and for someone so determined to follow a clear path north.

Could Clare have been *happy any where*? In a reduced life story where poetry operates as documentary evidence, the *genius loci* with no locus can be no genius poet at all. As commentators have often pointed out, the etymological relationship between 'spirit' and 'genius' is close indeed; in Latin 'genius' could – on its own without 'locus' – indicate the 'spirit of a place'. The word 'genius' is bandied about so much by writers in the Romantic period that Clare's particular access to it seems always to be inflected with one of its root Latin significations – that is, 'spirit of a place' – the indefinite article begging us to specify precisely what place it is that has inspired – in-spirited – the 'genius' poet in question. For Clare, however, if it were to secure permanence, literary genius simply had to lift up, up and away, way beyond place.

Clare Through Byron: Lift-off

Clare's particularly rooted variety of poetic genius, as criticism would generally have it, has a clear and shaping class dimension. The specific turn of the word 'genius' in Clare's case – its determinedly, geographically and socially stratified, 'placed' meaning – also serves to curtail what Clare's work could ever amount to. The manner in which Clare's sense of a 'spirit of a place' worked in support of early presentations of his work is testable by considering in tandem how Byron's 'genius' was never constructed as that of a particular or singular place, but was instead rare in its trans-continental, pan-European superhuman supremacy; and in its enriching multiplicity of places. The poet of metropolitan and international mobility – whose name and fame were made by the poetic presentation of a rootless subjectivity in exile, in the guise of Childe Harold initially – garners a claim to a supra-European genius which has little to do with a settled place at all. It is the sheer array of places in Byron – his assumption of the socio-economic confidence to exhibit mastery of places both classically old and recently battered by the Napoleonic wars, combined with his mastering of places way beyond the reach of most travellers and those recent spheres of conflict (therefore new both to him and to much of his audience) – that first generated a widely appreciated and excitedly testified sense that this was a poetic genius without precedent or equal. Clare's 1832 poem on masculine literary power, 'Genius', turns to Byron's posthumous position in a pantheon that seems to include only him and Walter Scott – the same two poets of whom Hazlitt thought that '[i]n their poetry, in their prose, in their politics, and in their tempers, no two men can be more unlike'.[93] Not so for Clare. His poem was prompted by the death of Scott in September of 1832,[94] yet it is Byron who soars 'like an eagle'.[95] On sending the poem to someone whose publishing help he wished to secure, Clare said that he was 'like a packhorse tied to the gate of an hedge alehouse on a winters day with nothing before him about him or above but hard fare & bad weather'[96] – tied to a place, alone, hedged, enslaved, exposed. Given the immiserated place Clare wrote from, it is remarkable that he could turn to thoughts of condors:

> He dared the world a war to wage
> He scorned the critics mock
> & soared the mightiest of the age
> The condor of the rock
>
> Screamed from the dizzy appenines
> As startled by his flight
> When Manfred sought the searing shrines
> Of demons in his might
>
> Fear left him to the thunder shock
> No fellow shared his throne
> The smaller birds in coveys flock
> The eagle soars alone
>
> He died as glory wills to die
> A martyr to its name
> A youth in manhoods majesty
> A patriarch in fame
>
> While Scott from historys visions won
> A heritage sublime
> Rising a jiant in the sun
> Too over grown for time...
>
> But genius soars above the dead
> Too mighty for his power
> & deserts where his journey led
> Beholds it still in flower
>
> A poesy spell for times unborn
> & when those times are gone
> The worth of a remoter dawn
> Shall find his name as one
>
> For poesy is verse or prose
> Nor bound to fashions thrall
> No matter where true genius grows
> Tis beautiful in all...
>
> Its voice grows thunders voice with age
> Till time turns back & looks

> Its breath embalms the flimsy page
> & gives a soul to books...
>
> The grave its mortal dust may keep
> Where tombs & ashes lie
> Death only may times harvest reap
> For genius cannot die[97]

From the start of these extracts from 'Genius', Byron is granted a global reach – challenging the whole 'world' and praised by Clare for his bravery from the outset of his career in his *English Bards*. The condor is of course not a bird native to the United Kingdom, nor to Europe, but to the mountainous regions of the North and South Americas, regions of great wonder and excitement in terms of natural history discoveries in the Romantic period. But the condor is not a bird that Clare chose arbitrarily for its geographical exoticism: by his time, these birds of prey were celebrated for their ability to survive all manner of violence, for the weight and size of the quarry upon which they could successfully prey, for the seemingly effortless nature of their flight, for their massive size and wingspan[98] and for the unparalleled heights to which they flew.[99] Supreme in its flight, its hunting, its size and lifting higher than any bird in the world (it was then thought), this animal of continents Clare would never know in person captures the poetic daring and abilities of Byron: for Clare, Byron could lift above and beyond any ordinary human place, and the realms he occupied were with unknowable gods (his Byronic heroes even more so, of course, but these figurations are all part and parcel of the elevation for Clare). Byron was an untouchable poet, a graceful predator, at the zenith of the literary food chain.

Returning to Europe in his poem, Clare places the hardiest rock-dwelling bird in mountainous regions Byron certainly did know and travel through – but the Apennines in Italy are not the home of either the condor or of the thoroughly Alpine aristocratic protagonist of *Manfred*. It is possible that Clare is wilfully conflating Byron with his play's protagonist (as readers overwhelmed by Byronmania were wont to do), yet the stanza reads like this was a mistake – and one not spotted by his various helpmeets during the production of *The Rural Muse* of 1835, in which an edited version of this poem was published.[100] Continuing the conflation of Byron with Manfred, the next stanza reiterates the poet's bravery and the concomitant lofty isolation. Clare buys into the heroic modelling of Byron as a 'martyr' and as regally masculine (two elements of Byronmania that Duncan Wu has been at great pains to 'correct'[101]), and further solidifies the supreme maleness with a rare use of the word 'patriarch'. Turning to Scott, Clare celebrates the novelist's 'history' and 'heritage' – and he deploys a similarly masculine 'sun' metaphor common in Clare's accounts of literary fame.

In Clare's 'Lord Byron', a poem published in the *Stamford Champion* in 1830, the poet is a 'splendid sun', his 'genius...a portion of eternity'.[102] Here in 'Genius', Scott is a sun too massive and permanent for 'time' to control. It is as if, through writing 'over grown' (long, sprawling, unclipped, unedited, 'natural'?) historical fiction, Scott himself has had an impact on culture so great that history could not cope with it, or weather it, or forget it, without plunging into darkness. The next stanza (beginning 'But genius soars above the dead') makes the point the poem closes with: that 'genius' is immortal, fertile and life-giving where other, presumably lesser, forms of art, and other artists, wither and bleach in old age.

Now Clare looks to the future – to 'times unborn', which fold into yet more historical periods where 'his name' is to be maintained inviolate. Clare reveals that for him 'poesy is verse or prose', meaning to include Scott's fiction alongside his and Byron's poetry; and that this inclusive trans-genre brilliance is not dictated to by 'fashions thrall' – another way of pointing to the cultural specificity of the high Romantic moment of the two authors. Their original genius means that they are in effect removed from historical relativism, just as they do not require a specific location ('No matter where...') to flourish for all time. Their triumph is in total displacement, and in effacement of the usual material foundations (time, place) of assessments of their influence.

In the next stanza quoted above, the titans of genius and time effectively fight; all that time can do is preserve the corpse of 'the flimsy page' and so lend the books into which the individual leaves are bound an eternal 'soul' (this having a rare appearance in Clare's conception of time and literature). The poem's final move asserts a triumphant end across three successive lines carrying 'grave', 'tombs' and 'death'. At its last, this poem is a 'public' memorial in the sense that it is about the public afterlife of two of the most famous male literary figures of an era swiftly retreating into the distant past by the time Clare is writing. This is also a public poem in its grandiloquent diction, and in the arch concepts of time, history and Clare's stylistically brittle assertions about a solid and certain futurity for the enduring genius of the two writers.

Crucially for our purposes in this chapter, Clare denies the significance of place in securing a future for the fame of these writers; he also denies the significance of the huge fame, sales and money both Scott and Byron (and their publishers) enjoyed. Clare builds the writers as eternal verities, beyond market, situation, historical or historicising evaluation: their quality is true and will be so for all time. Literary freedom – or real cultural power – requires an eternalising process of displacement. These two writers seem to need no 'place' to help to secure that fame or their genius for them; the implication is that 'place' would be a hindrance, a dead weight, that could only stultify these soaring posthumous careers.

How might we interpret Clare's pointed denial of place and situatedness as a constituent in the posthumous success and influence of 'poesy', when he himself is supposedly so committed to a singular locale, and so ruined when he was removed from it? It might be that, to use de Certeau's model, Scott and Byron's access to supreme cultural power affords their work dynamic movement through space – and mobile claims on many places as they cross that timeless, rootless space – rather than the disempowerment of situatedness in one, alienating place that cannot be controlled by Clare.

To compare the multiply displaced Byron with the singularly envillaged Clare is of course to reach across a broad socio-economic gulf, as well as a vast gap of geographical, mapped reach. Maybe we should not be so surprised. Clare's response to Byron was part of a wider class-crossing trend, a characteristic of the lord's influence of which Clare was aware when he witnessed Byron's funeral cortège in London,[103] but which is also reflected in the scholarship on his labouring-class peers. Summarising Byron's presence in the work of a host of poor poets he is introducing, Scott McEathron writes:

> Byron's role in this literary milieu may at first glance seem bewildering, given his contemptuous references to Lofft and the Bloomfields in *English Bards and Scotch Reviewers*. Yet, perhaps partly because of his avowed hostility, he served several of these figures as a force to grapple with, to imitate, and sometimes to impersonate. Further, the aggressive self-indulgence of his verse, especially *Don Juan* but including *Childe Harold's Pilgrimage*, seems to have suggested a new avenue of artistic empowerment, and his influence is clear (and often announced) in the vein of wit, satire, and iconoclasm that runs through the present collection.[104]

CLARE THROUGH BYRON: LIFT-OFF   37

There is no doubt that by 1841, Byron was a channel of 'artistic empowerment' for Clare. But before even the publication of Clare's first book, Byron was a significant presence in the poet's rapidly expanding literary horizons. Clare thoroughly enjoyed *Childe Harold's Pilgrimage* early on in his reading of Byron in 1819 – indicatively asking Gilchrist for a loan of more Byron at the same time as sending back Wordsworth after one reading.[105] While his subsequent and increasing fascination with the aristocrat seems not to have been maintained specifically by an envious attraction to Byron's restless urges (never mind his material freedoms) to travel, Clare's response was nevertheless informed by Byron's easy, bold and promiscuous facility to go beyond the strictures, conventions and expectations of a known, singular place. Before Clare had heard of Byron, and long before Gilchrist loaned him books, Clare had copied out the journal of a sailor who had been at sea with Byron who 'was known among the Sailors as a Traveller and not as a poet'.[106] Though this was not to be the only person Clare met who had known Byron, this early second-hand proximity was to be a defining encounter, because Byron was conveyed to Clare first as a 'Traveller and not as a poet'.[107]

As Stephen Cheeke has illustrated, Byron's fame, and much of his poetic originality, is informed by a rare commitment to being in, and writing out of, particular named places – places that are historically significant, culturally crucial or unknowably mysterious, but all of them real and locatable. For the touring Byron fan, the explicit verse situations meant they could be visited, meant that textuality could be reassuringly crunched into a gravelly materiality by the traveller's foot, the placed poetry ticked off against confirmations of the first-hand enriching experience of travel. Cheeke surmises:

> Byron wrote about historical places, about specific 'spots', as if they were sites in which direct connection with the buried subjectivity of the lived experiences associated with those places was somehow (supernaturally) possible... Byron's own subjectivity, which has occupied so much critical attention, is perhaps most available to us through place, or most open to our knowledge in those historical locales into which it is written[108]

Cheeke's account revalues Byron's own 'sense of place' against a Romanticism that has more often, and more traditionally, favoured inspiriting value in Wordsworthian constructs of named, sacrosanct and memorialised places, who might seem, like Clare, to be the model of a poet of a specific set of named, mapped places.

A distinction between Byron's 'sense of place' and that of someone like Clare might emerge in that for the former, the commitment is to a set of locales of historical significance – or of a poetic significance in a mythos invented, reborn or revoiced – which is tantamount to a self-willed narrative to explore: an intellectual, researched story of recent or distant history, to be resituated, once visited, in a subjective poetic journey all of Byron's own making, but one that is self-consciously paraded within a classically verified tradition. Byron's 'sense of place' is multiple, and highly resourced, in the sense that it flits from place to place and is driven and informed by recent and long-standing histories of European culture at its broadest reaches and beyond. Byron travelled, and his travel was enabled (and ennobled) by having money and social position, reading history and having servants. The multiple nodes that Cheeke and all Byron scholars have to follow on Byron's journeys from place to place construct an idea of place that is informed by the importance of 'being there', but also draws in textuality – myths, literature and histories – as a way of understanding, enlivening and expressing place. Cumulatively, Byron's mobility amounts to a dynamic mapping of spaces and an extension of ownership in the declarative poeticising act. This is *nothing like* Clare's 'sense of place' if we mean his lived experience of Helpston and its surrounds, and his accounts of its evolution as a lived and managed landscape – not to mention his sense of being an interloper. This would explain why Clare displaces – or de-places – Scott and Byron as he attempts to represent their fame, which for him will be eternal. In 1851, a special correspondent for *The Morning Chronicle* who visited the Northampton Asylum and met Clare reported that 'the bitterest complaint which he made to me was of the injustice done to him by the public in not recognizing him, instead of Scott and Byron, as the author of Marmion and of Don Juan'.[109] The two were still melded together, but by now Clare was piqued at his fame having not yet taken flight in their wake.

Clare's is a knowingly literary presentation of his place. Committing to and reworking traditions of various kinds, he draws on all manner of texts to make sense of, and sometimes to destabilise, the places he finds himself in. But of course the sheer quotidian, diurnal, iterative pre-writing depth of worked and familial familiarity with his places requires no texts to orientate, no maps to guide, no guidebooks to inform and warn, and no textual histories to access the stories and mythos of the place before it is arrived at in person. Byron might well have valued 'being in a place' in order to write about it, but the reason that was such a determined and artistic act was that, outside of forms of text, the place was otherwise alien and unknown. The choice to go to such places comes from a position of strategic power to choose; an artful and excited enactment of desire to build an empire of poetic territory. The 'sense of place', then, is a deliberative act of commitment.

In contrast, Clare's 'sense of place' was constructed by few if any choices as such. Conscious and artful he may well have been about his topic when he wrote about a place and its significance to his identity and knowledge, but nevertheless there is a sense in which the placing of Clare *in this place* is an accident of birth and restrictions, the social over-determination of which no other poet among the major Romantic writers could possibly attune to. Other than the itinerancy necessary in the hunt for work, wage labourers stayed where they were: the 'peasant' label was rooted deep, concreted over by a stagnant social and economic system which prevented and discouraged mobility of any kind, beyond the bounds of a tight circumscription. Travel, pedestrian leisure, the freedom to walk in working hours, bred suspicion, and not just in the heightened tension of the Napoleonic wars, during which every walking stranger was a potential French spy.[110] The awkwardness of Clare's landless occupancy of his place is sourced in an awareness that others in the poetic world exhibit some choice about the spaces they move through (if not always the opportunities to take up their desires). They can make of a singular place a plural set of spaces through the displacement of travel: Byron in a bespoke coach across Europe, Wordsworth the intrepid walker on foot, Keats in his various literary pilgrimages. Even a cursory consideration of the choice to pursue spaces in the movements of other writers of Clare's time throws a cold light on the sheer restrictions of Clare's own 'emplacement', and the tactics to which he could only have recourse in recompense. The fact that a village twenty-four miles away from Helpston took Clare beyond a comfort zone of known territory does not mean that he wanted to stay at home forever, no matter how discombobulating that first journey might have been. For example, he writes that 'Wisbeach was a foreign land to me for I had never been above 8 miles from my home in my life and I coud not fancy england much larger then the part I knew'.[111] This is an account of the changing territories of his youth – each journey taking him beyond the 'edge of the orison',[112] maturing him, changing him, as his world expanded. His sense of discombobulation when visiting other places does not equate with a *wilful* delimitation of his knowledge and experiences to the one village: any constriction on his experience was the result of his class-based scope for travelling.

To an extent, Clare is 'settled' in a place by the social sediment on top of him: grounded into rootedness by the lack of free movement around and above him; a poet of the earth (down to earth, singing the song of the earth, earthy); a mole who was not socially or economically permitted to fly as the eagle nor, indeed, as the condor. Clare is a poet of place because society deemed that to be the only possible positive outcome of his economic and geographical situation. We can – and critically we must – make a positive out of this restriction on Clare and the tactics he used to write beyond his situation; but alienating restriction it most certainly could be.

Clare could not move to London and probably did not want to, but he did wish London was closer to him. In a letter to his London publisher James Hessey, in which he is excited about Charles Lamb's 'Elia' essays of 1823,[113] he is also waiting on an artist to make a fresh engraving of his cottage as a frontispiece for publication in a repackaging of *The Village Minstrel*. Clare is therefore anxious about the appearance of the cottage – about the political and cultural dimensions of its representation:

> the trees have been [?bound] up like maypoles latly & my hut stands beneath them like a grotto or moss house or the rem[ains] of a London [?whim] a cockney cottage Artis considers the effect spoilt & declines giving an outline saying the old one is better then aught that can be taken now so let it pass & I expect to see the second Edit: out directly for I imagine New title pages & a wood engraving will not take long doing – my anxiety increases with the delay[114]

This passage betrays concern that a 'cockney cottage' would be a beflowered, stylised, effete, whimsical representation of his home; that such seeming luxury would stymie reception of the poems in the book; and that such associations would steer readers to think badly of him by association with the excesses and politics of that cockney scene. Or it implies that Clare is revelling in the idea that his cottage had become an outpost of cockney culture. Actually, the passage could be attesting to both: throughout the 1820s, Clare revelled in his cockney sociability, in his *London Magazine* friends and in his real friendships with his Taylor and Hessey stablemates, but this passage shows just how acute a sense of his own ruralised position in relation to that culture he held. It might be that, no matter how much he enjoyed his cockney friends on the *London*, as Richard Cronin writes, Clare was deployed 'as an antidote to its own Cockneyism';[115] his awareness of this role places pressure on ensuring that the pose of suburban, festive pastoral is not apparent in an engraving of his home at an atypical moment of the year. Clare's place was on the fringes of the cockney adventure – and that was a frustrating and precarious place to be. If claiming a place in cockney sociability was an uneasy stretch, by contrast social life in Helpston could be drudgery. A year earlier Clare had written to John Taylor of his despair at the poor sales of *The Village Minstrel* and at his own inability to be inspired to write, and the movement of place he wants to see in response is a remarkable fantasy:

> I wish I livd nearer you at least I wish London w[oud] creep within 20 miles of helpstone [ ] I dont wish helpstone to shift its station I live here among the ignorant like a lost man in fact like one whom the rest seems careless of having anything to do with – they hardly dare talk in my company for fear I shoud mention them in my writings & I find more pleasure in wandering the fields then in musing among my silent neighbours who are insensible to every thing but toiling & talking of it & that to no purpose[116]

As this passage reveals, Clare's responses to his own places – home, village, region, community, class – are never straightforward, and his concerns about them are never only sympathetic or sentimental.

Emplacement and Alienation: The Cottage and the Barn

The accepted story of Clare's located sensibility is used way beyond the ascetic confines of literary criticism. It has attracted UK government-run 'lottery' heritage funding to turn that most holy of holies in the route map of any poet's tour – the home in which he was born and raised – into a multi-million-pound museum and visitor centre.[117] British gamblers' losings[118] have been converted into the winnings of a peasant poet's mini-palace: a pristine venue far larger, and far more empty of noise, dirt, odour and work, than the thin slice of that original building Clare and his family rented. National funding implies that the poet is now a landmark of a nation-story of English poetry: Clare has been rehoused by the state, under the auspices of a project initiated by Clare scholar Paul Chirico and driven by his father-in-law, the veteran Labour

Member of Parliament and former Chair of the Education Select Committee,[119] Barry Sheerman. As Sheerman himself ambitiously put it, the cottage '"is both a place where you can worship John Clare, but also it's a national centre of learning outside the classroom"'.[120] This is to be a place of worshipful, respectful pilgrimage, and a grand centre for poetically (and politically) driven 'education', for the 'nation'. For these reasons and more, the cottage was greeted with suspicion by some Clare enthusiasts, but then that would surely be the kind of reception any big-capital project developing a sensitive area of specialised cultural interest would expect. Yet for all the early doubt, the development is a magnificent testament to Clare's status in the twenty-first century as a major feature of folk and rural histories, of the Romantic period, of early nature writing, of a working-class literary tradition increasingly writ large and now, as far as anyone can tell, permanently so. As Linda Young wittily puts it, '[t]oday's literary critics and historians squirm a little to find themselves being moved by the experience of a writer's house museum, but in the end, they won't deny it'.[121]

The cottage has been home to and stimulant of an array of artistic, historical, educational and community-based endeavours, and while the security of its finances might depend on the vagaries of the political and economic weather, at the time of writing its future appears secure. It marks Clare out as a literary hero, worthy of territory, worthy of a literary pilgrimage, in a country and a culture in which 'house museums' proliferate and are dominated by a preponderance of literary heroes' homes.[122] The Clare cottage is a grand demonstration of how the particularity of stories of a place can work well to generate and confirm a fascination with the locality of a writer – as of course could be said for many of the period's far more popular writers' homes, such as Dove Cottage and Rydal Mount for the Wordsworths; Jane Austen's House Museum in Chawton, Hampshire; the Keats House Museum in Hampstead and the Keats–Shelley Memorial House in Rome; and Newstead Abbey (partly) for Byron. All of these places are founded on the idea that an understanding of the one-time home of a writer is a significant and meaningful part of the process of grasping a set of texts, and that author's legacy. Gaston Bachelard would have it that anyone's first house 'has engraved within us the hierarchy of the various functions of inhabiting. We are the diagram of the functions of inhabiting that particular house.'[123] This myth of situation suggests that if you know the house, you will better know the former inhabitant, and this is the primary attraction of a place like the Clare cottage. The cottage is unquestionably a primary point of access to

Clare – habitable, welcoming, informative, open and interactive. Kate Soper writes that it 'has been suggested that heritage is to "cultural" preservation what environmentalism is to the preservation of "nature"',[124] and certainly the Clare cottage tries to bring both together under the same newly thatched roof.

To see an aspect of Clare's material 'legacy' go through that same process of domesticising memorialisation, of museumification, and to see 'his world' and work attract such vast riches from the government and politicians and their rich philanthropic associates, has been breath-taking and unsettling in equal measure. To see Clare artefacts under glass, to see the artificial renderings of a peasant's kitchen, with its models of apple slices, berries and pastry in mid-preparation on a sturdy wooden table, or the stipples of soot marks above a fake fireplace, or the broad-brimmed hat pinned to the back of a chair as if Clare had just stepped out – and to listen to the readings and instructions on the high-tech audio devices – can altogether seem rather curatorially packaged, managed, authorised; we might even say state sanctioned, given the source of much of the funding. A 'Clare experience' is channelled through brick, mortar and double-glazed refurbishments to the cause of a regional story (a story which, in the cottage-framed telling, evidently aspires to be of national purport).

Sit on the bench in the neatly parcelled garden, key the location number into the phone-like device, and the loco-specific recorded actorly voice instructs you to 'be inspired'. The place, as it is now, is technologically set up to work a narrative of locally specific effects: the sense of each place within the cottage, and even around the village, is authorised and explained by the voices on the visitor's big black handset. And the latent dissonance of the cottage rests in its relationship to place. Clare and his family never owned even their narrow rented slice of the cottage building, as detailed in information the cottage itself offers. The trust owns the entire building, has extended it, owns the neighbouring dovecote and territory beyond anything Clare could have understood as being 'his home'. The trust has even bought the Exeter Arms pub.[125] The business entities[126] that own the buildings necessarily have an empowered and controlling relation to the space of the cottage that is distinct and, in some ways, sits in opposition to that of Clare and his family. While the cottage does offer stories of Clare's dire poverty, the gulf between Clare's 'home' and this building as it is now cannot of course be foregrounded too much by the materials in the cottage itself, without distracting self-harm.

Use of a handset is optional. To sit on what was *possibly* Clare's own bedroom window sill, in silence, and look across the street at the barn that he *possibly* worked in with his father is an offering unique to the building, to the cottage project, and to the access to places and viewpoints that only it can afford the visitor. In this house, kids can even dress up as peasants and play with a mock child's-sized threshing flail. Like all writers' house museums, the cottage has to offer a *possibility* that we might locate and experience Clare's 'sense of place' here, might live momentarily through his sense of Heideggerian dwelling, metaphorically walk in his muddy peasants' boots and locate the truth that only an art experience can offer – 'the silent call of the earth'.[127] Clare finds locales and makes the nondescript described, and we tourists are to refind them in his home – time travel through being in a place, all labelled neatly and bound up in a contemporary Clare story. There is a more serious political claim on this image too. For Marxist playwright Edward Bond, writer of the celebrated play about the poet, *The Fool*, Clare 'talked about economic reality and wrote that you have mud on your boots if you cross a field'.[128]

Did he work there, in that old barn opposite? Given the proximity, it seems logical enough that both Clare and his father Parker threshed with flails in the barn across from their front door, but other than an accident of 'place' there is no evidence as such. Clare never mentions the building explicitly (it is now a part of what is called Woodgate Farm) or the Wright family who likely owned it at the time.[129] An early attempt to present Clare to the world, penned by the eager Edward Drury for John Taylor to use as the introduction for Clare's first edition (Taylor drew on it, but went his own way), describes Clare as 'an untaught, unassisted, poverty struck laboring man, who is the son of a thresher'.[130] Threshing together was a defining moment for Clare's father too. Clare recalls a moment of his father's pride as follows:

> surely it is a thrilling pleasure to hear a crippled father seated in his easy arm chair comparing the past with the present, saying 'Boy who coud have thought, when we was threshing together some years back, thou woudst be thus noticed and be enabled to make us all thus happy.'[131]

Although he might more accurately be described as a gardener, threshing first defined Clare in terms of labour, and in terms of his relationship with his father. While he might be sentimental, here the father is not proud of the threshing itself: rather, it is the family's nadir from which Clare's poetry establishes signs of distance. The social status of the thresher was low indeed. The denigrating local term 'whopstraw' – which *The Village Minstrel*'s own glossary defines as 'a contemptuous appellation for countrymen' – literally means thresher. As a term of abuse in the angry mouth of a military man, Clare makes its purpose and effect stark:

> The bumptious serjeant struts before his men,
> And "clear the road, young whopstraws!" will he say;
> And looks as big as if king George himsen,
> And wields his sword around to make a way[132]

There was no getting away from the status of threshing, or its perennial presence in the young Clare's family life. A threshing barn sat directly opposite Parker Clare's crippled thresher's body even as, from his chair, he glowed with pride about his son's poetic achievements. As Clare wrote in the 1830s with the by then characteristically muted social fury, for the thresher '[h]ard labour is the all his life enjoyed/His idlest leisure is to be employed'.[133]

The resonance of the particular place of the cottage, and the voyeuristic sense of cosy restitution it offers for the Clare pilgrim-tourist of the visual link between bedroom window and high-lintelled barn – between place of rest and place of work, both buildings listed[134] and so 'protected' from the supposed ravages of modernity – is made even more awkward and entirely discomfited by Clare's own prose account of what threshing in a barn meant to him:

> In cases of extreeme poverty my father took me to labour with him and made me a light flail for threshing, learing me betimes the hardship which adam and Eve inflicted on their childern by their inexperienced misdeeds, incuring the perpetual curse from god of labouring for a livlihood, which the teeming earth is said to have produced of itself before, but use is second nature, at least it learns us patience   I resignd myself willingly to the hardest toils and tho one of the weakest was stubbor[n] and stomachful and never flinched from the roughest labour... I believe I was not older then 10 when my father took me to seek the scanty rewards of industry   Winter was generally my season of imprisonment in the dusty barn[135]

This account changes somewhat in the hands of the early biographers. Frederick Martin has it that 'John was sent to the farmer's to thrash before he was twelve years old, his father making him a small flail suited to his weak arms'. J. L. Cherry, probably following Martin uncritically, says Clare was 'set to assist his father in the threshing barn', while the Tibbles say that to pay for his Glinton schooling he 'helped his father at threshing, with a small flail his father made for the purpose'.[136] The view of the barn from the cottage bedroom window can only be experienced in that specific place. What being in that place might mean is constructed entirely by the subject position (the reading, attitude, knowledge, prejudice, mood) of the sitter, just as the reading of all poetry and history is similarly so determined. But it is that location alone that offers the *possibility* of re-enactment of a simple view, from one old building to another.

It is an emplaced view that changes *entirely* the moment Clare's text intrudes – because what he is talking about is his first taste of child labour. He claims bravery and a stern and honourable commitment to hard work, yet in reaching first for the original biblical punishment to explain where this suffering came from, in suggesting resignation and then installing the sheer shock of recollection stylised through the negating, delicate staging of 'I believe I was not older then 10' towards the close of this account of early labour, Clare artfully builds towards a shocked revulsion in his own dramatised recollection, at what he and all labourers have to endure and will always have to endure. This is punishment from above – and is therefore inexplicable and ineluctable: a permanent God-given state of affairs. The 'sense of place' is despoiled only in the realisation that any 'sense' derived in experiencing the proximity of bedroom window to barn door is an ahistorical romanticisation. Clare's text has to spoil our touristic experience that the 'place' of the cottage has to offer – and sour our child's play at being a mini-thresher-cum-peasant – because while the barn represents a complex of historical meanings in relation to Clare's one-time home, the meaning of threshing for our poet overall is stunned alienation – and a child's confusion – over the need to labour, the urgency of social and familial pressure for a child to do physical work. Time in the barn threshing – in any other barn in Helpston if not that precise one – is 'imprisonment'. The threshing barn opposite with its massive iron threshold amounts to a solid threat: the threat of repetitive work, the threat of flailing pain, the threat of arduous boredom. The barn is a place of intense and prolonged suffering. Its place diagonally opposite Clare's window is now as bleak as the closing lines to 'November' in *The Shepherd's Calendar*. When all other labouring has stopped, threshing carries on, and on:

> At length the noise of busy toil is still
> & industry awhile her care forgoes
> When winter comes in earnest to fulfil

> Her yearly task at bleak novembers close
> & stops the plough & hides the field in snows
> When frost locks up the streams in chill delay
> & mellows on the hedge the purple sloes
> For little birds – then toil hath time for play
> & nought but threshers flails awake the dreary day[137]

The barn building is now protected by government order, and so what Clare classed as his first prison is preserved, in a face-off of preservation with the cottage-cum-museum.

Immediately following the recollection of his father's pride in Clare having moved so far away from threshing, quoted above, Clare writes:

> About this time, which my fathers bursts of feeling aludes too, I began to wean off from my companions and sholl about the woods and fields on Sundays alone   conjectures filld the village about my future destinations on the stage of life, some fanc[y]ing it symtoms of lunacy[138]

Is this the description of a traumatised child? In this prose autobiography, Clare gives the experience of threshing with his father a direct and causal relationship to his early solitary musings. The trauma of threshing forms the conditions for the beginnings of an intellectual consciousness that cleaves Clare from his community and casts him as an outsider. He writes that 'at this time my taste and pasion for reading began to be furious and I never sholld out on a Sabbath day but some scrap or other was pocketed for my amusement'.[139] Could it be that his 'furious' commitment to reading is somehow a refracted response to the miseries of threshing and the humiliation of working with his father?

Modernity was disparaging the barn even as Clare first picked up his bespoke child's-sized flail in his tenth year. Regarded by modernisers as tremendously hard and inefficient work, threshing was one of the areas under great pressure from the invention of a variety of mechanised replacements for precisely the kind of flail work in which Clare's labouring life painfully commenced. As staples of the British farm and its building complex, the thresher and his threshing barn were to be made redundant, as John Sinclair, the President of the Board of Agriculture, put it in 1813:

> Grain in the straw, keeps infinitely better in the open air, than in close barns; it is less apt to be destroyed by vermin, and saves the enormous expence of

constructing and repairing great barns. Threshing-mills, when generally introduced, will soon prove the absurdity of erecting such unnecessary buildings.[140]

For Romantic-period agricultural improvers, the barn is itself redolent of old-fashioned methods and farming cultures: it is on its way out. It is a building of nostalgia, even in Clare's time, and the job he first steps into is already becoming redundant, as water-, horse- and steam-powered machinery became ever more available and popular. That threshing machines were a particular focus of the violent ire of the Captain Swing riots of 1830 and 1831 was an indication that the barn-free village remained a distant dream for the mechanisers and modernisers.[141]

The barn is also a cornerstone of the map of Clare's alienated situation in relation to capital and culture, and his account is witness to the start of the battle for him between the place of his labour-intensive village life and the reach beyond his place of literature, which returns us directly to Cronin's model of Clare's binary estrangement, discussed above. This dialectic in Clare's understanding of experience of his place, productive of so much created textual life and of a profound alienation, which in turn generated more poetry through a compensatory attachment to the natural world, is outlined in an account nowhere bettered than as follows, by Merryn and Raymond Williams:

> This is the complication: a class consciousness which is most sharply experienced as an alienated individual consciousness; the knowledge of a spectrum of deprivation which, as he directly experiences it, really does run from the more readily acknowledged and recorded facts of low wages and high prices, the humiliation of hirings, to the more painful and sometimes more immediate recognition of limited knowledge, limited interests, limited tolerance of other possible ways.
>
> This complex is then interpreted, in an intensely personal way, as a double deprivation: at once poverty and a cultural block. It is also, in its outcome, a specific alienation: an alienation which he sought to overcome in the literary market, which then in turn alienated him...He attached himself to what was still, through all the changes, present: the specific and diverse physical world of his own place – the trees, the birds, the flowers, the weather: the midsummer cushion which he could make in his own way.[142]

Clare's Places: Cul-de-sacs, Car Parks and Songbooks

In Clare's contemporary story, beyond the cottage and the neighbouring buildings – such as the barn, the Blue Bell pub, St Botolph's Church and the Buttercross – are plaques, memorials, statues and headstones, and then the John Clare Primary School, the John Clare Theatre in Peterborough, even a John Clare Ale at one time. The list of John Clare's situations, placings, namings, within and beyond Helpston, is getting longer as his reputation grows, and as the desire to use his name to do something for a new place, or mark an old place, increases. There is even a blue plaque on a building in Epping Forest, courtesy of Waltham Abbey Town Council, that reads 'JOHN CLARE THE FAMOUS POET LIVED HERE IN LIPPITS HILL LODGE 1837–1841'. There is no mention of the fact that this was one of the buildings that housed Matthew Allen's asylum (this is the building behind the hedge, on the front cover of this book). It is not that kind of place now: it might have once been a lunatic asylum, but it is sane now, the insanity hidden from view, the asylum's history hidden by the plaque. Literary fame, though – that is allowed to characterise the place. What 'sense of place' does the name of 'THE FAMOUS POET' give this place? What does it offer any place?

There are buildings and streets far beyond Helpston, beyond Clare's walked horizons, which seem to use his poetic expression of rootedness to lay claim to be a special node on his uncommon mapping of common places. Some places claim his name for sites the poet could not have witnessed: the impressively brutalist concrete John Clare Car Park in Peterborough, for example (Fig. 1.1),[143] while new housing estates include a John Clare Close in Oakham, another John Clare Close in Brackley, a Clare Road in Wellingborough, and there is a Clare Street in Northampton and a John Clare Court in Kettering. Located in this way, Clare is the poet of cul-de-sac real estate, in English English *the close* – a usage which derives directly from the act of 'enclosing' a place previously unmanaged and uninhabited. Perfectly nice new streets are given a marker of the permanently extraordinary by a poet's nominal dedication to them. By no means is it only Clare's name that is deployed in this way. It is a testament to his status in the English canon that across from Clare Road in Wellingborough is Shelley Road, which links to Scott Road, which in turn is connected to roads called Ruskin, Pope, Burns, Shakespeare, Byron, Keats, Tennyson, Chaucer, Swinburne and even Cowper.

Fig. 1.1 Clare Green Car Park, Queensgate Shopping Centre, Peterborough, formerly known as John Clare Car Park

Before we sneer at the arbitrary meaninglessness of the adoption of these grand, old and exclusively male names, I should say that my own first *ever* conversation about William Blake – and possibly my first insight into Romantic poetry in any shape or form – was with my uncle Ron, a postman who lived in Blake Close, part of a poetically named council estate at the foot of Shooter's Hill, in Welling in south-east London. My discussion with him about the name of his close led us into a discussion of Blake's poetry, the wider Romantics and Georgian London. No matter how superficial and canonically hegemonic the mechanisms which generate the process, the naming of an inhabited place generates and proliferates meanings for inhabitants, if they choose to care. As a postman, street names fascinated Ron.

Repeatedly, then, a poet's name is placed in inoffensive celebration, as a hollow form of statist commemoration, concretising a British male tradition, at least in the case of the Wellingborough estate (and in Welling too, for that matter). In order to be applied at all the name has to be well known enough to be mobile, footloose, deracinated. Modern building style means that places like this are enclosed, tarmacked, flattened, clipped, housed, suburbanised – and demarcated as civilisation against the wide expanse of troubling green. Clare's sense of place is made into a town planner's branding tool – his name a kind of toponym giving to a new place that could be anywhere, and to new houses the developer hopes will all the more quickly become homes, an immediate sense of being somewhere identifiable with located, rooted meaning.

Clare's 'sense of place' might seem to have become a nonsense of no place, a senseless guarantor of placedness which actually offers nothing of the sort, other than to make both name and place blandly arbitrary in their nominal collocation. Most paradoxically of all, Clare's name legitimises and renders sacrosanct the determinedly human habitation of a suburbia retrieved from the rural and the natural: the street, the close, the enclosed. A poet so famous for protesting about the damage of enclosure – the action of demarcating then converting common land into private ownership – becomes the legitimiser of 'the close'.

If I read Clare Road in Wellingborough and similar such demarcations as inscribing Clare as the rootless poet of loss – loss of place, loss of natural landscape, loss of locatable meaning – then, oddly enough, I am arguing that the anonymous gods called 'town planners' get it right more often than Clare scholarship feels comfortable in acknowledging. A Clare road sign signals a poetry of a process of de-territorialisation. It might be that a generative presence which tussles in an uneasy dialectic with place in much of Clare's work is the undercutting sense that things found, places visited, animals unearthed, flowers caressed, hands held, lovers joined, songs sung, festivities celebrated, poems written and 'meetings' had are all immediately, ineluctably, threatened by loss, departure, disorientation, disintegration, dissolution, with theft and breakage, with violent termination and with vanishings. Broadly, Clare is aspirationally a materialist in a grounded non-human sense, but someone who could not securely rely on human aspects of materiality – hence his resort to tactics for an expressive route beyond his place, to the 'poor wanderer's lot' for example. Clare's poetry does not necessarily offer a countering of displacement or alienation through the seeking of security in the natural. For all the evident desire for such security and solidity, in Clare's poetry nature is often fluid and ungraspable, as moveable, as shifting and as dynamic, and sometimes as *unstable*, as the poet's subject position. As we shall see across this book, ground dissolves, nature fades and fogs, identities are loosened and sometimes lost. He meets a woman, a lane, a bird, a flower, near a natural body which he will express as a process, as dynamic and fluid – and that which is met threatens to dissolve almost in the same breath that it is gathered in to an insecure lyrical and ecological subjectivity. The first line of the first poem in his first book is 'HERE we meet, too soon to part,': the meeting is immediately a losing.

This continual process of 'losing' (Clare often spells it 'loosing' – see Chapter 2) was apparent to his first editor, John Taylor. In his introduction to the first collection *Poems Descriptive*, while establishing Clare as a poet of a particular place, of extreme poverty and exclusively as a poet of nature, Taylor says that Clare 'looks as anxiously on [nature's] face as if she were a living friend, whom he might lose'.[144] The slipping away is as immediately present as the poetic expression of connection. The immediacy of the threat of loss is for Taylor the reason Clare's vision is so acute, so sensitive, and his poetry so immediate:

> hence he has learnt to notice every change in her countenance, and to delineate all the delicate varieties of her character. Most of his poems were composed under the immediate impression of this feeling, in the fields, or on the road-sides.[145]

Loss generates everything: the way he thinks, the way he composes and when he writes. At the outset, Taylor casts Clare as 'nature lover' – which like so many early models remains dominant today. Yet actual human women, and human-to-human love, as a subject of interest in the poems that follow are not alluded to at all (more on this topic appears in Chapter 4). Paradoxically, then, after asserting the primacy of his place and of nature to Clare's existence, Taylor quotes 'The Meeting', which, as the editor says, 'came too late to be inserted in its proper place in this volume'.[146] This lyric is a quite traditional male love poem, which as Taylor rightly says reflects Burns's 'O, Were I on Parnassus' Hill', in both the quite rare stanza form[147] and in its theme of love. Clare would also have seen the stanza in Wordsworth's 'The Green Linnet', in *Poems* of 1815, albeit with a longer, iambic tetrameter line for the triplets.[148] Like 'The Green Linnet', 'The Meeting' has 'nature' in it – but that is not the focus at all. Nature is present only to forge an understanding of, and to place, the affection described. Nature, here, is ornate, almost baroque in its rusticated positioning. The sharpest focus is reserved for affection. Here is the poem in full as it appeared in the first edition of *Poems Descriptive*:

> HERE we meet, too soon to part,
> Here to leave will raise a smart,
> Here I'll press thee to my heart,
>   Where none have place above thee:
> Here I vow to love thee well,
> And could words unseal the spell,
> Had but language strength to tell,
>   I'd say how much I love thee.
>
> Here, the rose that decks thy door,
> Here, the thorn that spreads thy bow'r,
> Here, the willow on the moor,
>   The birds at rest above thee,
> Had they light of life to see,
> Sense of soul like thee and me
> Soon might each a witness be
>   How doatingly I love thee.
>
> By the night-sky's purple ether,
> And by even's sweetest weather,
> That oft has blest us both together, –
>   The moon that shines above thee,
> And shews thy beauteous cheek so blooming,
> And by pale age's winter coming,

> The charms, and casualties of woman,
>   I will for ever love thee.[149]

This is a poem of location; it structurally voices a resounding commitment to place: appearing seven times, 'here' is the commanding anaphora of the first two stanzas. But 'here' is a literary love landscape, so the topography is that of poetic tradition, not a map of Clare country. The second and third stanzas inscribe the love in a bedding of natural bodies such as plants, birds, sky and moon – but these operate as witnesses, guarantors the speaker swears by. They constitute a natural frame, are arranged to underwrite the pledge of committed love, and they are domesticated, cosy, situated by the woman's door. The 'place' of this poem is not Helpston.

In 'O, Were I on Parnassus Hill', Burns's speaker wants the muses of Parnassus to help him sing poetry to a woman, but admits he will have to do with local features instead of the classical originals; this central conceit is the comedic spine of the poem. Burns's wry, localised and Scottish trumping of grand classical precedents is taken a step further by 'The Meeting': removing all comedy as he does so, Clare erases all classical traces. Rather than relocating the scene to his own village, he situates the loving pledges in an anonymous rural everywhere, beyond the confines and stylisations of the pastoral. Clare de-localises a Burnsian precedent. Another distinction between the two is that while Burns's poem maintains the strength of the loving feeling '[t]ill my last weary sand was run',[150] Clare's poem structures a cleaving threat to the love from the first line, with the likelihood that the lovers will 'part', through to the penultimate line – at which point he introduces 'the casualties of woman'. Clare's is a poem which establishes loving connection in the same breath that it confirms that all human things fall apart. Loss is built into love: it is a necessary constituent of intimacy and connection. To interrelate is to lose.

To conclude this chapter on place, we will follow the trajectory of this poem with no placedness. This was a poem which lost touch with Clare almost as quickly as it was first printed. Across the first half of the nineteenth century, there is no doubt that this was Clare's single most successful poem – and that it took with it no sense of Clare's 'place', in any possible sense of that freighted word. And this is an aspect of its international flight that is worth noting, that might have been generative of its success: it is a poem of no place and as a result, perhaps, it ended up in a lot of places, sounded out in a wide variety of sites and situations – in print and in music, in anthologies and in broadsides. Clare did not know of its success, and the poem when sung as a song did not know of him either, uncoupled from him – as it was much of the time – into musical anonymity.

Music and song were more important to the culture in which Clare grew up than poetry, though the separation of song for singing from verse for reading is never distinct in Clare. Taking the phrase from a well-known Charles Dibdin naval song, Clare described himself as a 'desent scraper'.[151] His ability on the fiddle and his reading and writing of notation, together with music's centrality to his family and village life, meant that musicality was partner to his poetic development in ways that warrant more exploration, though pioneering work has been done in this area by George Deacon and Trevor Hold.[152] Some of those who nursed Clare's literary career, however, were not so happy about his delight in music. In March 1820, James Hessey warned Clare of the dangers of musical excess:

> I trust I need not warn you against devoting too much time to music – It is an infatuating luxury, and unless taken in moderation has a great tendency to weaken the mind and to render it unfit for serious application to study. But moderately used it is a delightful & rational mode of enjoyment[153]

Immediately Clare's work was made public, however, professional musicians evidently saw in it the potential for musical setting and performance. As many since Frederick Martin have recounted,[154] in 1820 the poem was set to originally composed music by Haydn Corri[155] and performed on stage at Drury Lane by Madame Vestris. Clare missed the performance, but wrote that he 'felt uncommonly pleased at the circumstance'.[156] This performance alone would make 'The Meeting' the most immediately impactful of Clare's poems in the first few months of his published career, but the story is more rich and extended than just this celebrated first gig. The poem-as-song was retitled 'Here we meet too soon to part' and set to an already famous aria called 'Di Tanti Palpiti', from the opera *Tancredi* by Gioachino Rossini. As Jonathan Bate recounts, it was then sung in 1821 by Covent Garden soprano Catherine Stephens.[157] Musical historian Philip Gossett states that Rossini was 'the greatest Italian composer of his time' and '[n]o composer in the first half of the nineteenth century enjoyed the measure of prestige, wealth, popular acclaim or artistic influence'. Gossett writes further that the fame of 'Tancredi appeared to rest on the cavatina "Tu che accendi", with its cabaletta "Di tanti palpiti"... Rossini's melody seems to capture the melodic beauty and innocence characteristic of Italian opera, while escaping naivety by its enchanting cadential phrase'.[158]

This, the most influential setting of 'The Meeting', seemed initially to draw on the pre-existing fame of Rossini's cabaletta, but the partnership of poem and tune worked even more popular wonders.

For most scholars, that is where the story stops. In fact, the song as 'Here we meet' continued to be reproduced and set afresh in all manner of broadsides, song-sheets, songsters, anthologies, chapbooks and guides to learning music. Indeed, it becomes such a touchstone that it appears in plays and stories across Britain and the United States. This was a common enough pattern for the work of Romantic-period poets, though. For example, in her introduction to a collection of songs by James Hogg, Kirsteen McCue summarises the dispersal of his songs in a way which (Scots context notwithstanding) could be directly applied to the fate of some of Clare's work:

> many of his songs appeared in single song-sheet format, with the names of notable contemporary performers associated with them, supplying evidence of popular performances in theatres and public leisure gardens... Hogg's songs also appeared across his literary works in all genres, and within text-only collections of Scots songs during this time and for many decades following his death.[159]

If we follow a similar fate for just one of Clare's songs, we find a quite incredible array of appearances. In the early years of its circulation, Clare's name stayed attached to 'Here we meet too soon to part'. As early as 1820, it was being sung by Mr Broadhurst at the Theatre Royal English Opera, to another original composition by John Waring.[160] A performance of another, separate, original musical setting was reviewed in August 1820. Placing Clare explicitly in terms of region and socio-economic position, the anonymous reviewer (quoted here in full) in the monthly *La Belle Assemblée* conveys a rich sense of how the new music and the poem work together, and in front of whom the song was performed:

> The words of this pleasing ballad are written by John Clare, a Northamptonshire peasant; we mention this because we think them very beautiful, and we have before had occasion most sincerely to applaud the compositions of Mr. Williams in making his notes harmonize with, and express the meaning of the words. The andantino at the commencement, with the flute accompaniment, is tender and pleasing, and the expression of

the music in the refraine of 'How much I love thee,' is well adapted to the sense, and gives room for a judicious ad libitum at the end of the second verse; and we know not any one who can better make use of this musical licence than Mr. Duruset, by whom this ballad has been delightfully sang at the private concerts of the nobility.[161]

In 1824, James Ely Taylor anthologises the whole poem as 'The Meeting' in his *The Beauties of the Poets, Lyric and Elegiac, Selected from the Most Admired Authors*.[162] Another London-based anthology of 1824, *Beauties of the British Poets*, collected by F. Campbell, copies the poem entire from its *Poems Descriptive* publication, with only small variations of punctuation. The poem is prefixed by Campbell with a page of quotations from John Taylor's introduction to *Poems Descriptive*, covering Clare's place of birth, his family's 'extreme poverty' and father's illness, his prospects, education, the circumstances of his first discovery by booksellers and so on. In this book, 'The Meeting' appears sandwiched between a Shakespeare fragment entitled 'Music' (uncredited, but taken from the words of Lorenzo in *The Merchant of Venice*) and James Merrick's oft-anthologised classical translation 'The Wish' on the brevity of life.[163] Also in 1824, the song as 'Here we meet too soon to part' is published in Philadelphia, 'adapted to Rossini's Beautiful Air Di Tanti Palpiti, with New Symphonies & Accompaniments for the Piano Forte, by T. B. Phipps'.[164]

In 1825 the song appears in simplified anonymous form in a musical teach-yourself book, *The Sky-Lark*, which subtitled itself *A Choice Selection of the Most Admired Popular Songs* – a forum which provides an insight into the song's sheer presence in popular culture by this point: the compiler assumed that people knew it and would want to play it.[165] With Clare's surname appended this time, the song was included in the mammoth three-volume *Universal Songster* of 1826; indicative, again, of its widespread popularity is the fact that in this collection a song entitled 'In these arms, my Julia, Rest' is said to be sung to the 'air' of 'Here we meet...'.[166] In 1829, Rossini's setting leads the otherwise anonymised presentation of the song in John Parry's *The Vocal Companion*, a collection of scores adapted to assist the self-improving amateur musician.[167] In 1830, having been anonymised, the song featured alongside other 'popular songs' in Dean and Munday's *London Songster*.[168] In 1831, the poem was selected for inclusion in *Hodgson's Fashionable Song Book*.[169] In 1832, James Catnach, 'leading broadsheet seller of his day' according to the *ODNB*, was listing 'How we meet too soon to part' as a broadside song for sale in his huge and influential catalogue. Like other songster publishers, Catnach included the poem in cheap songsters across the 1830s – such as the undated, unpaginated *The Harp*, also by Catnach, in which the lines are entitled 'The words from Clare's poems' (and are situated just beneath an illustrated gun-hunting poem).[170] But one of the most intriguing 1830s reprintings of the poem is as the closing text of the bawdy songbook *Tommarroo Songster*, published by Lovelace and Perkess in London, probably in 1833, recently discovered by Derek B. Scott.[171] The poem text itself is much the same as the two-stanza version that appears elsewhere and, other than repeating the first four lines of the first stanza at the end of each stanza and losing the third stanza entirely, considering the distance from the poem's first publication in 1820, this appearance remains remarkably faithful to Taylor's original 1820 setting. Beneath the title appears the italicised line 'Sung by Madame Pasta', indicating that the song was performed by celebrated soprano Giuditta Pasta, 'who performed regularly in London in the late 1820s and early 1830s', as editor Derek B. Scott points out.[172] An Italian soprano of the London stage, Madame Pasta was a far more highly regarded figure than Vestris, Stephens or Broadhurst; indeed, it could be that Pasta was the most highly regarded nineteenth-century singer ever to sing Clare's poem. In the publication, the poem is placed as if to raise the tone of an evening of rude comedy songs, closing with this song of a love more elevating and spiritual, and less driven by and towards the body, than the other songs, for the most part, in Lovelace and Perkess's *Tommarroo Songster*.

In 1845, in the United States, the poem is included, with yet another original score, in the *Boston Melodeon: A Collection of Secular Melodies*.[173] In 1846, 'Here we meet...' was included in (Edward) *Lloyd's Song Book* in London.[174] In 1847, the song appears in the Philadelphia-published *Grigg's Southern and Western Songster*, the geographical specificity of which reveals that the collectors somehow came to think this song an American regional folk original.[175] Two creative references to the song in late 1840s America show just how well known it must have been: there is a fleeting reference to just the song's title in 'We Are All Singing', a poem in S. M. Hewlett's *Temperance Songster* published in New York,[176] while in a Philadelphia-published collection the song is alluded to albeit briefly, in that the first line – which had become, by now, the title – is said to be sung, by a Mrs Lovely, in *Three Eras of a Woman's Life: A Dramatic Sketch, in Three Parts*, a play by James Rees.[177] For a poet and a playwright to include such fleeting references suggests the song was so well known in America that even a hint of it was sufficient to stimulate a clear and comforting nod of recognition in an audience. Back in London, the 1848 catalogue of the significant publisher Duncombe and Moon lists it as follows: 'Here we meet too soon to part, a favourite Song, the Words by Clare, the Music by Rossini, sung with universal applause at Public Concerts'.[178]

An anonymous article entitled 'Labour and the Poor' in *The Morning Chronicle* of January 1851 reports on a visit to Clare in the Northampton Asylum, stating that 'Clare was the writer, though not generally known as such, of the lines, "Here we meet too soon to part" – which, set to one of Rossini's most beautiful airs, were some time exceedingly popular'.[179] The report is immediately picked up by other papers, such as the *Aberdeen Journal*, which summarises Clare in a way (as already mentioned) that suggests the poem was by far his most prominent at that time. Here is the complete note:

> Clare, the Northamptonshire poet (author of 'Here we meet, too soon to part,' and other well-known pieces) is still an inmate of a lunatic asylum. He complains that he has been defrauded of the honour of writing 'Marmion' and 'Don Juan,' and winning the battle of Waterloo.[180]

This account (repeated in the *Dundee Courier* and the *Caledonian Mercury*) is the only suggestion that asylum-bound Clare claimed Walter Scott's work as his own, alongside the work of those we more commonly know about – Byron, Burns and Shakespeare. As if destined to be as successful as Scott, the spread of Clare's poem in print and in song continued. In 1853 the poem appears, with a version of the Rossini score, in *Davidson's Universal Melodist*, a collection of 'Popular, Standard, and Original Songs' published in London,[181] and with no name or score in the *Cyclopedia of Songs and Recitations*, published in London,[182] and in *Selkirk's Songs & Ballads for the People*, published in Newcastle.[183] In 1856 we find the song in Glasgow, in *The Popular Vocalist*.[184] The song was a standard on the stage of the Victorian music hall, according to its appearance in *Diprose's Music Hall Song Book* of c. 1859–1862 and the same publisher's flag-waving *Red White and Blue Monster Song Book* of about 1860.[185] In the year Clare died, the song appears, with his name reattached, in J. E. Carpenter's *Songs for All Ages*.[186] Potentially the widest single circulation the song would have received, however, and its most literary setting of the nineteenth century, was when it appeared as a full quotation and subsequent discussion in a

'Johnny Ludlow' story, written by the hugely popular bestselling writer and editor Mrs Henry Wood (Ellen Wood), in an issue of her monthly literary compendium *The Argosy*. The song is sung in a story called 'The Tragedy', serially published from January through to April 1886.[187] 'The Tragedy' sees a hapless Valentine Chandler sing it with his beautiful voice at a sociable evening at Colonel Letsom's, by way of continuing to charm Jane Preen. The narrator, Johnny Ludlow, introduces the song thus:

> The song he chose was a ridiculous old ditty about love; it went to the tune of 'Di tanti palpiti.' Val chose it for Miss Jane and sung it to her; to her alone, mind you; the rest of us went for nothing. [The narrator then quotes all four stanzas of the poem in full.]... Now, as you perceive, it is a most ridiculous song, foolish as lovesongs in general are. But had you been sitting there with us in all the subtle romance imparted by the witching hour of the evening twilight, the soft air floating around, the clear sky above, one large silver star trembling in its blue depths, you would have felt entranced. The wonderful melody of the singer's voice, his distinct enunciation, the tender passion breathing through his soft utterance, and the slight, yet unmistakable emphasis given to the avowal of his love, thrilled us all. It was as decided a declaration of what he felt for Jane Preen as he could well make in this world. Once he glanced at her, and only once throughout; it was where I have placed the pause, as he placed it himself, 'like thee – and me.' As if his glance drew hers by some irresistible fascination, Jane, who had been sitting beneath the rock just opposite to him, her eyes cast down – as he made that pause and glanced away at her, I say, she lifted them for a moment, and caught the glance. I may live to be an old man, but I shall never forget Val's song that night, or the charm it held for us. What, then, must it have held for Jane? And it is because that song and its charm lie still fresh on my memory, though many a year has since worn itself out, that I inscribe it here.[188]

As the serial story of gentle rural middle-class intrigue, money-induced familial strife and polite domestic affection draws to a close, Wood uses the song to ramp up to a crescendo of sentimental and communal nostalgia, just before an abrupt, suicidal and utterly isolated conclusion for the heroine's suffering brother. Clare's song is the story's core moment of loving innocence and sentimentality, in an otherwise complex and fraught world of rural manners, careerist opportunism and social disappointments. There are no doubt many other instances of the song still to be found, but we will part with the flight of 'The Meeting' for now.

As 'The Meeting' becomes 'How we meet too soon to part', the author's name mostly falls away along with the original title – only to reappear here and there across its varied life in print. In most of these references the song flies far away from the grounded and studied track of Clare's career. Clare therefore made no money from the song, and gained no practicable recognition from it either, though so famous was it, so much a part of traditional and common culture, that when it was attached to his name it led the manner by which he was recognised and recalled, if at all. The international nature of the song's weird prevalence, its pervasive volume in singing situations high, low and unknown, to various melodies, to various ends – educational, musicological, fictional, bawdy, clubbable, moralising or dramatic – and to audiences of all kinds, is a testament to just how significant Clare's work could be when let loose from the chains of nature and place. His most displaced and detached song – and the first printed in his first book – was by far his most successful and popular across the nineteenth century, in ways and in places which he never knew and which scholars have not considered. It is not a nature poem, and it is not a poem that places Clare, or needs Clare's place, his class or his biography as a reference point. It is an anonymised and declassified constituent of popular culture; it is a prop to – and sentimental reference point within – culture's broad structures of feeling, to use Raymond Williams's term. Given the right winds, Octavius Gilchrist's characterisation that 'Clare's genius is not framed for sustained or lofty flights' could be proven wrong.[189] Creative artists, singers, songbook and broadside makers and writers of fiction and drama – and singing audiences too – made sure that this first love poem, in Clare's first book, was the text that soared as high, and nearly as far, as the condor of the Americas, both during his lifetime and beyond.

Notes

1. Ronald Blythe, 'A Message from the President', *JCSJ*, 1 (1982), 5 (5).
2. There are numerous studies of place in relation to these writers. Exemplary responses can be found in Fiona Stafford, 'Wordsworth's Poetry of Place', in Richard Gravil and Daniel Robinson (eds), *The Oxford Handbook of William Wordsworth* (Oxford: Oxford University Press, 2015), pp. 309–24; Sally Bushell's short film *Wordsworth's Sense of Place: Home at Grasmere* (Lancaster: Lancaster University, Wordsworth Centre for the Study of Poetry, n.d.); and Lawrence Buell and Richard J. Schneider (eds), *Thoreau's Sense of Place: Essays in American Environmental Writing* (Lowa City: University of Iowa Press, 2000), which contains a comparative essay by

Greg Garrard, 'Wordsworth and Thoreau: Two Versions of Pastoral', pp. 194–206.
3. In the most textually detailed account of the ways in which Clare drew on these and many more such poets, Paul Chirico says that Clare forges 'sociable texts'. See *John Clare and the Imagination of the Reader* (Basingstoke: Palgrave, 2007) and for example, Chirico's account of Clare's engagement with Yearsley, pp. 24 and 33-4.
4. For an ever-growing annotated bibliography of labouring-class poets before and beyond Clare's time, see John Goodridge et al. (eds), *Database of British and Irish Labouring-Class Poets and Poetry, 1700–1900* https://lcpoets.wordpress.com [accessed 31 July 2016]. For selections from, and discussions of, a wide variety of labouring-class poets writing immediately before and contemporary with Clare, see Tim Burke (ed.), *Eighteenth-Century English Labouring-Class Poets*, vol. III: 1780–1800 (London: Pickering and Chatto, 2003) and Scott McEathron (ed.), *Nineteenth-Century English Labouring-Class Poets*, vol. I: 1800–1830 (London: Pickering and Chatto, 2006).
5. Elizabeth Helsinger, 'Clare and the Place of the Peasant Poet', *Critical Inquiry*, 13.3 (Spring, 1987), 509–31 (509).
6. 'Prospectus' (Market Deeping: J. B. Henson, 1818), *Critical Heritage*, p. 30. The quotation from Clare is in a letter written to Henson in 1818, *Critical Heritage*, p. 31.
7. Octavius Gilchrist, 'Some Account of John Clare, an Agricultural Labourer and Poet', *London Magazine*, January 1820, *Critical Heritage*, pp. 35–42 (40).
8. Tom Paulin, 'John Clare: A Bicentennial Celebration', in Richard Foulkes (ed.), *John Clare: A Bicentenary Celebration* (Northampton: University of Leicester, Department of Adult Education, 1994), pp. 69–78 (p. 74), and Elizabeth Helsinger, 'Clare and the Place of the Peasant Poet', *Critical Inquiry*, 13.3 (Spring, 1987), 509–31. For a recent consideration of Clare's 'displacement', see Sara Guyer, *Reading With John Clare: Biopoetics, Sovereignty, Romanticism* (New York: Fordham University Press, 2015), pp. 78–100. For an extended account of loss (of place and other things) in Clare's later poems, see Stephanie Kuduk Weiner, *Clare's Lyric: John Clare and Three Modern Poets* (Oxford: Oxford University Press, 2014), pp. 86–121.
9. The letter in Nor. 44 is transcribed by Margaret A. Powell, in 'Clare and his Patrons in 1820: Some Unpublished Papers', *JCSJ*, 6 (1987) 4–9 (4).
10. An example of this trait in Clare criticism, as symptomatic in its own way as Lord Milton's letter to Taylor, can be found in Eric Robinson's article, 'John Clare's Learning', *JCSJ*, 7 (1988), 10–25: 'The stereotype of John Clare today, even in academic circles, or perhaps I ought to say, more particularly in some academic circles, is that of a *naif*, a peasant poet, a

natural genius with all the limitations that the world "natural" implies. Just like the reviewers of 1820, many readers of today cannot get over their surprise that Clare's poems should have been written by an agricultural labourer' (10). Robinson was writing at a time when Clare's critical acceptance and profile were limited.

11. Mina Gorji, *John Clare and the Place of Poetry* (Liverpool: Liverpool University Press, 2008), pp. 7 and 122.
12. Richard Cronin's essay centres on Clare's bookish and literary stylisations of situation, and on the according critical 'placing' of his work. See 'In Place and Out of Place: Clare in *The Midsummer Cushion*', in John Goodridge and Simon Kövesi (eds), *John Clare: New Approaches* (Helpston: John Clare Society, 2000), pp. 133–48.
13. Nicholas Birns, '"The riddle nature could not prove": hidden landscapes in Clare's poetry', in *John Clare in Context*, pp. 189–220 (p. 189).
14. *Natural History*, pp. xlix and 11.
15. EPI, pp. x–xi.
16. Johanne Clare, *John Clare and the Bounds of Circumstance* (Kingston: McGill-Queen's University Press, 1987), p. 144.
17. Theresa M. Kelley, 'Postmodernism, Romanticism, and John Clare', in Thomas Pfau and Robert F. Gleckner (eds), *Lessons of Romanticism: A Critical Companion* (Durham, NC: Duke University Press, 1998), pp. 157–70 (p. 161).
18. Ian D. Whyte, *Landscape and History Since 1500* (London: Reaktion Books, 2002), p. 8.
19. Michael O'Neill, 'The Romantic Sonnet', in A. D. Cousins and Peter Howarth (eds), *The Cambridge Companion to the Sonnet* (Cambridge: Cambridge University Press, 2011), pp. 185–203.
20. Bate, *Biography*, p. 208.
21. Bate, *Biography*, p. 331.
22. Bate, *Biography*, p. 445.
23. See for example Jonathan Bate's *Romantic Ecology: Wordsworth and the Environmental Tradition* (London and New York: Routledge, 1991) and his *The Song of the Earth* (London: Picador, 2000), both of which contain pioneering environmental discussions of Clare and other Romantics.
24. J. L. Cherry, *The Life and Remains of John Clare* (London: F. Warne, 1873), p. 28.
25. Angus Fletcher, *A New Theory for American Poetry* (Cambridge, MA: Harvard University Press, 2004), p. 55. See also Mark Storey, criticising Edmund Gosse for seeing Clare 'as little more than a camera', in 'Clare and the Critics', *John Clare in Context*, pp. 28–50 (p. 47).
26. Though there are many 'naturalising' models of Romantic creation, which sometimes tend towards a degree of organicising passivity in the subject

position of the poet. Specifically here I am thinking of the model of the Aeolian lyre or wind harp, *pace* M. H. Abrams: '[t]he Aeolian lyre is the poet, and the poem is the chord of music which results from the reciprocation of external and internal elements, of both the changing wind and the constitution and tension of the strings', *The Mirror and the Lamp: Romantic Theory and the Critical Tradition* (Oxford: Oxford University Press, 1953), pp. 48–53 (p. 51). For an excellent account of the poetry and the science of the harp, see Shelley Trower, 'Nerves, Vibration and the Aeolian Harp', *Romanticism and Victorianism on the Net*, 54 (2009), http://www.erudit.org/revue/ravon/2009/v/n54/038761ar.html [accessed 4 December 2016].

27. See Juliet Schyrava's insightful application of Schiller to unpick Clare's critical reception, in *Schiller to Derrida: Idealism in Aesthetics* (Cambridge: Cambridge University Press, 1989), pp. 80–110, esp. pp. 82–3.
28. Wendy Mulford, 'John Clare's Mountain', in Denise Riley (ed.), *Poets on Writing: Britain, 1970–1991* (Basingstoke: Macmillan, 1992), pp. 114–20 (p. 115).
29. See Chirico, *John Clare and the Imagination of the Reader*, especially chapter 6, 'Imagination and Artifice', pp. 138–66; and *By Himself*, p. 101.
30. I am drawing here (and throughout this book) on two leading essays analysing the 'problem' of natural (and naturalised) genius: Bridget Keegan, 'Boys, Marvellous Boys: John Clare's "Natural Genius"', in John Goodridge and Simon Kövesi (eds), *John Clare: New Approaches* (Helpston: John Clare Society, 2000), pp. 65–76; and Simon J. White, 'Otaheite, Natural Genius and Robert Bloomfield's *The Farmer's Boy*', *Romanticism*, 17.2 (July 2011), 160–74.
31. Kim Taplin, *Tongues in Trees: Studies in Literature and Ecology* (Bideford: Green Books, 1989), pp. 49–50.
32. John Barrell, *The Idea of Landscape and the Sense of Place, 1730–1840: An Approach to the Poetry of John Clare* (Cambridge: Cambridge University Press, 1972).
33. Franco Moretti, *Graphs, Maps, Trees: Abstract Models for Literary History* (London and New York: Verso, 2007), especially pp. 35–64. Excited though he is about Barrell's mapping of Helpston, Moretti does not mention Clare once, skipping from Barrell straight to Mary Mitford.
34. A moving and self-reflective account of tracing Clare's footsteps in this manner can be found in James Canton, *Out of Essex: Re-imagining a Literary Landscape* (Oxford: Signal Books, 2013), pp. 18–45. For a parallel project, if on a larger psychogeographical scale, see Iain Sinclair, *Edge of the Orison: in the Traces of John Clare's 'Journey out of Essex'* (London: Penguin Books, 2005), discussed in the final chapter of this book.

35. Michel Foucault, 'Different Spaces', in *Aesthetics, Method, and Epistemology*, ed. James D. Faubon, trans. Robert Hurley et al. (New York: New Press, 1998), pp. 175–85 (pp. 175 and 177), first delivered as a lecture in 1967. Foucault does not cite it explicitly, but the Bachelard text he draws on in general would be *The Poetics of Space* (1958).
36. Henri Lefebvre, *The Production of Space*, trans. Donald Nicholson-Smith (Malden, MA, and Oxford: Blackwell, 1991). First published in French in 1974. For an incisive account of Foucault, Bachelard and Lefebvre – and every other major contributor to theorisations of space, for that matter – see Robert T. Tally Jr., *Spatiality* (London and New York: Routledge, 2013).
37. Yi-Fu Tuan, *Space and Place: The Perspective of Experience* (London: Edward Arnold, 1977).
38. Michel de Certeau, *The Practice of Everyday Life*, trans. Steven Rendall (Berkeley and Los Angeles: University of California Press, 1984), p. 117. First published in French in 1980.
39. Frederic Jameson, *Postmodernism, or, The Cultural Logic of Late Capitalism* (London and New York: Verso, 1991), pp. 154–80 (pp. 154 and 156).
40. Edward S. Casey, *The Fate of Place: A Philosophical History* (Berkeley: University of California Press, 1997), pp. 331–9 (p. 339).
41. J. E. Malpas, *Place and Experience: A Philosophical Topography* (Cambridge: Cambridge University Press, 1999), p. 27.
42. For a recent summary of developments in Clare criticism since the 1990s, see *New Essays on John Clare*, pp. 7–9. For an overview of how Clare studies has developed in the *John Clare Society Journal*, see Greg Crossan, 'Thirty Years of the *John Clare Society Journal*: A Retrospective Survey', *JCSJ*, 31 (2012), 5–22.
43. Ursula K. Heise, *Sense of Place and Sense of Planet: The Environmental Imagination of the Global* (Oxford: Oxford University Press, 2008), p. 21.
44. Yi-Fu Tuan, *Space and Place: The Perspective of Experience* (London: Edward Arnold, 1977), p. 149.
45. For a salient discussion of the problematic relationship (and relatability) of local and global frames for environmentalist criticism (and action), see the 'Introduction' to Tom Lynch, Cheryll Glotfelty, and Karla Armbruster (eds), *The Bioregional Imagination: Literature, Ecology, and Place* (Athens, GA: University of Georgia Press, 2012), pp. 1–29.
46. Kate Rigby, *Topographies of the Sacred: The Poetics of Place in European Romanticism* (Charlottesville and London: University of Virginia Press, 2004), pp. 60–1. The Edward S. Casey text referred to is *The Fate of Place: A Philosophical History*, cited above.
47. An insightful account of the erasure of class politics in ecocritical accounts of Wordsworth is offered by Scott Hess, *William Wordsworth and the Ecology of Authorship: The Roots of Environmentalism in Nineteenth-Century Culture*

(Charlottesville and London: University of Virginia Press, 2012), especially pp. 147–55. For Hess, 'an explicit environmental focus' appears to denigrate a critic's sensitivity to class politics: summarising his account of critical responses to Wordsworth and the Lake District railway protest, Hess writes that 'critics who come to the railway protest without an explicit environmental focus tend to be much more sensitive to these class politics, likely because they are not predisposed by their own affinity for a Wordsworthian version of nature' (p. 149).
48. This passage summarises the findings of the Appendix to Barrell's book, 'John Clare and the enclosure of Helpston', in Barrell, pp. 189–215.
49. Barrell, pp. 214–15.
50. Barrell, pp. 201–2.
51. See Bate, *Biography*, p. 50 and note, who cites E. P. Thompson, *Customs in Common* (London: Penguin, 1993), pp. 180–1, and Robert Waller, 'Enclosures: The Ecological Significance of a Poem by John Clare', *Mother Earth: The Journal of the Soil Association*, 13 (1964), 231–7. See also Edward Goldsmith, 'Robert Waller', http://www.edwardgoldsmith.org/914/robert-waller/, 15 November 2005 [accessed 30 July 2016].
52. *By Himself*, p. 90. A couple of these lines are quoted in Barrell, p. 212.
53. Barrell, pp. 212–13. Jonathan Bate mentions that Clare worked on enclosure, but the length of this period of work remains indefinite, the dating of events in Clare's teen years being so difficult. Some dates are available: his work as a gardener in the nursery at Burghley Park from 1816–1817, for example. See Bate, *Biography*, pp. 75, 80, 94, 106 and, for Burghley Park dates, p. 81.
54. 'Don Juan', LPI, p. 95, l. 151.
55. See H. W. Gardner and H. V. Garner, *The Use of Lime in British Agriculture* (London: Farmer & Stock-Breeder Publications Ltd., 1953), pp. 14–22; Michael Havinden, 'Lime as a Means of Agricultural Improvement: The Devon Example', in *Rural Change and Urban Growth 1500–1800*, ed. C. W. Chalklin and M. A. Havinden (London and New York: Longman, 1974), pp. 104–34; Richard Williams, *Limekilns and Limeburning* (Princes Risborough, Bucks.: Shire, 2004), pp. 3 and 7–8. My particular thanks go to John Goodridge and Robert Heyes here.
56. See Bate, *Biography*, pp. 83–7. For Clare's own accounts of the lime-kiln work and its social impact, see *By Himself*, pp. 21–22, 86, 92, 105 and 112.
57. Michel de Certeau, *The Practice of Everyday Life*, p. 30.
58. Michel de Certeau, *The Practice of Everyday Life*, p. 30.
59. The minoritarian position and the definition of a 'minor literature' – which they develop through their analysis of Franz Kafka – first appears in Gilles Deleuze and Félix Guattari, *Kafka: Toward a Minor* Literature, trans. Dana Polan (Minneapolis: University of Minnesota Press, 1986). Original French publication 1975.

60. Michel de Certeau, *The Practice of Everyday Life*, p. 30. De Certeau's italicised emphases.
61. Michel de Certeau, *The Practice of Everyday Life*, p. 36.
62. Michel de Certeau, *The Practice of Everyday Life*, pp. 36, 37 and 38. De Certeau's emphases.
63. John Goodridge and Kelsey Thornton, 'John Clare: the trespasser', in *John Clare in Context*, pp. 87–129. This essay has been substantially revised and published as a standalone book: John Goodridge and R. K. R. Thornton, *John Clare, The Trespasser* (Nottingham: Five Leaves Publications, 2016).
64. Robert Heyes, review of Simon J. White, *Romanticism and the Rural Community*, *Romanticism*, 21.3 (2015), 319–21 (321).
65. EPII, pp. 660–5.
66. *Lyrical Ballads* (Bristol: Longman, 1798), pp. 189–90.
67. Bate, *Biography*, pp. 81: 'When John was "discovered" as a poet late in 1818, the family owed two years' arrears and were going to have to leave the cottage the following year – Parker, Ann and grandmother Alice to the poor-house, John and Sophy into service.'
68. *By Himself*, p. 5.
69. *The Parish*, EPII, pp. 698–779; workhouse section pp. 764–6; quotation is l. 1790.
70. MPV, pp. 105–14 (p. 107, l. 79).
71. Two other poems – both of them love poems of desire with no mention of a workhouse or anything like it – feature the name of a loved addressee, 'Mary Lee': 'Mary Lee' of 1830 (MPIII, pp. 410–11) and an untitled lyric of forty-two lines, first line 'If I was bonny Mary Lee' of 1834–5 (MPV, pp. 237–8).
72. In July 1820 Clare was infuriated that 'false delicasy' meant the poem was extracted, meaning 'the gold is lickd off the gingerbread' that was his first collection (*Letters*, pp. 83–4). See also the discussion of 'Dolly's Mistake' and the popular song from which it derives, in Deacon, pp. 47 and 58. On Clare's patrons, editors and this song – along with others that similarly fell away from *Poems Descriptive* after the first edition – see Roger Sales, *John Clare: A Literary Life* (Basingstoke: Palgrave, 2002), pp. 56–7; Chirico, *John Clare and the Imagination of the Reader*, p. 9; Alan Vardy, *John Clare, Politics and Poetry* (Basingstoke: Palgrave Macmillan, 2003), pp. 96–7; and Bate, *Biography*, pp. 164–5.
73. *The Parish*, EPII, p. 765, ll. 1797–8.
74. This is Timothy Morton's term, developed in part out of his reading of Clare's 'I Am' – and pretty much only this poem – in 'John Clare's Dark Ecology', *Studies in Romanticism*, 47.2 (2008), 179–93; this is developed further in his *Ecology Without Nature: Rethinking Environmental Aesthetics* (Cambridge, MA: Harvard University Press, 2007), especially pp. 197–205.

For a sustained critique, see Emma Mason, 'Ecology with religion: kinship in John Clare', in *New Essays on John Clare*, pp. 97–117.
75. In Clare's first two collections we might also consider 'Helpstone' (*PD*), 'Helpstone Green' and 'Home' (*VM*) as poems about village and cottage comforts, though of course the home is present in many other poems too.
76. *VM*, 2, p. 152. For a manuscript-based transcription, see EPII, p. 28.
77. Gaston Bachelard, *The Poetics of Space*, trans. Maria Jolas (London: Penguin Books, 2014), p. 67. First published in French in 1958.
78. Valerie Pedlar, 'John Clare's Recollections of Home: The Poetics of Nostalgia', *JCSJ*, 33 (2014), 5–19 (11).
79. Yi-Fu Tuan, *Space and Place: The Perspective of Experience* (London: Edward Arnold, 1977), p. 22.
80. John Goodridge, *John Clare and Community* (Cambridge: Cambridge University Press, 2013), p. 169.
81. Transcribed from Pet. A61, p. 50. See also MPV, p. 271, ll. 1–5.
82. See Ronald Blythe, 'Clare in Hiding', *Talking About John Clare* (Nottingham: Trent Books, 1999), pp. 39–47.
83. Helen Feder makes a similar point in her fine essay, 'Ecocriticism, New Historicism, and Romantic Apostrophe', in Steven Rossendale (ed.), *The Greening of Literary Scholarship: Literature, Theory, and the Environment* (Iowa City: University of Iowa Press, 2002), pp. 42–58.
84. James C. McKusick, *Green Writing: Romanticism and Ecology* (Basingstoke: Macmillan, 2000), p. 79.
85. For a summary of the ways in which critics tend to see the move to Northborough as a catastrophe of displacement, see Simon J. White, 'John Clare's Sonnets and the Northborough Fens', *JCSJ*, 28 (2009), 55–70 (55–57). White suggests that any changes were more to do with altered topography rather than the mere fact of leaving Helpston.
86. Bate, *Biography*, p. 389.
87. Sara Guyer, *Reading With John Clare: Biopoetics, Sovereignty, Romanticism* (New York: Fordham University Press, 2015), pp. 98 and 98–9.
88. Shalon Noble, '"Homeless at Home": John Clare's Uncommon Ecology', *Romanticism*, 21.2 (July 2015), 171–81 (173).
89. James Reeves, 'The Savage Moon: A Meditation on John Clare', *Selected Poems* (London: Allison and Busby, 1967), pp. 31–8 (p. 36).
90. Cecil Scrimgeour, 'John Clare and the Price of Experience', *JCSJ*, 2 (1983), 28–39 (32).
91. Theresa M. Kelley, *Clandestine Marriage: Botany and Romantic Culture* (Baltimore: Johns Hopkins University Press, 2012), p. 128.
92. *Living Year, 1841*, p. 154.
93. William Hazlitt, 'Lord Byron' in *The Spirit of the Age: Or Contemporary Portraits*, 2nd edn (London: Henry Colburn, 1825), pp. 149–68 (p. 149).

94. This transcription of this quotation is from MPV, though it is also available in *Letters*. Clare first sent the poem to the sculptor Henry Behnes in November 1832, who did not like it at all. Clare's aim was to rouse Behnes's interest in his building subscriptions for a putative collection, and to help him find a publisher for his work. 10 November 1832, *Letters*, pp. 596–600 (p. 599n1).
95. MPV, p. 9, l. 21.
96. To Henry Behnes (later known as Burlowe), 10 November 1832, *Letters*, pp. 596–600 (pp. 599–600).
97. MPV, pp. 9–12, ll. 29–48, 57–68, 77–80, 85–8.
98. Oliver Goldsmith writes: 'if size and strength, combined with rapidity of flight and rapacity, deserve pre-eminence, no bird can be put in competition with it'. *A History of the Earth and Animated Nature*, 6 vols (London: Wingrave and Collingwood, et al., 1816), 4, pp. 77–81. Goldsmith cites tales about the condor's legendary ability to survive all manner of violence at the hands of man, and to pick up sheep, cattle and even children when hunting.
99. In Clare's time, the Andean Condor was thought remarkable for being one of the world's largest birds, but also the highest-flying bird, recorded at an estimated 20,000 feet. 'Of all living beings, it is without doubt the one that can rise at will to the greatest distance from the earth's surface' wrote the influential naturalist of South America, Alexander von Humboldt, 'On the Lofty Flight of the Condor', *Edinburgh New Philosophical Journal* (January–April 1830), 142–3 (143).
100. *The Rural Muse* (London: Whittaker & Co., 1835), pp. 94–8 (p. 95).
101. See Duncan Wu's chapters 'Byron was a great lover of women' and 'Byron was a "noble warrior" who died fighting for Greek freedom' in *30 Great Myths About the Romantics* (Chichester: Wiley Blackwell, 2015), pp. 140–8 and 156–64. If these are myths, they were foundational for Clare's appreciation of Byron, as was the other 'myth' Wu scorns, that 'Byron was a champion of democracy' (pp. 149–55). Wu has no patience with the idea that myths (if that is what these aspects of Byron are) can be as historically significant as facts; or that, sometimes, in literary history facts might not matter much at all in the appreciation and celebration of a poet and the work.
102. MPIV, pp. 158–9, ll. 1, 13–14. Here the Oxford editors note that 'Lord Byron' was published in the *Stamford Champion*, 16 March 1830, and in *The Rural Muse* (1835), p. 120.
103. *By Himself*, pp. 156–8.
104. 'Introduction', in Scott McEathron (ed.), *Nineteenth-Century English Labouring-Class Poets*, vol. I: 1800–1830 (London: Pickering and Chatto, 2006), p. xix.

105. In his first couple of letters to Octavius Gilchrist in late 1819 and early 1820, Clare asks for Byron, 'that Vol which has the smaller poems', and then asks to keep hold of a particular volume, 'a little longer wishing to read "Child Harold" a Second Time' (*Letters*, pp. 23–25).
106. *By Himself*, p. 65.
107. For example, John Hamilton Reynolds was Clare's favourite of the *London Magazine* scene and he seems to have got to know him well. Reynolds had received praise from Byron in rich correspondence, and then had dined with the lord and received advice from him on how to cope with reviewers. See Leonidas M. Jones, *The Life of John Hamilton Reynolds* (Hanover and London: University Press of New England, 1984), pp. 49–50. For Clare's account of Reynolds and his association with Byron, see *By Himself*, pp. 140–1.
108. Stephen Cheeke, *Byron and Place: History, Translation, Nostalgia* (Basingstoke: Palgrave Macmillan, 2003), p. 13.
109. Anonymous, 'Labour and the Poor', *The Morning Chronicle*, 16 January 1851, pp. 5–6 (p. 6).
110. See *By Himself*, pp. 11 and 93, for example.
111. *By Himself*, p. 70.
112. *By Himself*, p. 40.
113. For critical accounts of the relationship between Lamb and Clare, see Scott McEathron, 'John Clare and Charles Lamb: Friends in the Past', *Charles Lamb Bulletin*, 95 (July 1996), 98–109, and Simon Kövesi, 'John Clare, Charles Lamb and the London Magazine', *Charles Lamb Bulletin*, 135 (July 2006), 82–93.
114. To James Hessey, 7 January 1823, *Letters*, pp. 255–7 (p. 256).
115. Richard Cronin, 'John Clare and the *London Magazine*', in *New Essays on John Clare*, pp. 209–27 (p. 211).
116. To John Taylor, 8 February 1822, *Letters*, pp. 229–30 (p. 230).
117. In 2007, the John Clare Trust – set up to purchase the cottage in Helpston – was awarded £1.27m by the UK government's Heritage Lottery Fund. This was supplemented in 2013 by a £500,000 'matched funding' endowment grant. See http://www.hlf.org.uk/our-projects/john-clares-cottage-opening-door-countryside and http://www.clarecottage.org/pages/catalyst respectively [accessed 13 November 2016].
118. The 2010 report of the UK government's gambling commission revealed that the UK National Lottery Draw was by far the most popular form of gambling in the country. It is popularly thought that this is another form of tax on the poor (some sorts of gambling – football pools, bingo, betting shops – seeming to be more central to working-class culture), yet the 2010 report reveals that the lottery is fairly equally popular across all household income brackets and social classes. Helen Wardle et al., *British Gambling*

Prevalence Survey 2010 (London: Gambling Commission, 2010), http://www.gamblingcommission.gov.uk/PDF/British%20Gambling%20Prevalence%20Survey%202010.pdf especially 'Profile of Gamblers', pp. 37–51. Profits from the government-sanctioned lottery support the Heritage Lottery Fund, which is overseen by the Secretary of State for Culture, Media and Sport.

119. Barry Sheerman MP was Chairman of the Education Select Committee from 2007 to 2010.
120. Rebecca Cooney, 'Barry Sheerman: his story', *FE Week* (10 March 2014), http://feweek.co.uk/2014/03/10/barry-sheerman-his-story/ [accessed 1 September 2016].
121. Linda Young, 'Literature, Museums, and National Identity; or, Why are there So Many Writers' House Museums in Britain?', *Museum History Journal*, 8.2 (July 2015), 229–46 (242).
122. Linda Young estimates 'a ratio of nearly 60% of writers to little more than 40% of all other vocations among UK heroes' house museums' in her article, op. cit., 233.
123. Gaston Bachelard, *The Poetics of Space*, trans. Maria Jolas (London: Penguin Books, 2014), p. 36. First publishe d in French, 1958.
124. Kate Soper, *What is Nature? Culture, Politics and the non-Human* (Oxford: Blackwell, 1995), p. 199.
125. Tom Peck, 'Rhyme and reason for the MP who bought country pub in the village of the Peasant Poet', *The Independent* (7 April 2012), http://www.independent.co.uk/news/uk/politics/rhyme-and-reason-for-the-mp-who-bought-country-pub-in-the-village-of-the-peasant-poet-7624919.html [accessed 1 September 2016].
126. Sheerman is listed as director of two separate entities relating to the cottage: John Clare (Helpston) Limited and the John Clare Trust. http://companycheck.co.uk/director/904343900 [accessed 1 September 2016]. The net worth of the latter is £1.5m.
127. Famously, Martin Heidegger roots his sense of the truth that only art can evoke in Van Gogh's painting of a muddy peasant's boots. See 'The Origin of the Work of Art' in *Off the Beaten Track*, trans. Julian Young and Kenneth Haynes (Cambridge: Cambridge University Press, 2002), pp. 1–56. Reaching his climax, Heidegger writes: 'The shoes vibrate with the silent call of the earth, its silent gift of the ripening grain, its unexplained self-refusal in the certainty of bread, wordless joy at having once more understood want, trembling before the impending birth, and shivering at the surrounding menace of death. This equipment belongs to the earth and finds protection in the *world* of the peasant woman' (p. 14). For the best account of Heidegger and Clare, see Emma Mason, 'Ecology with religion: kinship in John Clare', in *New Essays on John Clare*, pp. 97–117.

128. David Tuaillon (ed.), *Edward Bond: The Playwright Speaks* (London: Bloomsbury Academic, 2015), p. 31.
129. Local historian of Helpston Peter Wordsworth, who has made a private but as yet unpublished study of the documentation attesting to property, ownership and enclosure in Helpston throughout the nineteenth century, is convinced that during Clare's time, what is now called Woodgate farm (one of whose buildings is the threshing barn opposite the cottage) yet is often referred to as Savidge farm would in fact have been owned by the Wright family, the male head of which was one William Wright. The Savidge family only took ownership in the 1880s. My sincere thanks to Peter Wordsworth for sharing this information with me. Clare does mention 'Hellen Wright', a 'cruel maid' who is the addressee of the late love 'Song' (first line, 'O Hellen Wright, O Hellen Wright', LPII, p. 892), but there is no evidence that she is any relation to the family from Helpston.
130. Mark Storey, 'Edward Drury's "Memoir" of Clare', *JCSJ*, 11 (1992), 14–16 (16).
131. *By Himself*, p. 5.
132. 'The Village Minstrel', *VM*, I, stanza LXVII, p. 36, ll. 1–4.
133. 'With hand in waistcoat thrust the thresher goes', MPV, pp. 276–7.
134. The official entry for this building on the UK's 'Statutory List of Buildings of Special Architectural or Historic Interest' reads: 'Probably early C18. Small coursed stone rubble barn with steeply pitched slate roof with coped gable ends. Facing road a central doorway with chamfered lintel and plank door. Date "1832" inscribed above door. Barn doors facing garden at rear. Square ventilation holes in north end and loft door in south end.' See *British Listed Buildings Online*, http://www.britishlistedbuildings.co.uk/en-50109-barn-immediately-south-west-of-no-17-spri#.VbgJuPlViko [accessed 29 November 2016].
135. *By Himself*, pp. 3–4.
136. Frederick Martin, *The Life of John Clare* (London and Cambridge: Macmillan, 1865), p. 9; J. L. Cherry, *The Life and Remains of John Clare* (London: F. Warne, 1873), p. 6; J. W. Tibble and Anne Tibble, *John Clare: A Life* (London: Cobden-Sanderson, 1932; revised edn., London: Michael Joseph, 1972), p. 11. See also Bate, *Biography*, p. 22–3.
137. Tim Chilcott (ed.), *Shepherd's Calendar*, pp. 180 and 182, ll. 173–81 (Chilcott's MS transcription). Interestingly, in the instance of this particular stanza, alterations in the published 1827 version – apart from the first line – are relatively light.
138. *By Himself*, p. 5.
139. *By Himself*, p. 5.

140. John Sinclair, *An Account of the Systems of Husbandry Adopted in the More Improved Districts of Scotland*, 2nd edn., 2 vols (Edinburgh: James Ballantyne, 1813), 2, p. 17. For an extended discussion of the problems of barn flail threshing and the improvements offered by threshing mills, see, for example, R. W. Dickson, *Practical Agriculture; or a Complete System of Modern Husbandry*, 2 vols (London: Richard Phillips, 1807), 2, pp. 294–301; and Anon., *The Complete Farmer; or General Dictionary of Agriculture and Husbandry*, 5th edn., 2 vols (London: R Baldwin, et al., 1807), 2: see entries for 'Thresher', 'Threshing' and 'Threshing Machine' (alphabetised entries; no pagination).
141. A comprehensive account by E. J. Hobsbawm and George Rudé of possible reasons behind the peculiar focus of the Swing rioters on the breaking of threshing machines appears as Appendix IV, 'The Problem of the Threshing Machines', *Captain Swing* (Old Woking: Lawrence and Wishart, 1969), pp. 359–64.
142. Merryn and Raymond Williams (eds), *John Clare: Selected Poetry and Prose* (London and New York: Methuen, 1986), p. 16.
143. Having been called the John Clare Car Park since 1982, the multi-storey facility of the Queensgate shopping centre in central Peterborough was renamed in 2011, with only one zone of it now retaining a trace of the poet in the name 'Green Clare Car Park'. The word 'Clare' was retained only after a public outcry that 'Green' should erase his name altogether. I was told all of this by a local resident, to whom I offer sincere thanks.
144. *PD*, p. xx.
145. *PD*, p. xx.
146. 'The Meeting', *PD*, pp. xiii–xiv (p. xiii). See *Letters*, pp. 20–21. For a full account of the development of this collection, see P. M. S. Dawson, 'The Making of Clare's "Poems Descriptive of Rural Life and Scenery" (1820)', *Review of English Studies*, n.s., 56.224 (April 2005), 276–312.
147. An *aaaabcccb* stanza – again with an iambic tetrameter line – is famously used by Tennyson in 'The Lady of Shallott', first published in *Poems* (London: Edward Moxon, 1833), pp. 8–19, while Christina Rossetti uses an *aaabcccb* octave but with a trimeter line for the triplets, and an even more abbreviated dimeter line for the *c* pair, in 'Dream Land', first published in *The Germ*, I (January 1850), 20. Thomas Hardy uses the rhyme scheme for the mournful pentameter poem 'The Mongrel', in *Winter Words; in Various Moods and Metres* (London: Macmillan, 1928), pp. 83–4.
148. William Wordsworth, *Poems, Including Lyrical Ballads, and the Miscellaneous Pieces of the Author*, 2 vols (London: Longman, Hurst, Rees, Orme, and Brown, 1815), 1, pp. 243–4. As mentioned above, in December 1819 Clare returned a loan of Wordsworth's poems from Octavius Gilchrist

(*Letters*, p. 23; p. 23, n. 2), which means he was reading Wordsworth at the behest of one of his closest admirers, across the time Taylor says he was writing this poem. Byron was looming large, but there is no doubting Wordsworth's presence in Clare's first collection too, perhaps most especially in the form of this poem written just before publication, in Taylor's account.

149. *PD*, pp. xxiii–xxiv.
150. 'O, Were I On Parnassus Hill!', *The Works of Robert Burns*, 4 vols (London: T. Cadell and W. Davies, 1813), 1, pp. 291–2 (p. 292).
151. *By Himself*, p. 82. Clare lifts the phrase from Charles Dibdin's staple ballad (first line 'We Tars are all for fun and glee'), which was known as 'Jack at Greenwich', and reproduced in songbooks throughout the nineteenth century:

>A fiddle soon I made my own,
>   That girls and tars might caper;
>Learn'd Rule Britannia, Bobbing Joan,
>   And grow'd a decent scraper…

The Professional Life of Mr. Dibdin, Written by Himself. Together with the words of six hundred songs [etc.], 4 vols (London: Charles Dibdin, 1803), 4, pp. 223–5 (p. 224).

152. See Deacon, pp. 37–68, and Trevor Hold, 'The Composer's Debt to John Clare', *JCSJ*, 1 (1982), 25–30.
153. Hessey to Clare, 14 March 1820, British Library, Egerton Manuscript 2245, fol. 57. My thanks to Erin Lafford for generously providing this transcription.
154. See Frederick Martin, *The Life of John Clare* (London and Cambridge: Macmillan, 1865), pp. 103 and 111; Bate, *Biography*, pp. 157 and 166; and Deacon, pp. 65–7. Deacon includes two facsimiles of the song: one an anonymised setting without music published by Catnach (undated, p. 65) and the other Corri's original score (p. 66).
155. Haydn Corri (1785–1860), was 'Pianist, organist and composer, son of Domenico Corri. In 1811 and 1819–1820 he travelled to Ireland as *maestro al cembalo* for a series of performances given by Italian opera singers from London, at Dublin's Crow Street Theatre. In 1821 he settled in Dublin, with his wife soprano Ann Adams (Adami) whom he had married in London on 15 July 1814… Quickly establishing himself as a teacher of the voice and piano, Haydn played a central role in the musical life of the city for many years… He published a singing tutor and wrote a number of glees and songs.' Peter Ward Jones and Rachel E. Cowgill, 'Haydn Corri', in Stanley Sadie et al. (eds), *The New Grove Dictionary of Music and Musicians*, 2nd edn., 29 vols (London: Grove, 2001), 6, p. 502.
156. *By Himself*, p. 136.

157. Bate, *Biography*, p. 214.
158. Philip Gossett, 'Gioachino Rossini', in *The New Grove Dictionary of Music and Musicians*, 21, pp. 734–68 (pp. 734 and 738). A 'cabaletta' specifically 'denotes the second, usually fast movement of a double aria in an Italian opera, consisting of a melodic period of two stanzas which is repeated with decorations added by the singer after an orchestral ritornello, often accompanied by choral or solo pertichini and followed by matching coda designed to stimulate applause', according to Julian Budden, in *The New Grove Dictionary of Music and Musicians*, 4, p. 759.
159. Kirsteen McCue (ed.), *James Hogg: Contributions to Musical Collections and Miscellaneous Songs* (Edinburgh: Edinburgh University Press, 2014), p. xxiv.
160. Published in London by I. Waring, Fleet Street. The Bodleian Library provides a date of 1820 for this item, though the music sheet itself is undated. As both Broadhurst and Waring go unrecorded by Clare or any of his associates, it might be that 1820 is too early (though the Williams and Duruset performance suggests 1820 was a busy year for this song, in ways as yet unregistered). Broadhurst was active at this time – and had been a busy if uncelebrated Regency singer. He is recorded as singing on the London stage as early as 1810. See, for example, *Teggs' Prime Song Book: Fifth Collection* (London: Thomas Tegg, 1810), p. 1, and *The Jovial Song-Book for 1810* (London: T. Hughes, 1810), p. 22. A reviewer of a performance at the English Opera House on 26 December 1821 notes 'the pleasure we shared with the audience in hearing the songs sung by Mr. Broadhurst in a style at once, sweet, simple, and pathetic'. This was the very same venue at which Broadhurst performed Waring's setting of Clare's song. *European Magazine* (January 1821), p. 71.
161. 'Review of New Music', *La Belle Assemblée; or, Bell's Court and Fashionable Magazine*, 139 (August 1820), p. 94.
162. James Ely Taylor (ed.), *The Beauties of the Poets, Lyric and Elegiac, Selected from the Most Admired Authors* (London: John Bumpus, 1824), p. 124. This is a companion volume to Ely Taylor's *The Beauties of the Poets, Moral and Sentimental, Selected from the Most Admired Authors* (London: John Bumpus, 1824) which includes the Clare poem 'What is Life?', pp. 81–2.
163. F. Campbell (ed.), *Beauties of the British Poets; with Notices, Biographical and Critical*, 2 vols (London: Richard Edwards, 1824). 'The Meeting' and note: 1, pp. 110–11.
164. Published in Philadelphia by G. E. Blake, 13 South 5th Street.
165. *The Sky-Lark: A Choice Selection of the Most Admired Popular Songs, Heroic, Plaintive, Sentimental, Humourous, and Baccanalian. Arranged for the Violin, Flute, and Voice.* (London: Thomas Tegg, 1825), pp. 112–13.

166. *The Universal Songster; or, Museum of Mirth*, 3 vols (London: John Fairburn; Simpkin and Marshall; Sherwood, Gilbert, and Piper, 1826): 'Here we meet...': 2, p. 57; 'In these arms, my Julia, Rest': 3, p. 151.
167. The long title of this work provides the context in which the song was appearing: John Parry, *The Vocal Companion, Consisting of Favourite Songs, Duets, Glees... Comprising Many Works by the Most Celebrated Composers, adapted for the Voice, Violin, or Flute*. Volume the First. (London: Goulding and D'Almaine, 1829), pp. 38–9. The second volume in Parry's series was *The British Minstrel* of 1830, while the third was *Flowers of Song*, 1837.
168. Again, the long title of this collection is worth reproducing in full, as it shows how the song was regarded by the collectors: *The London Songster; A Cabinet Edition of Naval, Military, Bacchanalian, Comic, Sentimental, Love, Patriotic, and Other Popular Songs, English, Irish, and Scotch: comprising those Singing at the Theatres, Private Concerts, and other Places of Fashionable Resort, we well as those held in General Estimation* (London: Dean and Munday, 1830), p. 59.
169. *Hodgson's Fashionable Song Book, for 1831: A Choice Collection of Nearly One Hundred Popular, Favourite, and Entirely New Songs* (London: Bernard Hodgson, 1831), [no pagination].
170. See *ODNB* on James Catnach (1792–1841). *Catalogue of Songs and Song books. Sheets, Half-Sheets, Christmas Carols, Children's Books, &c. &c. &c.* (London: J. Catnach, 1832), p. 3. See Steve Roud and Paul Smith (eds), *A Catalogue of Songs and Song Books Printed and Published by James Catnach 1832: A Facsimile Reprint with Indexes and Examples* (Doncaster: January Books, 1985), p. 19. *The Harp* was an illustrated collection published by 'J. Catnach, 2 Monmouth Street', which the Bodleian dates to *c.* 1830–1837. Many cheap songsters in which Clare's song appears are undated, in the Harding collection, Bodleian Library, Oxford, but are likely of the 1820s and 1830s.
171. *Tommarroo Songster* (London: Lovelace and Perkess, ?1833), in Patrick Spedding and Paul Watt, gen. (eds), *Bawdy Songbooks of the Romantic Period*, 4 vols (London: Pickering and Chatto, 2011), 4, Derek B. Scott (ed.), pp. 327–55 (pp. 354–5).
172. Derek B. Scott (ed.), *Bawdy Songbooks of the Romantic Period*, vol. 4 (London: Pickering and Chatto, 2011), pp. xix–xx.
173. E. L. White, *The Boston Melodeon: A Collection of Secular Melodies, Consisting of Songs, Glees, Rounds, Catches, &c., Including Many of the Most Popular Pieces of the Day Arranged and Harmonized For Four Voices*, 2 vols (Boston: Benjamin B. Mussey & Co., c. 1845), 1, p. 152.
174. *Lloyd's Song Book; containing upwards of Four Hundred Songs, Duets, Glees, & c., &c.* (London: E. Lloyd [1845]), p. 66.

175. *Grigg's Southern and Western Songster: Being a Choice Selection of the Most Fashionable Songs*... New edn. (Philadelphia [PA]: Grigg, Elliot & Co., 1847), p. 234.
176. S. M. Hewlett, 'We Are All Singing', *Hewlett's Temperance Songster. A Collection of Songs, Dedicated to All the Temperance Societies in the World*, 6th edn (Cooperstown [New York]: S. M. Hewlett, 1846), p. 11.
177. James Rees, 'Three Eras of a Woman's Life: A Dramatic Sketch, in Three Parts', in *Mysteries of City Life* (Philadelphia [PA]: J. W. Moore, 1849), pp. 182–198 (p. 191).
178. 'Here we meet...' appears as song 404 listed in the catalogue of *Duncombe's Music for the Million!* (London: Duncombe and Moon, c. 1848).
179. 'Labour and the Poor', *The Morning Chronicle*, 16 January 1851, pp. 5–6 (p. 6). This is one in a series of correspondents' letters covering the poor across rural areas, the full title in this instance being 'Labour and the Poor. Rural Districts [from our Special Correspondent.] Counties of Northampton, Leicester, Rutland, Nottingham, and Derby. Letter XLIV'.
180. 'The Income Tax (*From the Times*)', *The Aberdeen Journal*, 29 January 1851, p. 3. See also *Dundee Courier* 29 January 1851, p. 1, and *Caledonian Mercury*, 27 January 1851, p. 1.
181. *Davidson's Universal Melodist, Consisting of the Music and Words or Popular, Standard, and Original Songs, &c.*, 2 vols (London: G. H. Davidson, 1853) 1, p. 218.
182. *Cyclopedia of Songs and Recitations* (London: 'for the Booksellers', 1853), p. 58.
183. *Selkirk's Songs & Ballads for the People*, no. 9 (Newcastle: Selkirk, 1853), p. 192.
184. *The Popular Vocalist; Containing a Choice Selection of Favourite National Songs, as sung at the Different Places of Entertainment by the Most Eminent Singers* (Glasgow: George Cameron, 1856), p. 102.
185. *Diprose's Music Hall Song Book*, no. 5 (London: J. Diprose, c. 1859–1862) p. 34, and J. Diprose (ed.), *The Red White and Blue Monster Song Book* (London: J. Diprose, c. 1860), p. 19.
186. J. E. Carpenter (ed.), *Songs for All Ages* (London: Routledge, Warne, and Routledge, 1864), pp. 55–6. This book was reprinted by Routledge in New York in 1866.
187. Johnny Ludlow (nom de plume of Mrs Henry Wood), 'The Tragedy', *The Argosy*, January 1886, pp. 28–44; February 1886, pp. 112–28; March 1886, 192–208; and April 1886, pp. 269–85. The song appears in full in the April issue on p. 274, while the narrator's discussion quoted here follows on p. 275.
188. Ibid., pp. 274–5.
189. See note 7 above.

CHAPTER 2

Clare and Ecocentrism

The Context of Romantic Egotism

This chapter considers whether Clare's much-vaunted proto-ecologism – some of which was indicated in the preceding chapter – has any basis in theorisation beyond its celebrated practice in poetic demonstrations. To do this, the chapter contextualises Clare's supposed resistance to anthropocentrism by reading him in the contexts of literary Romantic egotism. We start with a *Blackwood's* review of Clare's 1835 volume of poetry, *The Rural Muse,* in which John Wilson (aka Christopher North) writes:

> It is right that every Poet, high or humble, should be an egotist. Clare speaks much – but not too much – of himself – for always in connection with his lot, which was a lot of labour from which his own genius – and we believe the kindness of his friends – have set him free.[1]

Though he is wrong about the change in Clare's circumstances, Wilson touches on an aspect of Clare's writing mode which now dominates the way Clare scholars think about the poet in comparison to his Romantic contemporaries: regardless that his most famous poem is entitled 'I Am', he is overall a less egotistical poet, less centred on the human self and more able to be 'ecocentric' – that is, to be more empathetic with the interrelatedness of natural bodies and beings. This assumption is part and parcel of the valuation of the 'ecological consciousness' for which Clare is increasingly turned to, and it is also a constituent of the manner in which he is critically and historically 'placed'. This chapter is designed to uncover any resistance in Clare to egotism, because that resistance appears so essential and politicising a theoretical foundation of his proto-ecological consciousness. It then assesses what happens aesthetically, structurally, in a poem which is symptomatic of that 'green' consciousness.

For the renowned Tory critic, journalist and philosopher Wilson, the lack of egotism in Clare's work is immediately related to the poet's social circumstances – to his place. The labouring-class poet cannot do anything else other than write 'in connection with his lot'. Chapter 1 made clear that Wilson is not alone: many well-meaning critics have done the same before and since. Wilson places Clare in a situation out of which his poetic wings alone are not deemed powerful enough to lift him; he needs his friends' help. For Wilson, the 'place' of production limits interpretative value in extremis. Continuing the discussion from Chapter 1, this chapter will argue that for Clare the constant struggle against place went hand in hand with his sporadic kicking against the over-determined literary styles of the period in which he wrote, and together they form the foundation of his ecologism.

The meaning and usage of the term 'egotism' were unstable throughout the Romantic period, and the associated term 'egoism' was often contrasted to it. That Wilson was influenced by Wordsworth is implicit in his review, but the egotism he extols was not always favoured by his peers. When Wilson wants to dismiss poets as inferior relative to Clare in the same review, he employs the term 'egoism':

> True descriptive poetry, however, does not at any time consist in the attributing to nature whatever qualities it may please a self-conceited coxcomb, in the superabundance of his egoism, to bestow upon our gracious mother – nor in the pouring out into her lap all the diseased feelings that may happen to have been generated in his – however *intense*. The inferior followers of Shelley, Keates, Hunt, and Tennysson, are all addicted to this disgusting practice – and show it chiefly in the sonnets. The men we have named are all poets – the creatures we have hinted are not even poetasters.[2]

Egotism is idealised, while egoism is cast as its nasty bastard relative. Wilson is confidently writing within a well-established if shifting pattern of usage. The root word 'ego', which in Latin functions as the first-person singular subject pronoun, enters the English language, according to the *OED*, in 1789, in a letter from William Cowper, incidentally a highly important poet in Clare's own development.[3] The quotation the *OED* provides is also quite acerbic: 'To thee both Ego and all that Ego does is interesting'; it is used here, it seems, to form an accusation of self-interest, of vanity, in the addressee. 'Egotism' and 'egoism' have been well explored by Romantic critics, most usefully by Stephen Bygrave. Bygrave notes that in the work of the philosopher Thomas Reid, and subsequently in Samuel Taylor Coleridge's usage, '"egoism" comes to refer to a passive state – thinking about oneself, while "egotism" is expressive and active – talking about or asserting oneself: the morally ambivalent quality for the Romantics of Shakespeare's Edmund and Milton's Satan, or of historical figures such as Napoleon or Milton himself'.[4] For Coleridge, egoism is the greater sin, as it compounds a limiting and narcissistic self-interestedness, whereas egotism consists of agency and agenda. Wilson follows this understanding of the separable terms. For some Romantics though, what was fresh and liberating in the young minds of Coleridge and Wordsworth in the 1790s – the belief that they could write in epic grandeur about themselves – was gradually negated and so egotism was engendered with a pejorative meaning (though clearly this was not the case for John Wilson in 1835). The *OED* includes only negative instances of the word 'egotism': it defines it as '[t]he obtrusive or too frequent use of the pronoun of the first person singular' and as '[t]he vice of thinking too much of oneself; self-conceit, boastfulness; also selfishness'. It even provides a quote from the *Lectures on Shakespeare* by a fifty-eight-year-old Coleridge; by 1830 he was using the word to mean 'intense selfishness'. Even in one individual's usage, then, we can see how much the concept changes through the course of the Romantic period.

The Romantic writer who made the concept of 'egotism' his own, particularly as a tool for ambivalently belittling the poets of his day, was William Hazlitt. Perhaps most famously, in his first published assessment of Wordsworth, a review of *The Excursion*, Hazlitt writes:

> An intense intellectual egotism swallows up every thing. Even the dialogues introduced in the present volume are soliloquies of the same character, taking different views of the subject. The recluse, the pastor, and the pedlar, are three persons in one poet... If the inhabitants of the mountainous districts described by Mr. Wordsworth are less gross and sensual than others, they are more selfish. Their egotism becomes more concentrated, as they are more insulated, and their purposes more inveterate, as they have less competition to struggle with. The weight of matter which surrounds them, crushes the finer sympathies... Their physiognomy expresses the materialism of their character,

which has only one principle – rigid self-will... There is nothing which excites so little sympathy in our minds as exclusive selfishness.[5]

For Hazlitt, Wordsworth's ego devours everything he writes about, thus rendering into one self those individual figures who should have been imbued with discrete personalities. Egotism is synonymous with 'exclusive selfishness'. While Hazlitt is firmly committed to the popular opinion that Wordsworth 'has described the love of nature better than any other poet',[6] still the poet's reading of his chosen 'mountainous districts' becomes an exercise in imperious monomaniacal imposition of the self, of the writing subject, on everything and everyone he attempts to represent. Instead of a representation of society and landscape, we are given a chartered map of the poet's mind. And for Hazlitt, this just will not do, though as John Kinnaird rightly states, overall the review is 'generally favorable'.[7] In assessing another poet, Hazlitt constructs egotism as having been generated by wealth and privilege. He writes:

> Perhaps the chief cause of most of Lord Byron's errors is, that he is that anomaly in letters and in society, a Noble Poet. It is a double privilege, almost too much for humanity. He has all the pride of birth and genius. The strength of his imagination leads him to indulge in fantastic opinions; the elevation of his rank sets censure at defiance. He becomes a pampered egotist. He has a seat in the House of Lords, a niche in the Temple of Fame. Every-day mortals, opinions, things are not good enough for him to touch or think of.[8]

Hazlitt reads a direct relationship between Byron's elevated position in the social hierarchy and what he sees as Byron's imperious and self-interested poetic manner. In other words, the elevated class position allows the poet to ignore self-censure and to indulge himself in himself. In the same collection, Hazlitt mounts a somewhat unconvincing defence of his friend Coleridge:

> Mr. Coleridge talks of himself, without being an egotist, for in him the individual is always merged in the abstract and general.[9]

Clare might have agreed that the 'abstract and general' were predominant in Coleridge, though he found a practised staginess on meeting the elder writer: 'you woud suppose he had learnt what he intended to say before he came'.[10]

Although the essays in *The Spirit of the Age* were collected some four years after Keats's death and Hazlitt's key essay 'On Egotism' appeared even later in 1826,[11] we can trace the echoes of the earlier Hazlitt's direct influence on Keats in Hazlitt's characterisation of the Bard – whom he holds up as a stark contrast to Wordsworth: 'We do not think our author has any very cordial sympathy with Shakespear. How should he? Shakespear was the least of an egotist of any body in the world.'[12] While it is important for a contextualisation of Clare's theories on egotism to recall Keats's anti-egotistical construction of the ideal poet, it is sufficient for the present purpose to quote the following from the famous Keats letter of October 1818:

> As to the poetical Character itself, (I mean that sort of which, if I am any thing, I am a Member; that sort distinguished from the wordsworthian or egotistical sublime; which is a thing per se and stands alone) it is not itself – it has no self – it is every thing and nothing – It has no character – it enjoys light and shade; it lives in gusto, be it foul or fair, high or low, rich or poor, mean or elevated – It has as much delight in conceiving an Iago as an Imogen. What shocks the virtuous philosop[h]er, delights the camelion Poet...A Poet is the most unpoetical of any thing in existence; because he has no Identity – he is continually in for – and filling some other body – The Sun, the Moon, the Sea and Men and Women who are creatures of impulse are poetical and have about them an unchangeable attribute – the poet has none; no identity.[13]

Keats boldly advocates the necessary precondition of a negation of the self in order that a poet might create. He opposes this negation of self to Wordsworth's enhancing expansion of the self through creative expression. As I hope to show, Clare's writing theory was equally as radical and idiosyncratic as Keats's, though hardly as celebrated. The link between Hazlitt, Keats and Clare is palpable: all three writers were published by John Taylor and James Hessey. Keats and Clare never met, but they read each other's work[14]; both poets read and met Hazlitt. Clare's library contained four collections of Hazlitt's essays and all of Keats's published volumes. In journal entries for 22 and 23 October 1824, Clare mentions that he is reading Hazlitt's *Lectures on the English Poets* (1818) and that the author is 'one of the very best prose writers of his day'. Clare continues:

> his works are always entertaining and may be taken up when ever one chuses or feels the want of amusement – his political writings are heated and empty full of sound and fury – I hate polotics and therefore I may be but a poor judge.[15]

This was in 1824. In the 1830s, Clare lists Hazlitt's 'Liber Amoris a New Pygmalion' (as he calls it) as being worth '7/6'[16] (and this work is not in his extant library), either to sell or to purchase. By 1830, the key year for the discussion below, Clare is much more charged politically, though still maintaining a distaste for political tribalism and denying any direct involvement in public debate. The network linking Hazlitt, Keats and Clare is crucial in forging an understanding of Clare's developing theoretical thoughts, his problems with Romantic egotism, and crucial too in the formation of his unique ecological consciousness. I am now going to focus on just one instance, in a draft letter, of Clare's engaging with these issues of ego, of the writer's own subject position and of the political implications of the first-person singular. The letter offers the most pointed example of Clare's problems with the politics of writing style, and his consideration of the relationship of style to content.

Before we move to the letter, we need to establish the context in which it was written. The letter, to Clare's London friend Eliza Emmerson, exists now only as a draft written between March and April 1830; if this draft was ever copied from the notebook and sent, the finished letter is lost, as are many of Clare's posted letters to Emmerson. Since 7 February 1820 when Emmerson wrote a fan letter with an enclosed gift of Edward Young's *Night Thoughts*, she had been Clare's most dependable correspondent and an increasingly important source of advice, patronage and connection to London literary and moneyed society. From the extant letters we can glean a flirtatious dimension to their relationship, certainly, but as Emma Trehane has established, beyond the practical support Emmerson gave Clare and his family across a sustained period, she was a serious reader and thinker. In the early 1830s Emmerson was assisting Clare with what was to be his final lifetime book publication, the one that eventually dwindled down to the thin 1835 volume, yet whose title *The Rural Muse* was even coined by Emmerson. After a decade of visits and correspondence, by 1830 Emmerson was so trusted by Clare, so learned, well read and, crucially, offering such a 'rich appreciation for language',[17] as Trehane puts it, that she was the trusted sounding board for an effusive, digressive, experimental letter from Clare in which he theorises language and style. Clare takes playful risks in this letter because of the relaxed and confident relationship he had with the recipient, but also because he respected her wide reading and intellectual disposition.

This was not the best of years for the poet. His relationship with his former publisher was at a low ebb, John Taylor having decided to abandon publishing poetry altogether. Clare despaired at how little money he had received over the years from his initially successful publications; after Taylor settled accounts and all 'unpleasant business' with him at the end of 1829, Clare was able to think that 'the situation of booksellers is somthing like that of lawyers & that the mystery of a many of their Items appear rather more consistant to custom then to fair play'.[18] He was also regularly too ill to keep up with correspondence, and by July 1830 was being treated thoroughly for nervous and physical exhaustion, as he frequently complained, for example: 'I have been bled blistered & cupped & have now a seaton in my neck & tho much better I have many fears as to recovery ... & the seaton tho I cannot bear it to be dressed for 3 or 4 mornings together discharges so much that I fear that I shall fall into a decline at last'.[19] In this same letter to Taylor, the poet implies that the lull in correspondence is however the publisher's fault; he is anxious too about losing contact with James Hessey, poet and former *London Magazine* contributor George Darley, and the landscape artist Peter DeWint. Clearly, Clare feels as if he is being left out in the parochial cold, his last trip to London having been from February to March 1828. He stayed in Emmerson's home off Oxford Street throughout this visit, and Henry Behnes worked on a bust of the poet during this stay.[20] The literary social life Clare briefly enjoyed across the 1820s, especially in the early years of the decade, had dwindled by 1830 to just a thin trickle of letters. He was quite isolated from London, was destined never to visit again, and the *London Magazine* scene had long since dispersed. Emmerson was the one friend in the capital upon whom he could still fully rely.

Beyond the Self: 'I am Growing Out of Myself into Many Existences'

To analyse Clare's dense draft letter of March–April 1830, I will quote from it in small sections and discuss each in turn. It begins:

> Had I not recieved your letter to remind me of my errors I should not have been with you in the shape of a letter untill the day after tomorrow for I was indulging in the gossip you desired of me & wishing to make it more commendable by variety I determined to speak in parables & that in past moods & tenses for I am growing out of myself into many existences & wish to become more entertaining in other genders[21]

In this first part, it is clear that Clare is in experimental mode: he writes 'I am growing out of myself into many existences'. The individuated writing self is a limitation which creative rewriting, through play with ancient and sacred narrative techniques, allows him to dispel as a creating agent seeking 'variety'. To 'speak in parables' also positions Clare as a Christ-like subject, suggesting that if the intended audience is Emmerson, he can talk metaphorically because of her sophisticated literary understanding. He can also talk as a cod Christ because of her sustained sympathy for his world-view. What he actually says, though, is that he wishes 'to make [the gossip] more commendable by variety'. The juxtaposition of 'parable' and 'gossip' seems odd. If Clare adopts a biblical narrative strategy and is thus positioned as Christ, but is reduced in his communication with Emmerson to mere 'gossip', then are we perhaps to acknowledge the gulf between the capability of this story-teller and the force of the circumstance of an irksome patron–poet relationship? Or is it rather a nod to their long-standing friendship? Is the disjunction between chatty 'gossip' and moralising 'parable' suggestive of a writer's sigh: that sigh at the burden of his audience; the sigh of despair that nothing gets taken the right way because of the weakness, the vanities, of his audience, which by the 1830s was limited in the extreme? As Christ used parables to speak 'unto the multitude' (Matt 13.34), we can read by contrast the narrowness of Clare's own audience (reduced to one, in this letter), together with the fetters of his literary martyrdom: by 1830, in publishing terms he was in the wilderness. Or, as the narrator does not go on to adopt parabolic allegory in this letter, is the laconic diffidence of the biblical gesture a joke? Is the writer poking fun at his own vain aspirations, which aim at the narrative ability of God on earth?

Maybe Clare is being hard on himself; as it says in the 'Proverbs' of Solomon, 'As a thorn goeth up into the hand of a drunkard, so is a parable in the mouth of fools' (Pr 26:9). Is Clare constructing himself as a 'holy fool' or is he making a broader point about his own god-like position as author? He goes on to resist the notion of the 'I', that marker of an author's authority, in part because it becomes god-like. As I shall show, such a hierarchy is something Clare wants to resist, even at the expense of his own position as authorial god.

The parabolic technique he says will help him to avoid 'past moods & tenses'; possibly these are meant to be typical characteristics of direct or prosaic narration. The odd thing is that only a few parables in the King James version of the Bible are voiced in the present tense; to write or speak in biblical parable does not equate with use of the present tense.

Conceivably, without using 'past moods & tenses' he wishes to evoke Psalm 78: 'I will open my mouth in a parable: I will utter dark sayings of old'. If by 'dark' we can understand 'mysterious', 'remote' or 'secret', then we are next led to the most confusing, most fascinating moment of 'darkness' in this letter so far, when he writes 'I am growing out of myself into many existences & wish to become more entertaining in other genders'. I think we expect 'genre' here: together with his wide range in verse, Clare had experimented with writing in drama and novel forms. But the manuscript in which this letter appears is clear: 'gender' is clearly written in standard spelling and seems not to be a slip of the pen. The final wish in the above excerpt is either a deliberate confounding of meaning or a classic Freudian slip; there are few moments in Clare's work in which he plays with biological gender. We might look forward to his 1841 'Don Juan', wherein he writes:

> I have two wives & I should like to see them
> Both by my side before another hour
> If both are honest *I should like to be them*
> For both are fair & bonny as a flower [my emphasis][22]

It is in this poem that Clare positions himself most deliberately as a bigamist Christ figure: the 'two wives' he mentions above are Martha (his real wife Patty) and Mary (an idealised lover of his youth). Also we should consider that Clare often has female speakers for his poems and has women story-tellers and wise-women as controlling subjects of his narrative verse.[23] It is evident here that there was in Clare's writing theory a semi-Keatsian desire to free himself of the shackles of his physical subject position, to free himself from his 'place'. Does the desire for plurality of gender conflict with the intention to use parable? Parable forms a recognisable biblical genre. And it is a gender-specific genre: Christ and all church-authorised preachers after him up to Clare's day were male. Likewise, all those who speak in parables in the Bible, in Old and New Testaments, are male. Clare seems to want to write beyond the limitation of gendered genres, and this desire has both a theological and a political dimension.

Of course, Clare might not have understood 'biological' or 'socialised' gender by the term at all; perhaps 'gender' would have had the broader meaning of a 'class' or 'genus'. Certainly Clare knew about the grammatical genders (masculine, feminine and neuter) of other languages.

In summary, then, we are left with a puzzle, but one of potential and desire for gendered liberation of one kind or another, be it from class or category, sex or language style and structure. This aspect of the letter relates to, though is noticeably distinct from, Keats's assertion that the poet 'has no Identity – he is continually in for – and filling some other body'; Clare instead wants a plurality of identities. Rather than a Keatsian negation of an individuated self, or a Wordsworthian involuted celebration and expansion of self as the subject of epic contemplation, Clare instead wants a free plurality of 'existances', a multiplicity of free writing selves. And it is this desired process that he organically defines as a 'growing out of myself'.

In the letter, we now arrive at what I think is the critical prose instance of Clare's resistance to authorial egotism:

> for that little personal pronoun 'I' is such a presumption ambitious swaggering little fellow that he thinks himself qualified for all company all places & all employments   go where you will there he is swaggering & bouncing   in the pulpit the parliment the bench aye every where even in this my letter he has intruded 5 several times already   who can tell me where he is not or one of his family thats his brother or from how many pen points he is at this moment dropping into his ambitions on humble extances   he is a sort of Deity over the rest of the alphabet being here there & everywhere [at one & the same time]   he is a mighty vapour in grammer   he grows into a pedantical nuisance & often an O would be a truer personification in philosophy a juggling gossip in oratory a consequential blusterer & in fashion a pretender to every thing –

Clare's attack on the first-person pronoun covers lots of ground, and I think suggests how endemic Romantic egotism – Hazlitt's and Keats's term, not Clare's – had become across all walks of life. Clare does not mention poetry, but since he effectively critiques his own style as much as everyone else's, counting the number of times 'I' has encroached already, we can take it as read that his criticisms are aimed at poetical as well as prose voices. Anthropomorphising the 'I' allows Clare to swipe at preachers, politicians and lawyers in one swoop. He does not employ the word 'egotism' in this letter at all; but he does provide us with characteristics such as the 'I' thinking 'himself qualified for all companys all places & all employments', which are resonant of Hazlitt's understanding of egotism and the *OED*'s too: Clare is criticising '[t]he obtrusive or too frequent use of the pronoun of the first person singular'.[24]

In a parallel fashion, Percy Shelley regards pronouns as artificially divisive and argues that if we could see beyond the limits of linguistic individuation, we would experience a kind of transcendent unity:

> The words, *I, you, they* are not signs of any actual difference subsisting between the assemblages of thoughts thus indicated, but are merely marks employed to denote the different modifications of the one mind...The words *I*, and *you* and *they* are grammatical devices invented simply for arrangement and totally devoid of the intense and exclusive sense usually attached to them.[25]

Consideration of the first-person singular pronoun also leads Clare to discuss standard language practices in general. The use of the 'I' is as rigidly adhered to, and as irritating an encumbrance, as punctuation practice, or 'points' as Clare calls it. The letter continues:

> next to points this 'I' is the most consequential in correspondence but he surpasses points   he keeps his place but they ramble any where & change places as often as they change writers so that no two puts them in the same posts of honour – where one points with a colon another will afix a semi-colon & where another thrusts in a comma another will deprive him of his consequence & put nothing in his place showing that he was a nothing there   so much for the pomposity of gramarians but in such a place he cannot be ambitious – he is an absolute Paul Pry – I <therefore hope to get rid of his company for> wish there he is agen – for varietys sake the english language like some of the oriental ones had no present tense & to come at this variety was the very cause of my delay

As was the practice for many Romantic poets, educated and self-taught alike, for Clare punctuation was something better left for the presentational concerns of editors. On the reverse page of this letter in the notebook, in a famous passage from another draft letter, he is more acerbic: 'I am generally understood tho I do not use that awkward squad of pointings called commas colons semicolons &c & for the very reason that although they are drilled hourly daily & weekly by every boarding school Miss.'[26] Like Byron, Clare is fond of the dash – the long line indicating a syntactical break or a parenthetical digression – but, as he proudly declares, by and large he avoids standard punctuation. As Barbara M. H. Strang puts it supportively, in verse Clare 'writes in such a way that this troublesome device [punctuation] can be dispensed with'.[27] Though Clare is writing in an era of grammatical and orthographical prescription after the strenuous attempts at codification of the eighteenth century, punctuation was still to some degree in unsettled flux.[28] What is clear from this letter is that the rules of standardising grammarians seemed 'pompous' to Clare; this word has class dimensions, in as much as it signifies an elevated sense of self-importance and pretentiousness. 'Pomposity' seems to link with the overall assessment in this letter of egotistical writing; it might normally be an innocuous word, but in context it seems charged with all the class resentment that we can find in other works of Clare around the same time.

I have already suggested that 1830 was not the best year for the poet. For rural life all around Clare and across the midlands, East Anglia and the south, it was a time of tension and even bursts of political agitation. E. J. Hobsbawm and George Rudé summarise the context in which Clare wrote, specifically from the perspective of the rural labourer:

> What sort of year was 1830? As the labourers saw it, it was first and foremost the year that followed one of the hardest periods in their appalling history... The harvest of 1828 was poor, though the winter was mild; the harvest of 1829 was worse, and not gathered in until the snow was already on the barn in early October. Eighteen-twenty-nine was... an entirely disastrous year, as bad... as 1817. The labourers must have faced the spring of 1830 with the memory of cold, hunger and unemployment.[29]

From soapboxes local politicians filled the masses with a desire for political change, while violent outbreaks of agitation among rural labourers tore across the south and midlands of England in the latter months of 1830 – including in villages close to Helpston.[30] Workhouses, threshing machines and wealthy landowners were targeted. Clare published political poems in response in local newspapers, as John Lucas and Alan Vardy have discussed.[31] But it is specifically Clare's disgruntlement with, and distrust of, political self-interestedness that is pertinent here. Even in the early 1820s when Clare was writing his lengthy heroic-couplet satire *The Parish*, the self-interest of local politicians enraged him: 'Thus village politics – and hopes for pelf/Live in one word and centre all in "self."'[32] Self-centredness was always a bugbear for Clare, and made him wary of groupthink of all kinds, across the whole developing political spectrum (his approach to politics is discussed further below).

What could Clare mean though by his wish that 'the English language like some of the oriental ones had no present tense'? He could have been referring to any one of a number of languages east of Europe: Chinese, Arabic and Hebrew have no present tense as English users might think of it. What they have instead are more like aspects (completed and uncompleted actions). Arabic and Hebrew also avoid the verb 'to be' altogether in the situations where English speakers most use it. Arabic has sixteen moods instead of tenses. Also of note is that many languages which Clare might have thought of as constituting the 'orient' *very* rarely use the first-person subject pronoun. Where Clare received his knowledge of languages of the east is difficult to discern, but by 1830 the ideas of orientalists and linguists like William Jones were in wide circulation.[33] Clare also read contemporary writers engaged in the mythology and philosophies of the east, particularly of India, such as Coleridge, Southey, Byron, Percy Shelley and De Quincey. But his use of the word 'oriental' might have a more general, subtextual meaning in the context of this letter, with its concerns about the implementation of the self in writing: as John James Clarke points out, in the hands of orientalists the East offered '... the idea that the self is not given by nature, but constructed, not stable and permanent but painfully fractured'.[34] It is exactly that instability, artifice and impermanence that Clare seeks for his poetic self's 'growing'. In the light too of his resistance to the organisers of organised religion (revealed especially in *The Parish*), it could be that Clare is suggesting that the Judaeo-Christian tradition has its limits, and that he might have to look to other theological traditions, to other languages, to experience creative freedom. From the start of his writing career he seems to have been enabled in part through resisting the trammels and orthodoxies of the Anglican church[35]; equally, village Sunday customs seem to have made him feel ill at ease about writing. In the essay 'My First Attempts at Poetry' he writes:

> I went on writing my thoughts down and correcting them at leisure spending my sundays in the woods or heaths to be alone for that purpose and I got a bad name among the weekly church goers forsaking the 'church going bell' and seeking the religion of the fields tho I did it for no dislike to church for I felt uncomfortable very often but my heart burnt over the pleasures of solitude and the restless revels of ryhme that was eternaly sapping my memorys like the summer sun over the tinkling brook... tho I was not known as a poet my odd habits did not escape notice[36]

Writing this essay for Taylor with the anticipation of polite publication, Clare is careful not to upset his audience, neither the intrusive Sunday villagers nor the urban middle classes, but he is determined nevertheless to pursue the 'religion of the fields'. In a subtle way, the act of writing poetry is constructed as resistance to both social organisation and to ordinary routine human behaviour. Poetry becomes the freedom to access a natural world far from what should in orthodox terms be Clare's place, on a pew, in St Botolph's, in Helpston. His subtle resistance to customary religion is more aggressively conveyed in *The Parish* of the early 1820s, which remained unpublished in his lifetime. Of the 'tribe' of church-going parishioners he writes:

> While half the tribes at bottom are no more
> Then saints skin deep and devils at the core
> Who act by customs and as custom shows
> Lay bye religion with their sunday cloaths.[37]

In the manuscript of this draft letter to Emmerson, which occupies one-and-a-third pages of the large notebook, appear draft versions of an essay entitled 'Apology for the Poor'. While the editors of *By Himself* present it in a relatively coherent form,[38] in manuscript the essay appears as a sporadic, disjointed set of draft notes. It seems to have been written for publication, but whether or not it was published in a local newspaper is not known. One of its main concerns is to expose the self-interestedness of political agitators, such as in the following extract, which appears directly opposite the letter at the centre of our attention, written with what looks like the same pen and ink:

> I never meddle with politics in fact you would laugh at my idea of that branch of art for I consider it nothing more or less than a game at hide & seek for self interest & the terms wig & tory are nothing more or less in my mind than the left & right hand of that monster [indecipherable word] for self interest then the other – that there are [blank space] some & many who have the good of the people at heart is not to be doubted but with the others who have only the good of themselves in view when balloted I fear that they will always be the few.[39]

Hazlitt's, and then Keats's, idealised notion of a complete annihilation of the self for poetical creation develops into a political ideal for Clare in

1830. The only answer to his political worries seems to have been to advocate a complete, idealistically artificial, lack of self-interestedness: to remove the 'I' from political discourse. Most importantly, it is clear that he wants to effect a change in language to enable concrete social changes for the poor. As discussed above, by 1830 Coleridge was using 'egotism' to mean not an ideally self-conscious and self-aware writing style, but instead 'intense selfishness'. What early Romantic writers had unwittingly enabled and legitimised was the use of the self, the explicit writing subject, as a rhetorical and political tool, a device which, in Clare's eyes, could mask self-interestedness. He saw a connection too between the increasing acceptance of the oppressive strictures of standardised linguistic practices and political hypocrisy and tyranny, and this link is more than mere analogy. His desire to write in other genders, in other voices, in other traditions, even in other tense-free languages, is indicative of a poet who feels trapped by social circumstance, his audience and a stifling and stylised contemporary discourse; and of a poet who feels stymied by an emplaced subject position and the modes available to him for free expression, beyond the confined self. At the core Clare feels the limitations of his own subject position, dictated to by that pompous deity of style, the first-person singular subject pronoun. He imagines a whole gamut of enlivening tactics of resistance, many of which he seems never to have pursued.

Clare's resistance to egotism should be central to forging an understanding of him as a proto-environmentalist, or as an ecological poet. The critique of egotism in this letter amounts to a theorisation of the ways in which his 'vision' of the natural world can be anti-anthropocentric; the critique is an attempt to bring into question the centring of discourse on the human individual. This might mean that Clare's position is quite extreme, even in contemporary terms. Influential ecocritic Kate Soper thinks that '[a]ll the "parties of nature" need to recognize ... the element of human self-interest that underlies their preservationist concerns',[40] yet that is one of the specific elements of discourse that Clare wants to critique. Similarly from an environmentalist's position, Jonathan Bate writes that 'what the life and work of John Clare can show us is that even in terms of pragmatic self-interest it is to our benefit to care for nature's rights – our inner ecology cannot be sustained without the health of ecosystems'.[41] I would suggest that Clare systematically argued along different lines that make him more akin to ecologism rather than the environmentalism that Bate suggests is the lesson the poet offers. For theorists of green political positions, there is a clear distinction between the human-centred pragmatism of environmentalism – which seeks to manage and moderate human impact on nature, because not to do so would be against human interests – and ecologism – which works to shift the self and human subjectivity ethically onto broader, anti-anthropocentric, ecocentric moral conceptions of the value of all natural things and processes.[42]

This letter offers evidence that for Clare, self-interest was precisely what damaged man's relationship with his fellow man and, by extension through his poetic practice, with nature. For Clare, egotism and self-interest are antithetical to both social equality and what we might now regard as his proto-ecologism. Central to current understandings of ecologism is a critique of anthropocentrism.[43] So if Clare is more hesitant to put himself in the frame than his contemporaries, perhaps it is not, as John Wilson would have it, simply because he is humble before his audience and aware of his social place; rather, it may be the radicalising act of an ecologically aware social leveller who questions the placing of humanity in a hierarchy above all other beings and natural processes.

In Clare's vision trees, animals, grasses, flowers can all have a song without the poet's presence; this distinguishes Clare quite markedly from his contemporary Romantic poets. When Percy Shelley goes to Mont Blanc and fills the unbearable vacancy with the 'human mind's imaginings',[44] he is admitting that man is at the centre of his perspective and concerns and that humanity provides nature with meaning, if interrogatively so. Clare, on the other hand, does not need to make his hunted badger or his singing nightingale into metaphors for humankind. Nor does nature seem to need his voice – and this decentring distinguishes him from all of the major Romantic poets. Our anthropocentric impulse is a legacy of post-Romantic egotism. Students trained in the seeking of literary metaphor and analogy often assume, on encountering Clare for the first time, that a poem can only be interesting if it is actually, *really* about the human: about Clare and his critics, or Clare as a poet, or how humans should preserve nature, or more broadly about the human condition. Clare is odd in that a poem about a badger, a nightingale, a tree or a weed might 'just' be about those flora and fauna in and of themselves; and this constitutes more than a gesture towards ecocentricity.[45] For the most part without explicitly moralising, Clare manages to *dehumanise* nature: in Clare's world ecosystems can work without the presence of man. Of course Clare personifies nature, anthropomorphises natural beings and the landscape at times, and he relates things natural to things human in order to understand and convey them; certainly, he writes about himself and his lyrical subject position in self-reflexive poems where the first-person singular is the platform of consideration – Clare can be self-obsessed as a poet (and a letter writer too). His most famous poem is, after all, 'I Am' (though it is hardly a statement of secure or assertive identity). But rarely does Clare position himself *above* the natural world in any way: even in 'I Am' he is level with the grass, down low and supine, looking skyward.

As we will see in the analysis that follows, in his poetic structures Clare can model what we might consider to be the position of a modern ecologist, ideologically speaking; if, that is, we are to accept that fundamentally modern ecologism is based on an assertion that 'human beings are part of a more complex system and no longer sit at the top of the ethical hierarchy', as Mark J. Smith conceives of it.[46] Clare's awareness of 'green' landscape (which in his pluralising vision can be many other colours) is a 'poetics of process', as Tom Paulin insightfully described it.[47] It always tends to offer a possibility that humanity can be an integral part of nature, though more often than not Clare implies that it should remain respectfully separate. In other words, man is not the god of nature, just as the 'I' should not necessarily be the 'Deity over the rest of the alphabet'. Clare's resistance to egotism in the 1830 letter is a political act of creative defiance which seeks to dispel the arrogant 'I' and become all 'eye': the pure observer, the social, pluralising poetic spirit who tries not to disturb the green life it encounters on its passage through the landscape. I am not suggesting that Clare achieves this, or that he is consistent even in the attempt – not at all. Instead, I am suggesting that what we can readily call an idealising 'eco-centric' intention constitutes Clare's aspirations as a mature poet of the early 1830s. As we will see below, the poetic practices that emerge from ego-resistant writing, and idealistic levelling, are complex structurally and lead to qualities in Clare's poetry that are quite distinct.

Poetic Structures of Ecocentricity and Green Textual Politics

Above, we considered briefly Clare's life-long distrust of the grandstanding of political positions. If we are to approach Clare as a proto-ecological thinker, his politics need some further consideration. If Clare delivers a clarion call of the beginnings of 'green' thought – a politicised colour that would have been entirely unknown to him, of course – the outlines of his politics cannot so straightforwardly be coloured red or blue, though many of his most significant promoters have attempted to do precisely that. It is true that Clare honed sharp resentments against the corruption of entrenched social hierarchies, capitalist greed, self-righteous elitism and individualistic self-promotion (some of which is indicated above). But equally, Clare was nervous about 'radical' movements which peppered – and sometimes disrupted – rural and national affairs. In the next chapter we will consider the politics of the editorial projects that have shaped Clare in the twentieth and twenty-first centuries. In the remaining part of this chapter, we will consider the politics and ethics that inform Clare's aesthetics. Extending from the theorisation analysed above, here we will focus on the Northborough-period sonnet 'The shepherds almost wonder where they dwell'. This poem delivers upon Clare's desire – in relation to the 'I' – to 'get rid of his company' altogether and to develop an ecocentric aesthetic of interconnectivity.

If the poet's role had been broadly idealised in the eighteenth century as that of a gentleman pursuing a literary hobby, ideally in the care of a good patron, by the 1820s it was transforming into a professional career, much to the distaste of anyone with eighteenth-century tastes and a patron's wealth, such as Byron. Clare was therefore unfortunate in being in continual and desperate need of financial assistance at a time when patronage was becoming unfashionable. A relatively threadbare form of patronage is what he received; as many critics have suggested, perhaps the limitation on his money was designed to keep his *genius loci* fixed in its original social and geographical place. Nevertheless, while Clare resented the genuflecting and pandering central to the process of courting power, the necessary moderation and qualification of his precarious political subjectivity must have given some steer to the politics of his poetic voice overall. Even if Clare is determined to satirise all manner of corrupting social ills from what we today might want simplistically to call a 'left' position, he also writes solidly celebratory poems about king and country, military victory and heroes, and writes against popular radicalism.[48] While such works might seem formulaic and relatively hollow in comparison to other elements of his work which attract more serious critical treatment, they must be included in any assessment or summary of Clare's political colour. There is indeed evidence to support Richard Heath's notorious characterisation of Clare in his survey *The English Peasant* of 1893:

> With a love for his native scenes, capable of being developed into the intensest patriotism, with a love of old customs and old institutions – in fact, a Conservative by nature – he is driven to cry –
> O England! boasted land of liberty.[49]

This conservative reading of Clare at the end of the nineteenth century was by no means dominant subsequent to Heath's claim. The relatively apolitical approaches of scholar-poets and editors such as Arthur Symons, Edmund Blunden and Geoffrey Grigson were gradually replaced in the 1960s to 1980s by a more openly leftist accommodation of Clare's work, notably by Raymond Williams and E. P. Thompson. Following in this line are important responses to Clare from the likes of John Lucas and Roger Sales, who continued to claim Clare for a loosely left-leaning agenda.[50] There have been more centrist and conservative takes on the poet, most usefully by Paul Dawson,[51] though the dominant critical current reads Clare as having a more politically nuanced and multifarious set of mobile positions – Zachary Leader and Alan Vardy's work is central here.[52]

Yet it remains unsurprising that Clare is a central part of Jonathan Bate's determination to switch the colour of our general literary critical lens from red to green, which he followed up purposefully with his influential biography and a selection of Clare's work.[53] Since Bate's *Romantic Ecology*, Romantic-period ecocriticism has argued that the relationship between red and green could be less oppositional. For Karl Kroeber, green politics does not have to *replace* red, but can work symbiotically. Adopting an unashamedly Romantic critical position in his attack on high theory and new historicism, Kroeber sees critical oppositionalism as being the unfortunate and politicised product of a cold-war mindset. For Kroeber, history and nature, historicising criticism and aesthetic green readings, should go hand in hand in the pursuit of a complicating and energising understanding of the literature of the natural world. This process, he claims, would enable 'us to interact in a responsible manner with our environment'.[54] Kroeber's idealising version of Romanticism is unapologetically canonical and so he ignores Clare. Nevertheless, he is provocative. His critique of entrenched oppositionist critical positions should give us pause when considering the critical world of Clare studies, which, as I will discuss in the next chapter, is coping with its own – often tacit – legacy of embattled critical positions and politically informed editorial approaches.

Clare himself, of course, made no reference to the set of opposing British political wings which we now deploy freely – blue, red or green – and which for him, as a political spectrum running left to right, would only recently have developed out of the model of the National Assembly in Paris. He was consistently resistant to any large-scale political affiliation. In the key year of 1830 discussed above, for example, in a political poem where the central resistance is to 'self interest', 'cant', sycophancy and hypocrisy, Clare writes:

> Im neither wig nor tory clean
>   To swear knaves act uprightly
> But just a water mark between
>   That skims opinions lightly
> I guess nones got their game to seek
>   With all their raving bother
> & one thing both will often speak
>   & as often mean another[55]

This sort of cynicism about all political agitation is a constant in Clare's works when politics surface explicitly, so the discerning of a codified set of rigid commitments from him is a project to be treated with caution. Yet we can say that as a natural historian, and as a nostalgic elegist for times past and worlds lost, there was plenty he wanted to *conserve*, and lots of cultural as well as natural forms he thought might be, or were already, lost forever without active efforts of *conservation* (though again, this is not a term Clare used). But as a working-class critic of human activity and social structure, there was much he would like to have changed, and much he thought should change. Not radically, not violently and ostensibly not at the macro level of the state; still, the sheer amount of protest in Clare's work overall – especially about poverty – means we have at least to accept him broadly as an agitator for progress and change.

As evidence of Clare's radicalism, many critics have turned to the famous response of his patron, the Tory Lord Radstock, who bridled at what he called Clare's 'radical Slang' – though Robert Heyes is certain that the actual penmanship of the extant marginal comment in Clare's fair manuscript was Taylor's rather than Radstock's. Taylor was passing on a comment that Radstock had made, both in a letter and, perhaps, on another manuscript. Taylor's own opinion of Radstock's meddling, even as he passed it on, was clear: '... in The Peasant Boy, Lord R. has put his Mark "This is Radical Slang" against 2 of the best Stanzas ... I think we must not compliment Lord R. with a Sonnet'.[56] Taylor was caught in the middle, but clearly siding with Clare and offering ways of resisting supine cap-doffing passivity in the face of the excessive intrusions of old-fashioned patronage. In his compelling account of Radstock, Roger

Sales surmises that the patron 'combined his obsessive crusade against radicalism with philanthropic concern for the poor', but was also 'a bully and an interfering busybody'.[57] But just because Radstock was so committed and clear in political terms does not mean that Clare was too – nor does it mean that Clare stands in clear and constant opposition to Radstock's positions. As Sam Ward has pointed out in his analysis of Clare and the Queen Caroline affair, 'political allegiances in this period were seldom as clearly defined as ideologues such as Radstock desired them to be'.[58] On balance, it is a testament to the precarious line that Clare and his liberally minded publisher John Taylor walked that Radstock did *not* withdraw his patronage, but maintained a supportive interest until he died in 1825, an interest that was to be materially and socially significant for Clare, which even Sales admits. Clare's publications *were* altered – censored even – at the behest of Radstock, but the relationship carried on, Clare continued as a publishing poet and Taylor maintained faith, even if publishing Clare with burdensome patrons meant managing an act of diplomacy for the risk-taking publisher.

Clare's political lubricity can be summarised by the following symptomatic example: one of the stanzas of 'The Village Minstrel' to which Radstock objected in the 1820s is the same one quoted by Richard Heath above, in support of his claim in the 1890s that Clare was uncomplicatedly Conservative. If nothing else definitive emerges from the 'radical Slang' episode, it is apparent that – in conjunction with his risk-taking editors – Clare played a pretty sophisticated political game. He might well have been 'neither wig nor tory', but in the turbulent 1820s he did little to trouble either camp. This strategy kept his options as open as they could be and secured some level of independence, given the severe constrictions of his social place.

However, social limits on Clare did not simply carry through in an unaltered fashion into the deep structures of his verse. Of course, many critics before now have implied that the poet's politics rest not just in what he says, but in how he says it. The most radical Clare is embedded in the latent structures of his poetry – and, as I hope to show, this root-level politicisation is almost anarchic in its levelling of hierarchies and squarely 'green' (in our contemporary sense) in its purposeful rendering of decentred interconnection. Below, I will suggest that Clare's poetic tendency to build levelling connections – applied to human life and natural life without recourse to the staple division of humankind from nature – is radical, because it posits a root-level sociality between all subjects and bodies in the material world. Radical stems from the Latin *radix*, the roots of a plant, the origin, base or source. The argument will further contend that society, for Clare, does not imply the workings of a world of humanity alone; instead, society for Clare is forged in relationships with other beings, processes and bodies, and is based on interconnection, intra-species relation and the dynamic processing of mutualities.

There is nothing particularly new in finding such structures in Clare's work. For John Barrell, Clare's vision delivers a natural simultaneity and resists the ordered linearity of eighteenth-century landscape art and poetry. Clare resists existing models through connectivity, and at the grammatical level Barrell tracks a resistance to syntactical subordination, enabling Clare to deliver a scene all at once, with no element necessarily taking precedence. To Barrell, this structural framework reflects Clare's 'open-field sense of space',[59] which resists the clipped linearity of post-enclosure landscape. In an open-field landscape, the 'field would thus present itself to the observer as a scene of continuous and simultaneous activity, carried on in all parts of the field yet visible "at a glance", and in which almost the entire village was engaged'.[60] For Barrell, Clare's engagement with locality, with the tight Helpston environs, is also a resistance to the 'ideology of enclosure, which sought to de-localize, to take away the individuality of a place'.[61] Barrell interlocks readings of Clare's resistance to existing aesthetic models, grammatical subordination and the parcelling lines of enclosure. The approach of the present chapter is similarly to locate meaning through the structure of Clare's work, and to extend Barrell's establishment of the relation between land and line into a green social connectivity. The establishing of connection and co-ordination between humans and nature; the narrowing of the space between definitions of culture and nature, human and environment; the resisting of anthropocentrism and subordination of the natural world to human needs – all of these ongoing intentions are central to the ethical promise of ecocriticism. And they emerge out of the following reading of a Clare sonnet.

Before we get to the poem in isolation, it is worth considering the manuscript context in which it appears: context in terms of the writer's location and environment, the date and time of year and the paper on which the poem is written. The title-less poem in question has the first line 'The shepherds almost wonder where they dwell' (hereafter, 'The shepherds...'). It is one of many sonnets written between 1832 and 1837, when Clare was living with his family at Northborough, a village just four miles' walk north-east of Helpston. Northborough is not far away, yet is closer to the Fens and so – as Simon J. White has pointed out[62] – sits in a more open, lower (in terms of height above sea level) and certainly flatter landscape. Carrying on beyond Northborough, in the same direction north-east for thirty miles or so, would take you across Fenland to the huge bay called The Wash.

The dating of this particular poem might be made more precise if we follow the 10 November 1835 date offered by a draft letter written in the same run of pages, in the fascicles of papers in Peterborough manuscript A61.[63] November is the month mentioned in 'The shepherds...' and is the implied season of the sonnet 'I love to hear the evening crows go bye'[64] written on the same page, because this is roughly the time of year when British starlings (Clare's 'starnels') are likely to group into large roosts and the famous murmurations, in the poem's words, 'darken down the sky'.[65]

Before we get to the poem 'The shepherds...' on its own terms, we have work to do on the poetic context in which this sonnet appears, and this is not quite as straightforward as simply following the immediate manuscript context. The particular type of paper on which 'The shepherds...' appears is very distinct, and thirty-two other poems,[66] fragments and the 10 November dated draft letter appear on this same paper (the Oxford editors choose either to present fragments separately or else move them to be integral parts of other poems[67]). It is good-quality, thick paper, of 'small post quarto' size, a standard and fairly wide shape of cut writing paper of the time (roughly 7 inches by 9 inches). The handwriting and ink used on this type of paper in manuscript A61 are very similar. It appears that 'The shepherds...' was written in conjunction with this specific gathering of sonnets. But, other than the four wasp sonnets mentioned above and – possibly, though not conclusively – a collection of sonnets focused on shouting maids, lines written on the same kind of paper as 'The shepherds...' in A61 do not form any sort of narrative pattern. Yet there is a discernible network of thematic and structural commonalities which I will trace now, the significance of which will become more apparent when we focus in on just 'The shepherds...'.[68] These pages are dispersed across the setting of sheets in the six A61 fascicle books, something which might have happened rather arbitrarily, especially if the archivist doing the original preservation work was faced with a mountain of loose sheets in no particular order or binding.[69] If Clare did write these thirty-two poems on this same paper at around the same time, as seems likely, the manuscript fascicle setting has ruptured the relationships between them. The Oxford edition has replicated that rupture by following the order of the poems as they have been set in manuscript. So I will now treat these thirty-two poems of November 1835 discretely as the tightest creative context in which 'The shepherds...' was composed. Part of the reason to do so is that following John Barrell's lead, critics such as Joseph Phelan have assumed a structural arbitrariness both within these Northborough-period sonnets themselves, but also thematically across the sonnets.[70] The intention here is to determine the thematics of the specific manuscript context of 'The shepherds...' and to look across a specific gathering of the sonnets, to better inform the close reading of that singular poem and to throw light upon the structural integrity of the patterns uncovered within it.

The thirty-two sonnets written on the small post quarto paper in manuscript A61 range across a dynamic and wide community of animals, birds and people mostly at work: ploughmen, milkmaids, cowboys, shepherds, hunters. The poems amount to rich evidence that John Goodridge is right to explore at length Clare's 'capacity to represent a communitarian tradition'.[71] For all the active, communal and mostly content husbandry and labour, there also appear travellers and isolated, seemingly homeless figures, who are busy nonetheless, with active survival in exposed conditions, or with drinking too much and alienating all. These poems also reconfirm Goodridge's reading of a productive dichotomy in Clare, between the sociable and the isolated.[72] The weather in these sonnets is persistently wintery (with a clear exception being the 'wasp' series) – with mists, floods, frosts, snow and freezing temperatures. And these sonnets tend to move through active sociability towards evening, towards dinner, towards bed: a returning father is welcomed on his return from work by food and children; a shepherd guides his sheep back home; a meal is lubricated by drink and drawn to a close by song and tale; a robin nestles down for the night in a cows' shed.

Even when a poem seems not to be a part of this presentation of communal and relational rural activity, its specific manuscript context tends to bring it into the fold of these poems. For example, a uniquely haunting poem (first line 'There is a place scarce known that well may claim') about a neglected burial site of French prisoners of war appears on the same page in manuscript with a poem (first line 'There is a place scarce known that well may claim') about a 'fowler' with a 'gun of monstrous length' who hunts 'the watery fen' and enacts 'vast slaughter'. While lucky birds in the latter poem 'fly far distant from the haunts of men' at the end, the 'frenchmen' in the former are not so lucky: 'england was their prison & their graves'.[73] The poems serve as a chilling counterpoint to one another. Sarah Houghton-Walker rightly says that the Northborough sonnets are 'distinguished by their factual observation and lack of judgement'.[74] Sure enough, here the neutral narrator of each poem offers scant moral direction over either scenario. Yet the sense that a murderous military conflict buried in the landscape is set out by Clare in part to reflect an ongoing 'vast slaughter' of birds is made clear by their collocation on the same page in the manuscript. In both poems human figures are incorporated as much into a dynamic landscape in process – albeit with distracting and mortal results – as they are in a poem about a village settling down to bed for the night, or one where 'maidens' are chatting after finishing their work milking, or another where everyone, and everywhere, is flooded.[75]

These poems explicitly mention 'labour' and its derivatives. The perspective of the narrator is often detached enough to talk about labour in quite an abstracted if still tangible manner, as in the following examples:

> Tis late the labouring men come dropping in
>
> Thus labour closes at the close of day
> & all the working tools are put away
>
> Labour fled home & rivers hurried bye
> & still it felt as it would never stop
>
> The reeking supper waits the labourer home
> Who daily goes to labour far away
>
> He labours hard & never lacks a job
> & owns a descent suit & nothing more[76]

The appearance of labour in this manner makes of it a process of communal and common activity that is almost always shared: labour is reliant on others for its proper operation, and if it is to be endured through frequently hard conditions. Labour operates as a collective noun for labourers too. Yet labour can also be isolating. The poem 'He never knew a book & never bought',[77] from which the final quotation above is taken, amounts to a subtle critique of someone who does not engage in communal relations at all, is 'stubborn' and 'never heeds discourse', and is essentially and miserably self-isolated. Here, the narrator is far from neutral in his judgement of this selfish man. The final two words of this poem are 'nothing more': there is nothing more beyond this individual – he extends nowhere – and can be fitted completely into this tight sonnet form, just as he squeezes everything he owns – 'his little store' – into his pocket and his fob. This diminished, pinched, arrogant man does not connect with anything other than hard work – no community, no thought, no love – and there are no bonds extended from or towards him of any kind. No animals are mentioned, no friends, no family. He embodies meaningless disconnection. He negates knowledge of anything, Clare masterfully, negatively punning on 'no' and 'know' here[78]: '& scarcely knowing nothing thinks he knows/More then the very wisest in his way'. Clare positions him deliberately in this sequence as a point of opposition to the communality of poems like 'The shepherds...' that follows, a poem in which connection is everything.

Like many sonnets in this run of thirty-two, that which appears right above 'The shepherds...' on the same page – 'I love to hear the evening crows go bye' – is highly populated: crows, starnels, sparrows, pigeons, hawks, 'stranger birds', robins, a maiden, a boy and cows all fly past in this dense sonnet of seven couplets:

> I love to hear the evening crows go bye
> & see the starnels darken down the sky
> The bleaching stack the bustling sparrow leaves
> & plops with merry note beneath the eaves
> The odd & lated pigeon bounces bye
> As if a wary watching hawk was nigh
> While far & fearing nothing high & slow
> The stranger birds to distant places go
> While short of flight the evening robin comes
> To watch the maiden sweeping out the crumbs
> Nor fears the idle shout of passing boy
> But pecks about the door & sings for joy
> Then in the hovel where the cows are fed
> Finds till the morning comes a pleasant bed[79]

While the opening octave of couplets is given over to a wide population of named and 'stranger birds', the final sestet of couplets focuses upon the more domestic nestling of the territorial robin. The listening of the narrator switches to the robin who watches the maiden at her close-of-day work, comprehends the lack of threat in the boy's noise and participates fully in an intimate domestic scene. Finally, the robin – the perfect embodiment of that busy and independent Clarean 'joy' – seeks further communal comfort for the night in the cows' accommodation. Populous, shared, crowded, busy and dynamic: guaranteed by that initial 'I love to hear', this is to be a comfortable – and comforting – sonnet of uncomplicated, unknowing rural connection and communion.

On the same page, just below 'I love to hear the evening crows go bye', appears this text of 'The shepherds...', Clare's handwritten presentation of which opens up some problems:

> The shepherds almost wonder where they dwell
> & the old dog for his night journey stares
> The path leads somewhere but they cannot tell
> & neighbour meets with neighbour unawares
> The maiden passes close beside her cow
> & wonders on & think her far away
> The ploughman goes unseen behind his plough
> & seems to loose his horses half the day[80]
>   The lazy morning wakens up a mist
>   The place we occupy seems all the world

> The lazy mist creeps on in journey slow
> The maidens shout & wonder where they go
> So dull & dark are the november days
> The lazy mist high up the evening curled
> & now the morn quite hides in smokey haze
> The place we occupy seems all the world

As my transcription of this poem approximating its layout in manuscript shows, 'The shepherds...' begs an interpretation that needs firstly to assume that there is a drafting process on offer here, not a completely finished text; this means that interpretation is needed to produce a 'reading text'. In the particular case of 'The shepherds...', the supplanting of some lines over others is required – if, that is, we are in pursuit of a straightforwardly tidy sonnet. Yet the manuscript page reveals just how insecure must remain this stage of text formation, if it wants to move beyond Clare's handwritten words. The manuscript shows how the proportions of the page might have informed the composition, as the poet reached the bottom edge and so turned the paper ninety degrees to write vertically – transversally – in the relatively fat margins of this relatively squarer page shape. This switch of writing direction forces a pause – and an apparent (if not certain, for us) rewriting – of the two potent last lines of the horizontal block of script. And this switch in turn means that 'The place we occupy seems all the world' (the crucial line of the poem, as will become apparent) in fact appears twice on the page, across two different textual planes: it 'occupies' two places, running horizontally and vertically. The first appearance of the repeated line is not indicated for deletion with a through line, though the two final lines of horizontal writing are indented and written in a slightly lighter hand (suggesting some kind of pause, a shift in pen or alteration in the composition somehow). An editor has to work out whether the repetition of the line beginning 'The place we occupy...' works, or whether the poem coheres only if those two indented lines are written out, leaving fourteen lines of a fairly coherent and separable sonnet, when the six marginal, vertical lines are bolted on to the first eight. This latter option is taken by the Oxford editors – and with solid and informed justification, not least because the end result is a potent and coherent poem indeed. Still, it is important to note that the coherent sonnet is the end product of a keen and interventive method of editorial interpretation and reconstruction. What is produced in the end, and in print, is not precisely the same text that appears in Clare's manuscript (though the Oxford editors meticulously provide notes illustrating what they have decided to do with the manuscript version: their choices are made evident).

Any editor of such a text is in an impossible bind: there is no 'purely' textually primitivistic way to reproduce such a sonnet with its repetition, and transversal writing, in transcribed print with its host of conventions – horizontal text being just one – unless we elide the evident compositional process and the textual direction change only available in the sole extant handwritten version. The unfinishable, provisional nature of such poems – the holographical fact that so many of Clare's poems seem to be held in process and never quite finalised for print – is something all textual critics either wrestle with or ignore and so rely on the printed versions. But such manuscript complexities offer a wealth of opportunities for critical interpretation, albeit interpretation built upon possibility rather than certainty; upon quizzical and relativising deferral rather than concrete definition; upon a networked, developing comprehension of relations and connections between poems (thematic, material, historical...) rather than localising and singularly fixed-text determinations; upon text in process rather than text as finished product. This kind of exploratory journey is not everyone's cup of tea, especially when it comes to editing – because traditional printed editions almost always require a finalised, reliable text of some kind and in no small part it is what readers want (the editing of Clare is a focus of the next chapter). Wilfully eschewing the determination of a final and steady textual base editorially can seem destabilising, deracinating and discombobulating in the lack of a centre or of a final, closing textual authority. But I would advocate – and hope to demonstrate – that precisely this textually critical approach is enabled by Clare's texts themselves – *required* by them, almost – and most evidently so in the succession of sonnet forms he composed at Northborough, one of which I will focus on below. Early on in his editing project, Robinson became aware that '[i]n Clare's manuscripts the poems are intertwined in a way that it is impossible to present except through a facsimile edition'.[81] The example we are considering here is a perfect case in point.

The Mystery of Mist: Ampersands and Rhizomes

After the last line of 'I love to hear the evening crows go bye' there is a space in the manuscript and 'The shepherds...' begins. Initially it appears that the setting is that same 'night' with which 'I love to hear...' ends, in which the robin sleeps with the cows. But appearances in 'The shepherds...' are to be deceived from the outset. For clarity, I now quote what might fairly be called the 'reading text'[82] offered by the Oxford editors:

> The shepherds almost wonder where they dwell
> & the old dog for his night journey stares
> The path leads somewhere but they cannot tell
> & neighbour meets with neighbour unawares
> The maiden passes close beside her cow
> & wonders on & think her far away
> The ploughman goes unseen behind his plough
> & seems to loose his horses half the day
> The lazy mist creeps on in journey slow
> The maidens shout & wonder where they go
> So dull & dark are the november days
> The lazy mist high up the evening curled
> & now the morn quite hides in smokey haze
> The place we occupy seems all the world

There is no introduction, no slow ramp-up, no scene-setting, no narrator leading us in with the gentle springboard of his sensory perception as in the first sonnet on this page: the scene here is immediate; or, rather, the occupants of the scene determine where we are immediately, and they are the pluralised 'shepherds'. What seems certain via the introductory definite article in fact defines a group noun 'shepherds' which by the third word 'almost' is rendered indeterminate, indefinite. The first line then begs an unanswerable question: what is it to *almost* wonder?

The first line is a complete sentence, as so many of Clare's sonnet lines are (this is a style characteristic of his verse beyond the sonnet, and it was with purpose that he mocked the awkwardness of enjambment in Wordsworth[83]). Therefore a connective bridge, the innocent, often ignored ampersand, begins the sentence following. Next we are given a singular 'old dog' on a 'night journey', suggesting that the setting overall is in the darkness of night. We do not know why, or at what, the dog is 'staring' in the dark. The third line does not resolve the mystery: 'they' must be the shepherds and the dog, and they are lost. Shepherds and dog have been formed into an alliance by perplexity, and by this third line things are becoming a little spooky, worrying, unstable and more indeterminate.

The fourth line adds to the indeterminacy in a moment of strangeness quite typical of the poet. Clare, developing a mode redolent of Wordsworth's 'encounter' poems[84] in *Lyrical Ballads*, is a poet of strange, defamiliarising and discombobulating encounters. Here, however, there is no 'I': no ostensible subject position to be perplexed. Instead we have half encounters between people and animals who do, and then almost do not, know each other. The fourth line is introduced with yet another '&'. Another two figures are introduced in the fifth and sixth lines: the maiden and the cow, in close proximity, but the maiden (though possibly the cow) 'wonders on'. This is the second instance of 'wonder' so far. The maiden thinks that the cow, or herself, is 'far away'. Wondering – meaning surprise, astonishment or marvel – carries with it the activity of 'wandering', and this poem is particularly directed towards sauntering, uncertain direction, roaming and rambling or, as the *OED* has it, moving 'hither and thither without fixed course or certain aim; to be in motion without control or direction; to roam, ramble, go idly or restlessly about; to have no fixed abode or station'. This is an overall effect brought about by this poem: it makes many elements, usually rooted in work and diurnal procedure, nomadic, loosened from locale, freed from determinism. Space, time of day, relation, purpose – all seem troubled and vexed, mystified and perplexed. The ghostly train of characters in the scene is trailed by the ploughman who is 'unseen', and so a driverless plough half appears. The second repetition of 'plough' in the same line, but now without the attached 'man', is exactly what seems to have happened – the man has been mysteriously dissolved away from his plough. The word 'seems' following an ampersand in the eighth line adds to the developing mystification of perception. In this same line, the doubling of the meaning of 'lose' through the given 'loose' (a common appearance in Clare[85]) is central to the meaning of the poem: all of these characters, human and animal alike, have lost their way and have had their grip on their locations, directions and associations loosened – both relaxed and troubled, perplexed and released – by whatever agent is doing the mystification; the agent of disarray is yet to reveal itself. The line is then followed by the manuscript poem itself loosening from its direction: the next two indented lines peter out and there is a switch vertically for the remaining six lines, where the subject moves, finally, to the lazy mist. This is the personified agent of the whole poem – the magically mystifying mist – and it enters late, in this ninth, vertical line. And it enters directly from Robert Burns's sixteen-line couplet sonnet (of sorts), 'The Lazy Mist'.[86] But where Burns's opening contemplation of an outward autumnal scene flips inwards to a *tempus fugit*-style extended contemplation of loss and mutability – and demonstrably isolates the poet into self-reflection ('Apart let me wander, apart let me muse') – in Clare's poem the poet's ego is never a concern and the poem maintains 'the lazy mist' as the ecocentric agent – half supernatural, half natural – throughout.

Ecolinguistic theory suggests that modern discourse – especially scientific – does not readily allow natural elements to take a subject position, nor does it tend to allow them much independent agency. Predominantly nature is acted upon and does not act itself; if it has a voice it is often passive; and when nature is given verbs they are often nominalised (processes are recoded into nouns).[87] By contrast, Clare repeatedly allows natural elements to take centre stage and, rather than being the stage upon which human subjects speak, instead nature offers separate *dramatis personae*. At times Clare allows a natural locality actively to voice a whole poem, most famously in the extended prosopopoeia of 'The Lament of Swordy Well'.[88] In a sense, in 'The shepherds...' the mist is a natural agent of the unnatural. Nature has the power to mystify everything, even itself (though the word 'nature' is a critical imposition, simplifying the attempt in this poem to render the 'natural world' as a complex system of independent bodies rather than one unifying force). The process and progress of the diurnal rural world here are contingent upon so many stabilities, such an interrelated set of assumed sureties, that the removal of one – in this instance full daylight – perplexes and retards the usual movement and affiliations of all natural things. All the conjoining &s that structure the poem are at full stretch, are high tensile; in Deleuze and Guattari's terms, the ampersand is a 'tensor'.[89] Each unit, each noun phrase, is threatened with breaking away into individualising fragmentation. All the little elements in this huge scene are troubled by their own loose lostness, lost looseness – yet they are also always intertwined and interrelated, affiliated in life and labour. The final four lines of the sonnet broaden the perspective out into a reflective, more omniscient position – the anonymous eye opens out to a veiled horizon. The mist's laziness is reiterated in these final lines. This mist is nature without work, without the coercion and pressure of husbandry and labour. Softly dominant here is the flocculent ease of a natural occurrence which defamiliarises everything, relaxes and merges every relation, every bond, every purpose.

The final four lines, with their preponderance of long open vowel sounds, slow down to the quietly triumphant closing line which is the crux of this odd sonnet – and the only line to appear twice, of course, if only provisionally so. This is a poem about place, about role and function, about occupation and veneration for the natural. But it is also a poem which is indeterminate even in its final, gentle assertion. Its closing effect is the assertion of a positive representation of location, suggesting that this location, this situation, is everywhere, and that everyone is similarly levelled everywhere in relation to their natural relations. This is a poem which dislocates location, turns location into the process of wondering and wandering. It turns relation into consideration, turns surety into reflection. Clare's characteristic 'sense of place' becomes a loosened, enlightened sense of everywhere.

Although the language of the poem could be described as predominantly 'standard', actually at the key moment expressing both the loosening, and the possible *almost* losing, of relation it doubles up, uses relaxed, unforced wordplay in a fully non-standard, unfixed manner. It is important to point out that 'loose' is not simply Clare's poor spelling of 'lose' that editors should correct. Animals are often made 'loose' from reins or plough in Clare, though the meaning of 'lose' can be carried with it: examples appear across his work, from the 1810s poem 'Summer Evening' – 'Plough men from their furrowy seams/Loose the weary fainting team' – through to the 1830 political poem 'Hue & Cry' – 'Till the farmer in fear loosed the team from his plough...', for example (there are many more, as noted earlier).[90]

One way of understanding the deep structures at play in 'The shepherds...' is to read it as being founded upon a 'rhizomatic' conception of experience. Deleuze and Guattari's rhizome is a metaphor loosely based on the botanical term first used in 1845 and defined in that scientific discipline as 'a prostrate or subterranean root-like stem emitting roots and usually producing leaves at its apex; a rootstock' (*OED*). The rhizomic (or rhizomatic) plant can reproduce vegetatively as well as sexually; that is, it can clone itself. Crucially for Deleuze and Guattari, it can spread and reproduce underground as well as above ground. As Felicity J. Colman puts it, the Deleuze and Guattari rhizome

> ...describes the connections that occur between the most disparate and the most similar of objects, places and people...the rhizome is a concept that maps a process of networked, relational and transversal thought...Ordered lineages of bodies and ideas that trace their originary and individual bases are considered as forms of 'aborescent thought', and this metaphor of a tree-like structure that orders epistemologies and forms historical frames and homogeneous schemata, is invoked by Deleuze and Guattari to describe everything that rhizomatic thought is not.[91]

The rhizome is a model of relation that is outwith fixed power structures, that works between and through determined systems, that multiplies and levels, that works on planes that intersect transversally and forms conjunctions, rather than asserting systems of hierarchy, deference, coercion or censure. The more specific link that substantiates the relevance of Deleuze and Guattari to Clare appears in their own definition of the rhizome. This includes an idealisation of co-ordination through the conjunctive 'and', as follows:

> A rhizome has no beginning or end; it is always in the middle, between things, interbeing, *intermezzo*. The tree is filiation, but the rhizome is alliance, uniquely alliance. The tree imposes the verb 'to be,' but the fabric of the rhizome is the conjunction, 'and...and...and...' This conjunction carries enough force to shake and uproot the verb 'to be.' Where are you going? Where are you coming from? What are you heading for? These are totally useless questions. Making a clean slate, starting or beginning again from ground zero, seeking a beginning or a foundation – all imply a false conception of voyage and movement (a conception that is methodical, pedagogical, initiatory, symbolic...). [But there is] another way of traveling and moving: proceeding from the middle, through the middle, coming and going rather than starting and finishing. American literature, and already

English literature, manifest this rhizomatic direction to an even greater extent; they know how to move between things, establish a logic of the AND, overthrow ontology, do away with foundations, nullify endings and beginnings... *Between* things does not designate a localizable relation going from one thing to the other and back again, but a perpendicular direction, a transversal movement that sweeps one *and* the other away, a stream without beginning or end that undermines its banks and picks up speed in the middle.[92]

In dialogue with Claire Parnet, Deleuze offers another relevant definition of the rhizome, in contrast to the dominant model of the tree:

You set about opposing the rhizome to trees. And trees are not a metaphor at all, but an image of thought, a functioning, a whole apparatus that is planted in thought in order to make it go in a straight line and produce the famous correct ideas. There are all kinds of characteristics in the tree: there is a point of origin, seed or centre; it is a binary machine or principle of dichotomy, with its perpetually divided and reproduced branchings, its points of arborescence; it is an axis of rotation which organizes things in a circle, and the circles round the centre; it is a structure, a system of points and positions which fix all of the possible within a grid, a hierarchical system or transmission of orders, with a central instance and recapitulative memory; it has a future and a past, roots and a peak, a whole history, an evolution, a development; it can be cut up by cuts which are said to be significant in so far as they follow its aborescences, its branchings, its concentricities, its moments of development. Now, there is no doubt that trees are planted in our heads: the tree of life, the tree of knowledge, etc. The whole world demands roots. Power is always arborescent... There are multiplicities which constantly go beyond binary machines and do not let themselves be dichotomized. There are centres everywhere, like multiplicities of black holes which do not let themselves be agglomerated. There are lines which do not amount to the path of a point, which break free from structure – lines of flight, becomings, without future or past, without memory, which resist the binary machine – woman-becoming which is neither man nor woman, animal-becoming which is neither beast nor man. Non-parallel evolutions, which do not proceed by differentiation, but which leap from one line to another, between completely heterogeneous beings; cracks, imperceptible ruptures, which break the lines even if they resume elsewhere, leaping over significant breaks... The rhizome is all this. Thinking in things, among things – this is producing a rhizome and not a root, producing the line and not the point.[93]

The route into the use of Deleuze and Guattari to help unlock Clare's eco-aesthetic starts via their positivistic presentation of 'and'. Use of this conjunction has been a pitfall in Clare's reception. In an otherwise positive appreciation, Robert Lynd says Clare's 'poetry is largely a list of things he loves'. With more distaste, Edmund Gosse reads Clare's 'redundant flow of verses... Clare wrote with inexhaustible fluency'.[94] This perceived lack of control or narrative ordering, and the tendency of Clare to list, means that Zachary Leader thinks that the editorial interventions of John Taylor in the 1820s are fully supportable. Leader's argument is insightful, but I would like to argue that Clare's manuscript ampersands – and his uses of polysyndeton overall – have an effect more central to his project than merely restricting poetic impact or leading to 'Clare's sameness', Leader's characterisation of this widespread tendency in his work.[95]

For a specific example, we will turn again to the ampersands in 'The shepherds...' sonnet. There are eight ampersands across the fourteen lines and the poem is overall dominated by a structuring polysyndeton. There are a few other non-standard linguistic features here, but the use of the ampersand, much more commonly apparent in Clare's manuscript than 'and', is key. To abbreviate the word 'and' to the logogram and ligature '&' symbolises the present-tense immediacy of Clare's response to, and construction of, the indeterminacy of this misty scene, a scene muffled by the wonder and blurred boundaries of a levelling nature. The ampersand is an icon of conjunction, rather than a word; yes, it is shorthand, but it is also an intensifying scriptive device. As Jan Tschichold puts it, the 'ampersand is always a particularly intimate merging of letters in which part of one letter either runs on into the next, or simultaneously forms it'.[96] The ampersand is a conjunction conjoined. To overlook its significance in earlier literary usage might also be a mistake, according to Alan Loney:

> Early modernist poets did however use the ampersand as a deliberate intervention in the smooth reading process. The intention was *precisely* to interrupt the flow, slow the reading down, and bring attention to bear on the means by which meaning is conveyed.[97]

Clare's predominant use of the ampersand when representing the natural shows affinity with the rhizome in terms of its co-ordinated, levelled, planar, anti-hierarchical shape. This structure embeds the poem in a full engagement with this particular Northborough landscape, on the edge of the Fens, that by November 1835 Clare knew intimately (though he had always been a keen wetland naturalist[98]). As Bridget Keegan has keenly illustrated, the local topography of the Fens is foundational to understanding how Clare's poetic vision is structured:

> Clare levels the hierarchy of the senses generally found in locodescriptive poetry. The wetlandscape offers no elevated prospect from which the speaker can place himself above nature, looking down upon it to describe it. The unstable ground, neither water nor earth, provides no place for the speaker to stop long enough to consume a picturesque view.[99]

In this particular poem, this same landscape-sympathetic levelling of any superior human perspective is combined with a world-view which is fluid, decentring, in flux and always in the process of slow becoming. Such co-ordination of relation between things does not merely establish an ecocentric interconnectedness, as deep ecologists might have it. It also creates relations of being between objects and subjects. It destabilises and problematises not just object/subject relations, but also subject/object definitions. This sonnet does not just enact a programme of ecological interconnectivity, but decentralises and *mist*ifies each constituent part, blending, liquefying and making an amalgam of the whole scene as it does so. While it maintains boundaries of activity through relations of husbandry which do not suggest a complete rejection of capital-driven farming – this is not a misanthropic poem at all – each relation becomes as significant as each node on the chain of relationship. The fraught issue of relationship in this sonnet throws light upon the dependence that each constituent part of the rural scene has upon the other components: interconnectedness is revealed to be the site of secure meaning for each of the component parts. Each component part only becomes aware of its state and status through the slight disabling of the familiar connections it habitually relies upon with other entities of the dynamic, yet hesitant, scene. Each body is shown to be not meaningfully a separable component: that is, it cannot maintain its relational identity without a continual process of becoming something other than itself. It relies for its meaning on becoming other things, not just on co-ordination with many things, but on a continual movement of being towards those things. All of the constituents lose subject positions and of necessity enter machinic processes of the rural, without which form, function and secure identity might be lost. Identity in this poem *is* relation, is connection, is fluidity, and is inherently reliant on the social. There is no separation between man and nature here, no reliance on binary opposition or fixed position, or position of judgement or power for man. There is no anthropomorphism any more than there is a becoming-animal or rather a becoming-mist that promises, in its total saturation, to enchant all the elements of the scene.

As I have said above, it has been a persistent criticism of Clare's verse that he has a tendency to list, that his descriptions never seem to be progressing, seem to lack order or coherent direction. In summarising the reception of this aspect of Clare, Zachary Leader quotes Clare's publisher James Hessey, whose editorialising letter to Clare of 1824 parodies this stylistic feature:

> Clare, he complains, once again describes 'the Morning & the Noon & the Evening & the Summer & the Winter, & the Sheep & Cattle & Poultry & Pigs & Milking Maid & Foddering Boys... the world will now expect something more than these; let them come in incidentally, but they must be subordinate to higher objects'.[100]

It is significant that Hessey's desire for subordination is prompted by his parodying of Clare's ampersand-co-ordinated lists: this was and remains a sticking point for anyone considering Clare's poetic abilities, and is an aspect of his verse that even his most positive supporters concede to – and some celebrate. But the ideas of progress, of ordering structure, of direction, all emerge from a capitalist imperative and an anthropomorphising drive that takes the shape of narrative order, an imperative to narrate, an impulse to make sense of, to resolve, to show explicit apprehension and progress towards rather than becoming among. In other words, to plot a story as a landowner is to lay claim to a 'plot' of ground. Plot is fixity, ownership, requiring fences that split and end, the product of controlling strategy. Clare has distinctly different structures in his writing, in which tactical lines of relation and response engage in ongoing processes.

Clare's narrative strategies are the product of a restless becoming-animal,[101] to use Deleuze and Guattari's terminology for ongoing processes which deny fixed subject positions, which are always becomings and never happenings, and which are forever shifting, never still, never resolved, never done, never completed. At times Clare's language structures, the resistance to grammatical, compositional, presentational and poetical standards, the reliance on a polysyndeton of anaphoric ampersands, the seemingly arbitrary disordering of multiple subjects, his resistance to the ordering first-person subject – and his resistance to (or inability to work with) John Taylor's dictum to philosophise – combine to suggest that he is deliberately avoiding poetry's human drive because the subject he seeks is not centred on the human. Humanity is not excluded – far from it – but is one part of a set of dynamic processes rather than apart and in charge; man and woman are links in a chain of &s rather than wielders of hammer and anvil that made the chain, nodes in a tentative root system rather than the trunk of the rooted tree. As such, humanity is as frail and fragile, as readily thrown and as harmoniously drawn, as the animals and crops humans tend to and work with. Woman is as decentralised as man in this equalising, yet disconcerting, poem.

This sonnet articulates Clare's green grammar not through the odd deviant spelling or through a sole focus on one animal or plant, but instead through its reaching for the complex and levelling map that is at the heart of current ecological theory: interrelationships between; co-ordination among. The poem grapples with a rhizomatic interdependency theory of green structure all of its own and local seeing, but with a final line which opens it into global and current relevance. The locality of the last line is exactly the place where so many ecological thinkers argue the green revolution must begin – locally, in small communities, in the place we occupy – and yet it opens out in scale to the whole world of the apprehending human subject. Although the verb 'occupy' can suggest possession, territory and plot, the 'we' cannot be solely human, because the logic of the poem's community is human and animal, agricultural and natural, perceptual and material, conceptual and material.

Each element, each body, assembled and disassembled here is no more and no less significant or central than the others around it. The focus becomes not the bodies, but the links between. The ampersands uncertainly join hands in the mist, as nature levels all. And strictly speaking, while everything seems almost to interrelate, Clare's vision here cannot be said to be organicist: no unified tree fixes the scene as a maypole around which the minor players dance. The generative idea of this scene – the wandering wonder of it – emerges in its restlessness, its lack of settlement, its nomadic, decentred and fundamentally planar shape. Any attempt to grasp, to pin down, to order and codify, to emplace, is shaken off by the deviant doubleness of a lost looseness. The rural plural here is not a single organic entity but a diverse set of lines criss-crossing in and among one another. This world is not separable, not classifiable: it is neither human, nor animal, nor vegetable. It is all of these together and none of them alone. The radical resistance here sets itself not just against classifying order, but also against simplifying union, the excessively simplistic idea that, ideally, 'we are all one' in 'harmony', the infantilising silliness of ecomysticism. Here each body is worryingly, perhaps enticingly, separable; the poem's activity precisely threatens that separation – the separation from routine and predictability, but also from reliability, from conscious comprehension of the material world. The mist moves among the bodies, arousing an awareness of ecological and existential fragility. The thick soup of November mist and the darkness it brings serve to remind each body of its reliance upon other bodies, while illustrating the delicate nature of tumbling sets of reliances and relations. November mist conveys this through silence, through an inarticulate, ungraspable pervasiveness. The mist itself becomes the medium through which all bodies are reminded of their dependency, while at the same time it is illustrative that they occupy the same plane: all are mystified, so all are levelled. The poem is a supremely sophisticated statement of social ecology because it is a flattened vision, with the moisture in the air acting as a medium of linkage, of pervasive interdependency, of rhizomatic relations. The poem presents social ecosystem in action. Its final move means both to delimit human environmental consciousness to a local sphere, while also imbricating within that intimate, if diffuse, ecological awareness a modelling of, and an extension to, a wider, unseen world, beyond the horizon.

NOTES

1. Unsigned review in *Blackwood's Edinburgh Magazine*, XXXVIII (July 1835), 231–47, in *Critical Heritage*, pp. 235–6.
2. John Wilson in *Critical Heritage*, p. 228 [Wilson's emphasis and spelling].
3. See Adam Rounce, 'John Clare, William Cowper and the eighteenth century', in *New Essays on John Clare*, pp. 38–56.
4. Stephen Bygrave, *Coleridge and the Self: Romantic Egotism* (New York: St. Martin's Press, 1986), pp. 3–4.
5. William Hazlitt, 'Observations on Mr. Wordsworth's Poem, "The Excursion"', in *The Round Table: A Collection of Essays on Literature, Men, and Manners*, 2 vols (Edinburgh: Archibald Constable; London: Longman et al., 1817), 2, pp. 95–122 (pp. 99, 120 and 121).
6. Hazlitt, 'Observations on Mr. Wordsworth's poem, "The Excursion"', p. 114.

7. John Kinnaird, *William Hazlitt: Critic of Power* (New York: Columbia University Press, 1978), p. 225.
8. William Hazlitt, *The Spirit of the Age: Or Contemporary Portraits*, 2nd edn (London: Henry Colburn, 1825), p. 165.
9. William Hazlitt, 'Mr. Coleridge', in *The Spirit of the Age: Or Contemporary Portraits*, 2nd edn (London: Henry Colburn, 1825), pp. 57–75 (p. 62).
10. *By Himself*, p. 144.
11. William Hazlitt, 'On Egotism', in *The Plain Speaker: Opinions on Books, Men, and Things*, 2 vols (London: Henry Colburn, 1826), 1, pp. 377–403.
12. William Hazlitt, 'Mr. Wordsworth', in *The Spirit of the Age*, pp. 189–206 (p. 201).
13. John Keats, 'Letter to Richard Woodhouse, 27 October 1818', in Hyder E. Rollins (ed.), *The Letters of John Keats* 2 vols (Cambridge: Cambridge University Press, 1958), 1, pp. 386–7.
14. There are many accounts of Clare's indirect relationship with Keats, but the most thoroughgoing is by John Goodridge, *John Clare and Community* (Cambridge: Cambridge University Press, 2013), pp. 59–82.
15. *By Himself*, p. 188.
16. Pet. A61, p. 3. See chapter 4, p. 225n97 for a transcription of this costed list of books.
17. Emma Trehane, '"Emma and Johnny": The Friendship between Eliza Emmerson and John Clare', *JCSJ*, 24 (2005), 69–77 (76). See also Bate, *Biography*, pp. 163–4, and *passim*.
18. Letter to George Darley, January–February 1830, *Letters*, p. 502.
19. Letter to John Taylor, before 15 September 1830, *Letters*, pp. 512–13. A 'seton' is a skein of cotton passed below the skin and left with the ends protruding to promote drainage. What Clare was being treated for by the London doctor George Darling remains unclear.
20. All the details of Clare's visit to London are drawn from Bate, *Biography*, p. 332.
21. *Letters*, p. 504. For a discussion of this letter as a precursor to a similar critique of the narrator's first-person singular in Virginia Woolf, see John Goodridge, *John Clare and Community* (Cambridge: Cambridge University Press, 2013), pp. 2–3. See also a brief discussion and excerpt of it in Dan Piepenbring, 'That Swaggering, Bouncing Pronoun', *Paris Review*, 13 July 2015 http://www.theparisreview.org/blog/2015/07/13/that-swaggering-bouncing-pronoun/ [accessed August 27 2016].
22. 'Don Juan', in *Living Year, 1841*, p. 53, ll. 255–8.
23. See John Goodridge, '"Now Wenches, Listen, and Let Lovers Lie": Women's Storytelling in Bloomfield and Clare', *JCSJ*, 22 (2003), 77–92.
24. In Jamaican Rastafarian patois, 'I' ideally replaces singular subject and object pronouns, which are regarded as being divisive. 'I and I' (or 'I&I')

symbolises the highest form of unity. By way of contrast, in Clare's theory the 'I' is a cause of hierarchical division.
25. Percy Bysshe Shelley, 'On Life' in Donald H. Reiman and Neil Fraistat (eds), *Shelley's Poetry and Prose* (New York and London: W. W. Norton, 2002), pp. 505–9 (p. 508). Shelley's italicised emphases.
26. Pet. A46, p.41; *Letters*, p. 491.
27. Barbara M. H. Strang, 'John Clare's Language', in R. K. R. Thornton (ed.), *The Rural Muse: Poems by John Clare* (Ashington: MidNAG and Carcanet, 1982), pp. 159–73 (p. 161).
28. For a summary of eighteenth-century English-language debates over standardisation, regulation and then prescription, see Albert C. Baugh and Thomas Cable, *A History of the English Language*, 3rd edn (London and New York: Routledge, 1978), pp. 253–93. For an accessible discussion of the dash, see Keith Houston, *Shady Characters: The Secret Life of Punctuation, Symbols & Other Typographical Marks* (New York and London: W. W. Norton, 2013), pp. 145–65.
29. E. J. Hobsbawm and George Rudé, *Captain Swing* (Old Woking: Lawrence and Wishart, 1969), p. 85.
30. In their *Captain Swing*, Hobsbawm and Rudé provide a comprehensive assessment of the twenty-two counties in which the riots, machine-breaking and rick-burning broke out across 1830 and into 1831, including in villages close to Helpston, across Northamptonshire, Cambridgeshire, Lincolnshire and Norfolk.
31. Lucas assesses key poems Clare wrote in response to the rural troubles across 1830 and 1831, in 'Clare's politics', *John Clare in Context*, pp. 148–77 (pp. 166–8). Alan Vardy's account is essential reading in this regard: *John Clare, Politics and Poetry* (Basingstoke: Palgrave Macmillan, 2003), especially pp. 169–75.
32. Eric Robinson and David Powell (eds), *The Parish*, ll. 1014–15 (Harmondsworth: Penguin, 1985), p. 56.
33. See Alexander Murray (ed.), *Sir William Jones, 1746–1794: A Commemoration* (Oxford: Oxford University Press, 1998). I owe a debt of gratitude to the late Bob Cummings for extensive direction on this front.
34. John James Clarke, *Oriental Enlightenment: The Encounter Between Asian and Western Thought* (London and New York: Routledge, 1997), p. 213.
35. The most comprehensive study of this area of Clare's life and work is offered by Sarah Houghton-Walker, *John Clare's Religion* (Farnham: Ashgate, 2009).
36. *By Himself*, p. 78.
37. *The Parish*, p. 45, ll. 545–8.

38. See P. M. S. Dawson, Eric Robinson and David Powell (eds), *A Champion for the Poor; Political Verse and Prose* (Ashington and Manchester: MidNAG/Carcanet, 2000), pp. 267–80.
39. Pet. A46, p. 43.
40. Kate Soper, *What Is Nature? Culture, Politics and the non-Human* (Oxford: Blackwell, 1995), p. 207.
41. Jonathan Bate, *The Song of the Earth* (London: Picador, 2000), p. 174.
42. For a delineation of the two positions, see Andrew Dobson, *Green Political Thought*, 4th edn (London and New York: Routledge, 2007), pp. 10–27. For a balanced overview of ecologism, see Andrew Vincent, *Modern Political Ideologies*, 3rd edn (Chichester: Wiley-Blackwell, 2010), pp. 198–225.
43. Mark J. Smith, *Ecologism: Towards Ecological Citizenship* (Buckingham: Open University Press, 1998), pp. 4–8.
44. Percy Bysshe Shelley, 'Mont Blanc. Lines Written in the Vale of Chamouni', in Thomas Hutchinson (ed.), *The Complete Poetical Works of Shelley* (Oxford: Oxford University Press, 1904), p. 586, l. 143.
45. There are many recent definitions of ecocentrism, but a fine literary analysis, alongside a consideration of the tradition of literary anthropomorphism, is offered by Bryan L. Moore, *Ecology and Literature: Ecocentric Personification from Antiquity to the Twenty-first Century* (New York: Palgrave Macmillan, 2008), especially pp. 5–21.
46. Mark J. Smith, *Ecologism*, p. 5.
47. Tom Paulin, 'John Clare: A Bicentennial Celebration', in Richard Foulkes (ed.), *John Clare: A Bicentenary Celebration* (Northampton: University of Leicester, Department of Adult Education, 1994), pp. 69–78 (p. 75).
48. For four indicative examples, see 'Waterloo', EPI, pp. 208–11; 'Sonnet' (first line: 'England with pride I name thee...'), EPII, p. 599; 'Nelson & the Nile', MPIV, pp. 100–4; 'On Seeing the Bust of Princess Victoria by Behnes', MPIV, pp. 160–1. See also Sam Ward, '"This is radical slang": John Clare, Admiral Lord Radstock and the Queen Caroline Affair', in *New Essays on John Clare*, pp. 189–208 (p. 203).
49. Richard Heath, *The English Peasant* (1893), extracted in *Critical Heritage*, p. 294.
50. See for example: John Lucas, *England and Englishness: Ideas of Nationhood in English Poetry, 1688–1900* (London: Hogarth Press, 1990), pp. 135–60; John Lucas, *John Clare* (Plymouth: Northcote House, 1994); Roger Sales, *John Clare: A Literary Life* (Basingstoke: Palgrave, 2002).
51. P.M.S. Dawson, 'John Clare—Radical?', *JCSJ*, 11 (1992), 17–27, and 'Common Sense or Radicalism? Some Reflections on Clare's Politics', *Romanticism*, 2.1 (1996), 81–97.

52. Zachary Leader, *Revision and Romantic Authorship* (Oxford: Oxford University Press, 1996), pp. 206–61. Alan Vardy, *John Clare, Politics and Poetry* (Basingstoke: Palgrave, 2003).
53. Jonathan Bate, *Romantic Ecology: Wordsworth and the Environmental Tradition* (London and New York: Routledge, 1991) pp. 8–9; *Biography; "I Am": The Selected Poetry of John Clare* (New York: Farrar, Straus and Giroux, 2003) and *John Clare: Selected Poems* (London: Faber and Faber, 2004).
54. Karl Kroeber, *Ecological Literary Criticism: Romantic Imagining and the Biology of Mind* (New York: Columbia University Press, 1994), p. 21.
55. 'Familiar Epistle to a Friend', MPIV, pp. 508–17 (p. 509, ll. 25–32).
56. Taylor to Clare, 6 January 1821, *Letters*, p. 135. Like other commentators before him, Jonathan Bate seems to imply (Bate, *Biography*, pp. 218–9) that the marginal pencilled words '*This is radical slang' alongside stanzas 107 and 108 in a fair manuscript copy of 'The Village Minstrel' (previously entitled 'The Peasant Boy') are Radstock's (Nor. 3, p. 186b). But Robert Heyes is certain the hand is Taylor's. See John Goodridge and R.K.R. Thornton, *John Clare, The Trespasser* (Nottingham: Five Leaves Publications, 2016), p. 85n76. I offer, yet again, my thanks to Robert Heyes for once again complicating another foundational Clare myth.
57. Sales, *John Clare*, pp. 51–9 (pp. 53 and 56).
58. Ward, '"This is radical slang": John Clare, Admiral Lord Radstock and the Queen Caroline Affair', p. 203. Ward concludes that '... if Clare's most anti-aristocratic seeming verse might have been viewed as contiguous with the wider radical discourse centred around Caroline, it did so because of the implicit challenge his writing posed to contemporary definitions of legitimate plebeian discourse and not because he was in any direct sense an active proponent of radical reform' (p. 203).
59. Barrell, p. 103.
60. Barrell, p. 105.
61. Barrell, p. 120.
62. Simon J. White, 'John Clare's Sonnets and the Northborough Fens', *JCSJ*, 28 (2009), 55–70 (56). For wider contexts of Clare as a Fenland poet, see Bridget Keegan, *British Labouring-Class Nature Poetry, 1730–1837* (Basingstoke: Palgrave Macmillan, 2008), pp. 148–71. For an analysis of the language patterns in Fenland poems, see Helen Pownall, 'Syntax and World-view in John Clare's Fen poems', *JCSJ*, 34 (2015), 37–50.
63. Pet. A61, p. 83. For a transcription, see *Letters*, p. 629.
64. MPV, p. 267.

65. The starnels also 'darken like a cloud the evening sky' in the poem appearing just two pages later in this manuscript, the first line of which is 'The wild duck startles like a sudden thought'. MPV, p. 269–70.
66. The Oxford editors decide to collect together as if one poem three sonnets which feature maids shouting to call farmhands to breakfast (see MPV, pp. 327–8). Page 127 of A61 features the first two sonnets of this supposed series, penned on paper with a rough tear at the bottom, approximately 10 inches long and 4 inches wide. Then on page 128 of A61 we are on distinctly different paper (the same size as that of 'The shepherds...'), in a script that is clearly Clare's hand but with a different pen (and/or ink) to page 127. In the Oxford edition, the sonnet 'The maiden shout to breakfast round the yard' (first line) is positioned as the third and final sonnet in this supposed series about maidens shouting (see MPV p. 328, l. 29). To further complicate matters, some (though not all) of the lines of this group of poems can be found in Nor. 7 (see headnote to the poems in MPV, p. 327). It is a remarkable achievement that the Oxford editors managed any coherence in this array of diverse materials. But it is also problematic that to an extent (though not entirely), these poems' position – and their narrative-derived relatability – in the definitive edition is being dictated to by an archivist's decisions on the order in which they have been pasted into manuscript fascicles based on mentions of maidens shouting and the appearance of the clumsy, hungry labourer Hodge (cf. my discussion of Hodge as the staple stereotype of male labouring idiocy below), but not (it would seem) on the material qualities of the paper on which they are written. It might be that the third sonnet is a rewrite of the first two of A61, or vice versa.
67. The lead example here is in the two isolated lines on page 54 of A61 – 'As stubborn as the oak that cannot bend/He recks no master & he has no friend'. The Oxford editors (MPV, pp. 290–1) install these lines as the closing couplet to an otherwise twelve-line sonnet which appears on page 77 of the A61 manuscript, first line 'From place to place they go afar they roam', a poem about lone travellers whom the shepherds of the closing lines regard as 'field marauders', even if the poem itself seems rather in awe of them. The final two lines that the editors import here do work (even if the 'oak' is an odd simile for the travelling kind), yet there is no evidence presented that this couplet on page 54 was in fact written as the close of the twelve of page 77. Page 77 is quite distinct paper from page 54 too, not that this would be conclusive evidence in either direction. The editors have created a poem that simply does not exist in manuscript. For fragments in A61 the editors decide have no home, see MPV, pp. 330–1.
68. The thirty-two sonnets I am identifying as a discrete subsection of the wider 'Northborough sonnet' project (if project is was what it was) appear in MPV, pp. 267–76; 292–98; 327–30. Their first lines and page numbers in the A61 Pet. manuscript are 'I love to hear the evening crows go bye' and

'The shepherds almost wonder where they dwell', p. 47; 'The horses are took out the cows are fed' and 'When milking comes then home the maiden wends', p. 48; 'The wild duck startles like a sudden thought' and 'He eats a moments stoppage to his song', p. 49; 'The noisy blathering calves are fed & all' and 'Tis late the labouring men come dropping in', p. 50; 'The cowboy shuns the shower & seeks the mat' and 'He waits all day beside his little flock', p. 51; 'With hands in pocket hid & buttoned up' and 'Lapt up in sacks to shun the rain & wind', p. 52; 'With careful step to keep his balance up' and 'The cowboys hut of straw neglected lies', p. 53; 'With hook tucked neath his arm that now & then' and 'He finds his old knife where the gipseys lay', p. 54; 'The maiden ran away to fetch the cloaths' and 'Among the orchard weeds from every search', p. 79; 'With boots of monstrous leg & massy strength' and 'There is a place scarce known that well may claim', p. 80; 'They pelt about the snow the birds to scare' and 'The cloudy morning brought a pleasant day', p. 81; 'The reeking supper waits the labourer home' and 'The crows drive onward through the storm of snow', p. 82; 'Close by the road the traveller set his cart', p. 83; 'He never knew a book & never bought' and 'He smokes his pipe & drinks his pint of ale', p. 84; 'The maiden shout to breakfast round the yard', p. 128; 'He fights with all the whasps nests in his way' and 'The school boy sets his basket down to play', p. 129; 'Maids set their buckets down & run the while' and '& every morning passing gives a call', p. 130. Page 54 also contains the two-line fragment discussed in the preceding note.

69. For his insights into the potentially arbitrary order of pages in the process of preservation of Clare manuscripts into fascicles, I am indebted to Richard Hunt, Director of Culture at Vivacity, Peterborough City Council, and former archives manager of Peterborough Central Library.

70. Following Barrell's lead, Joseph Phelan reads a diminution in the move to Northborough in the quality of Clare's supposedly Keatsian ability to complicate the sonnet form, the standard story of 'an increasing sense of alienation from the natural world' on that move away from Helpston, and he finds 'a poetry in which the boundaries between poems seem to have dissolved altogether' – which for him appears to be a weakness. See Joseph Phelan, *The Nineteenth-Century Sonnet* (Basingstoke: Palgrave Macmillan, 2005), 39–42 (41). He picks up on Barrell, pp. 177–80.

71. John Goodridge, *John Clare and Community* (Cambridge: Cambridge University Press, 2013), p. 6.

72. Goodridge, *John Clare and Community*, pp. 3–7.

73. Pet. A61, p. 80; MPV, pp. 293–4.

74. Sarah Houghton-Walker, *Representations of the Gypsy in the Romantic Period* (Oxford: Oxford University Press, 2014), p. 103.

75. See 'When milking comes then home the maiden wends', 'Tis late the labouring men come dropping in' and 'The maiden ran away to fetch the cloaths', MPV, pp. 270, 271, and 292 respectively.
76. All MPV (all untitled; first lines): 'Tis late the labouring men come dropping in', pp. 271–2, l. 1 and ll. 15–16 (a rare sixteen-line sonnet in this particular series); 'The maiden ran away to fetch the cloaths', p. 292, ll. 11–12; 'The reeking supper waits the labourer home', p. 294, ll. 1–2; 'He never knew a book & never bought', p. 298, ll. 13–14.
77. 'He never knew a book & never bought', MPV, pp. 297–8.
78. Somewhat more sardonically, Clare plays with the ambivalent possibilities of 'nothing' in a line about Byron: 'Who with his pen lies like the mist disperses /& makes all nothing as it was before', 'Don Juan', *Living Year 1841*, p. 51, ll. 233–4.
79. Pet. A61, p. 47. See also MPV, p. 267 and Eric Robinson, David Powell and P. M. S. Dawson (eds), *Northborough Sonnets* (Ashington and Manchester: MidNAG/Carcanet, 1995), p. 67.
80. Pet. A61, p. 47. See also MPV, p. 268 and *Northborough Sonnets*, p. 67.
81. LPI, p. xvii.
82. A clean critical-apparatus-free 'reading text' was one of the innovations – along with facsimiles of manuscripts, 'primitivist' transcriptions and inclusion of variants – of the influential twenty-one-volume Cornell University Press edition of the works of William Wordsworth (1975–2007). For a history of this edition, see Jared Curtis, 'The Cornell Wordsworth: A History', [Cornell University Press, n.d.], http://www.cornellpress.cornell.edu/html/WYSIWYGfiles/files/Cornell_Wordsworth_History.pdf [accessed 28 August 2016].
83. See 'Sonnet After the Manner of X X X X X', MPII, p. 7.
84. I am thinking specifically here of Wordsworth's poems such as 'Simon Lee', 'We Are Seven', 'The Last of the Flock', 'Old Man Travelling' – all of them in *Lyrical Ballads* (1798). In terms of its 'wedding guest' frame, Coleridge's 'The Rime of the Ancyent Marinere' is an 'encounter' poem – though this is not a poem in which Clare ever expressed an interest; he was not impressed by Coleridge as a poet or as a man. Clare noted that he thought Coleridge's 'sonnets are not happy ones', though he thought 'Monody on the Death of Chatterton' 'beautiful'. His journal records that he read these poems in October 1824, in *Poems by S.T. Coleridge, to which are now added Poems by Charles Lamb and Charles Lloyd* (London: Cottle, et al., 1797), the book having been a gift from Lord Radstock. See Clare's unimpressed account of meeting Coleridge, and of reading the poems, in *By Himself*, pp. 144 and 186.
85. Here are some examples among many where 'loose' operates as 'lose' from across the length of Clare's writing career: 'Plough men from their furrowy seams/Loose the weary fainting team' in the very early poem 'Summer

Evening' (EPI, p. 7, ll. 67-8); '& others driving loose their herds at will' in 'Rural Morning' (EPII, p. 616, l. 119); 'The sun een seems to loose its way' in 'The Flitting' (MPIII, p. 481, l. 55); '... birds scarce loose a nest the season through' in 'The Woodman' (MPIV, p. 212, l. 14); 'The tempest could not loose her when he tried' in the untitled Northborough double sonnet, first line 'The f[l]aggy forrest beat the willows breast' (MPV, p. 261, l. 23); 'The knot is tied – & then we loose the honey' in 'Don Juan' (*Living Year 1841*, p. 57, l. 298).

86. This poem appears in a Burns collection Clare owned: *The Poetical Works of Robert Burns* (London: T. Cadell and W. Davies, et al., 1817), p. 356. Item 134 in [David Powell], *Catalogue of the John Clare Collection in the Northampton Public Library* (Northampton: County Borough of Northampton Public Libraries, Museums and Art Gallery Committee, 1964).

87. See, for example, Andrew Goatly, 'Green Grammar and Grammatical Metaphor, or Language and Myth of Power, or Metaphors We Die By', in Alwin Fill and Peter Mühlhäusler (eds), *The Ecolinguistics Reader: Language, Ecology and Environment* (London and New York: Continuum, 2001), pp. 203-25. In the same collection, see Mary Kahn, 'The Passive Voice of Science: Language Abuse in the Wildlife Profession', pp. 241-4.

88. MPV, pp. 105-14.

89. 'The tensor effects a kind of transitivization of the phrase, causing the last term to react upon the preceding term, back through the entire chain ... An expression as simple as and ... can play the role of tensor for all of language.' Gilles Deleuze and Félix Guattari, *A Thousand Plateaus: Capitalism and Schizophrenia*, trans. Brian Massumi (London and New York: Continuum, 2004), p. 110.

90. 'Summer Evening', EPI, p. 7, ll. 67-8; 'The Hue & Cry. A Tale of the Times', MPIV, p. 520, l. 45.

91. Felicity J. Colman, 'Rhizome', in Adrian Parr (ed.), *The Deleuze Dictionary* (Edinburgh: Edinburgh University Press, 2005), pp. 231-3 (p. 231). For wider considerations of Deleuze and Guattari in relation to ecocritical thought, see Bernd Herzogenarth (ed.), *Deleuze| Guattari & Ecology* (Basingstoke: Palgrave, 2009), and Bernd Herzogenarth (ed.), *An [Un] Likely Alliance: Thinking Environment[s] with Deleuze| Guattari* (Cambridge: Cambridge Scholars Publishing, 2008). See also Félix Guattari, *The Three Ecologies*, trans. Ian Pindar and Paul Sutton (London and New York: Continuum, 2000).

92. Deleuze and Guattari, *A Thousand Plateaus*, pp. 27-8. Authors' italicised emphases.

93. Gilles Deleuze and Claire Parnet, *Dialogues II*, trans. Hugh Tomlinson and Barbara Habberjam (London and New York: Continuum, 2002), pp. 25-6.

94. Robert Lynd, 'Review of *Poems, Chiefly from Manuscript*', 22 January 1921, in *Critical Heritage*, pp. 340–3 (p. 342). Edmund Gosse, 'Review of *Poems, Chiefly from Manuscript*', 23 January 1921, in *Critical Heritage*, pp. 343–6 (p. 344).
95. Leader, *Revision and Romantic Authorship*, pp. 244–52.
96. Jan Tschichold, *The Ampersand: Its Origin and Development*, trans. Frederick Plaat (London: Woudhuysen, 1957), p. 5.
97. Alan Loney, *& The Ampersand* (Wellington: Black Light, 1990), no pagination; Loney's emphasis.
98. It is impossible to list all of Clare's references here, but his typical enthusiasm and knowledge of watery and wetland environments can be found in the index to *Natural History*, under items such as Crowland Wash, Deeping Fen, Holme Fen, North Fen, Welland Ford and Whittlesey Mere.
99. Bridget Keegan, *British Labouring-Class Nature Poetry, 1730–1837* (Basingstoke: Palgrave Macmillan, 2008), pp. 149–50.
100. Zachary Leader, *Revision and Romantic Authorship*, p. 247. See also *Critical Heritage*, p. 195.
101. For an extended discussion of 'becoming-animal', see Deleuze and Guattari, *A Thousand Plateaus*, pp. 265–78.

CHAPTER 3

Clare Making Text; Making Text of Clare

'The Judgment of Others': Editing Wars

So far, we have explored some of the ways in which Clare's texts can be complex in their manuscript form, and we have touched upon the issues facing anyone attempting to make editorial sense of them. We have also seen that if Clare's political leanings are ambivalent, he secures for himself an idiosyncratic platform for aesthetic explorations of, and critiques of, modes of being in and amongst the natural world. There is of course a relationship between the kinds of texts Clare writes and has left to us and the ecopolitics of structural and thematic coherences and patterns in his work, some of which I have tried to trace in previous chapters. All of the issues that feed into the way we receive and interpret his texts – textual, biographical, material, socio-economic, historical, ethical, political – also inform the way in which Clare has been edited and presented to the world. In the history of his presentation to the world of letters through a variety of editions and textually critical practices, the political lines of editors and critics became entrenched.

This chapter will consider the ways in which Clare's texts have been pressed into presentational moulds predetermined by quite severely politicised versions of his aesthetic and linguistic values and practices. Through the reading of a talismanic poem in which Clare lays claim to a mode in which he makes, or rather 'finds', his texts, this chapter will then consider whether a reading of his green politics can help inform new modes of presenting his texts, more in line with how we find them and how we might want to see them. First, we turn to Clare's seeming ambivalence over the procedures of editing:

> Get Taylor to Copy it out for me if he pleases with *remarks* as soon as leisure permits him as I have no Copy by me   his opinion will soon set me at rights   I wish I had him near me & I shoud do
>   I am obliged to trust to the judgment of others who mangle & spoil them very often & the Ballad that I wrote to the 'Souvenir' is so polished & altered that I did not scarcly know it was my own.[1]

These two symptomatic quotations, from letters by John Clare to his publishers James Hessey and John Taylor, respectively, show how difficult it could be for Clare to negotiate over his texts as they entered the machinery of print culture. They also show how varied his responses could be to the process of change which took his texts from manuscript to printed collection. In the first quotation from 1822, Clare wants the close, intimate help of Taylor, whose 'opinion' will put his texts at 'rights' – which implies he thought his texts were at some 'wrongs' before Taylor's help. In other words, Clare is submitting to the standardising procedures and demands of publication and print culture – and seemingly he is submitting willingly, gregariously and humbly. At this moment, he trusts his publishers with his texts and is happy for their editing to proceed. Three years later in 1825, in the second quotation, Clare shows another aspect of his trust in Taylor when he condemns the editor of the *Literary Souvenir* for the unauthorised publication of two poems[2] in a state which reveals them to have been 'polished & altered' on their way through the 'mangle' of despoiling publication. Clare is alienated from his own creation: the horror at his lack of authorial control is fully realised in his own creature being now barely recognisable to him. This comment was made in a letter which worries at the increasing estrangement and neglect Clare felt from Taylor, due to the delayed process of getting *The Shepherd's Calendar* into print, which was beginning to get troublesome.[3]

My point here lies in the differing contexts of the two quotations: differing publishing processes and differing editors. One known and authorised; one hidden and unauthorised; and finally each letter has a different recipient, and produces wholly different responses from Clare to basically the same issue. Unsurprisingly, contrasting contexts produce contrasting responses from Clare over editing and over the standardisation procedures that every single one of his published texts went through. Yet it is clear that he had a varying attitude to linguistic standardisation over the course of his long writing life – ranging across a whole spectrum from extreme to extreme. It is unfortunate for readers today that most editions of Clare's texts have not represented the instability and variation of his responses to linguistic standardisation.

The editing of Clare is constructed by two opposing and mutually exclusive views of what his attitude to language was. Editors' clashes over the poet's attitude to language essentially follow the same entrenched contours as the debate over standard language in the 1980s and 1990s, which were conflictual but more explicitly political. This wider debate continues as a politicised fight about linguistic and national histories, about education, about ideologies, about class and about the history of the historians of the English language. The debate is well rehearsed, but perhaps we should remind ourselves of its polarities.

From the blue corner emerges the argument that any nation needs a standard and widely understood language for its smooth running, for its economy, for its cohesion and its social unity. This position maintains that the version of the English language which in the nineteenth century became the standard way of writing and speaking was the best choice, the most sophisticated, the most complex, the most accurate, the most respected. From the opposing red corner emerges a belief that the language legitimised and enforced by hegemony and its education system inherently carries the values of the class which legitimises it – the class which speaks the language of choice, and in the case of English that is the language of exclusive, expensive, southern public schools, which therefore privileges and further empowers the speakers and writers of that version of English. The red corner would have it that any repression of local accent and dialect is tantamount to political oppression and the deliberate demonisation and inferiorisation of cultures; and that the enforced learning of a standard language facilitates indoctrination, pacification, colonisation. In the blue corner standard language is the bearer of morality, rationality, nationality; in the red corner standard language is the arbiter of state oppression, a marker of compromise and a tool of propaganda and distortion. In the blue corner standard language is a natural right and a social necessity which grants access to power, which levels society, which includes everyone who uses it. In the red corner it is argued that standard language has been naturalised through an artificial process of codification, and is enforced by language missionaries in the classroom and by rewriters of linguistic history in the universities; further, processes and enforcers of standardisation suppress local vernacular variation, seek to subsume all regional variances, and work to de-legitimise and stymie linguistic difference, rendering one variant 'better' than all others and so excluding and castigating those speakers and writers – and learners – who do not adhere to its rules. The blue corner would have it that nationally accepted 'rules' of language are exactly what the country needs for the sane running of its affairs.

The pair of colours I have used to describe this fight are entirely political. In debates which entrenched across the early 1980s language became a battleground, as conservative thinkers sought to 'rescue' the classroom from what they saw as linguistic social liberalism gone mad in the 1960s and 1970s. Marxist linguists and cultural and social theorists and educationalists stood their ground, dug in and had recourse to a reassessment of the history of language study, to investigate the manner of naturalisation of the standard, to reveal the artifice and social construction of its codification and dominance. This was, and to an extent remains, war, over that most important cultural everyman's land: language.[4]

This is a crude mapping, of course, but the fact is that the oppositional nature of the wars between left and right in the 1980s and 1990s takes exactly the same shape, and includes many of the same issues, as the directly conflictive, intransigent and impassioned debate which developed between editors over the presentation, editing and repackaging of John Clare's texts (though most involved would seek not to politicise their own positions in the blatant or tribal way described here). I will not look at the 'evidence' in Clare's own words in support of either case, nor at the resultant editorial practices, because both issues have been analysed in detail in two judicious essays by R. K. R. Thornton.[5] Instead, this chapter will focus on the narratives that editors of Clare construct to announce, proclaim and defend their own methods and texts, while denouncing the methodologies of others. We will then consider whether there is a way to break the deadlock.

Since the 1960s, Clare has been published for the most part by the Oxford University Clarendon Press editing team of Paul Dawson, David Powell and Eric Robinson – a team which has also included Geoffrey Summerfield and Margaret Grainger at times. In 2003 they published their ninth and final volume of the complete poetry, bringing to an end a colossal feat of scholarship. Without doubt the most prolific, comprehensive and powerful grouping of all Clare's editors, this team has also edited cheaper and essential paperback editions of the poetry and prose for

Oxford and the MidNAG/Carcanet partnership. The editors of the Oxford complete poetry were joined in their 'textual primitivism' by Anne Tibble and Kelsey Thornton in *The Midsummer Cushion* (1979), Margaret Grainger in *Natural History Prose Writings* (1983) and Mark Storey in *Letters* (1985).[6] All of the editorial work across this impressive range of collections underpins this book, as it does for many another critical study that has emerged in the last thirty years or more. The editorial methodology of the team editing the nine volumes of poetry especially requires some discussion. From the off, the editorial team asserted its belief that Clare was a radical about the way in which he would present his language in print. Here they are introducing the last volume of the Oxford complete edition:

> What we decided *not* to do, was to publish corrected versions of Clare. We came to the conclusion that Taylor's and Hessey's corrections took far more away from Clare's poetry than they contributed to its clarification. We do not accept the argument that, because Clare had sometimes passed proof for Taylor and Hessey, we should accept the corrected readings. We believe that Clare's genius is rooted in his language – in his vocabulary, his spelling, his syntax; his idiom, his tone and his use of dialect; even when this results in crude names for flowers or other natural phenomena. We believe that to change Clare's language is to alter his social and economic status and to destroy his local culture... In reading modernized editions of Clare, we are more often struck by the distortions of Clare's meanings that occur in them, than by the improvements made in the readings.[7]

This is more than a platform for an editorial methodology: it is a manifesto, a creed, a set of foundational, fundamental beliefs, with all the organicist, naturalising, rhetorical repetition of a national and political constitution. Their Clare is anti-standard grammar, anti-standard punctuation and a resister of the hegemonic, enforced codification and standardisation of language. Their Clare was never happy with editorial intervention, advice or correction of any kind, even when he said he was. For the purposes of this admittedly simplifying discussion, they are squarely, some might say oddly, in the red corner. Fundamentally their resultant claimed intention is to transcribe from Clare's manuscripts *exactly* as the poet wrote them. And this means that they denounce, and editorially ignore, the authority of any of the texts published in Clare's lifetime, even those which he oversaw and approved. Spelling, punctuation and capitalisation are often referred to as 'accidentals' in standard editing practice and, as such, 'not substantive',[8] but they are the central concern here. Because of the sheer range and importance of the editions following this method it is has become the orthodoxy. These books together form the scholarly foundations of all Clare research: they are the 'standard' editions, and rightly so. Many of the texts they present were never published before, and certainly never with such scholarly rigour.

If the various Oxford teams publishing poems, prose and letters – and their critical followers – are in the red corner, defending Clare's right to linguistic idiosyncrasy, then Jonathan Bate's recent paperback selection (Farrar, Straus and Giroux, 2003; Faber and Faber, 2004) and his celebrated Clare biography (Picador, 2003), as well as those who have advocated for a presentationally altered text, are in the blue corner, likewise claiming to do right by Clare, likewise asserting the moral high ground. Bate's Clare is a different authorial creature entirely and promotes a different programme of editorial intervention. In the biography, if the poet gets political at all, Bate claims that he does so '[a]lmost without realising it'.[9] In this subtle way, while providing the fullest account yet of Clare's life as a writer, Bate denies him active political agency. In his edition, Bate makes a case for his regularising and standardising of Clare's texts. He adds his name to a long list of dissenters from the Oxford editors' orthodoxy – a list which includes critical work by Zachary Leader, Tim Chilcott, Roger Sales, M. M. Mahood and Hugh Haughton, and editorial work by Kelsey Thornton in his Everyman edition, myself in two prefatory selections, and of course the names of many editors who worked on Clare manuscripts before the Oxford team's radical change of methodological direction in the 1960s. In short, this list of editors argues for and enacts a varied set of policies which broadly claim that it is a necessary part of the editorial process for Clare's texts to be regularised and standardised to varying degrees, not least because that was what he expected of his 'raw' manuscripts, once submitted – even though the manner in which editors in his own day proceeded did not always accord with his own oversight of the final pre-print presentation. The argument continues that for all his anger about grammar being 'like Tyranny in government',[10] actually he often appreciated 'help' from his editors to make his verse more accessible, so why should modern editors not continue to do so? In fact, the context of the 'grammer in learning is like Tyranny in government' line suggests that a full-scale resistance to standard grammatical agreements (and so on) was far from being resolute:

> I may alter but I cannot mend   grammer in learning is like Tyranny in government – confound the bitch Ill never be her slave & have a vast good mind not to alter the verse in question – by g—d Ive tryd an hour & cannot do a syllable so do your best or let it pass

Though furious and seemingly politicised over standard language practice here, Clare asks for editorial assistance – 'do your best', he instructs – meaning that this quotation can be marshalled in support of either side of the debate. But for this group, editorial interference is not necessarily a negative, invasive or destructive act, and the claims of a radical politicisation of Clare's language use have been much exaggerated. Here is an extract from latest in this line, Jonathan Bate:

> Clare indicated in a note to his publishers that he expected his editors to normalize his spelling ('I'm' for 'Im', 'used' for 'usd', etc.) and to introduce punctuation for the sake of clarity, but he did not want them to over-regularize his grammar or remove the regional dialect words that were so essential to his voice... [The] nine volumes of the Oxford University Press [published] between 1984 and 2003, [were] based rigorously on the original unpunctuated and erratically spelt manuscripts.
>
> But, as I show in my biography of Clare, the poet positively wanted his friends and publishers to assist him in the preparation of his work for the press. The final wording of many lines was reached via a process of dialogue that is frequently recoverable from surviving correspondence... Clare was glad to be given advice, but did not always take it. Sometimes he acknowledged that his work was improved by his editors, whilst sometimes he stood by his own first thoughts.
>
> As Clare used his critical self-judgement, so the modern editor should use critical judgement and analytical bibliography to decide on the status of the variations between manuscripts and printed texts – to distinguish between errors based on misreading of Clare's hand or misinterpretation of his sense, alterations that go against his spirit, and improvements of which he approved or is likely to have approved. This anthology is accordingly the first substantial selection from Clare's entire oeuvre to be prepared according to the principles that the poet himself wished to be applied to his work: the errors and unapproved alterations of earlier editors are removed, but light punctuation is provided and spelling is regularized without diluting the dialect voice.[11]

Bate's Clare spells 'erratically' and was 'glad to be given advice' by his friends, and so Bate puts himself in that same position, as a friend, as an advisor even. He then adopts something more appropriate to an authorial position: 'As Clare used his critical self-judgement, so the modern editor should use critical judgement and analytical bibliography to decide...' Here Bate claims to be doing more than merely interpreting text: the position he asserts for his editing has untroubled similitude, through that simple bridging 'so', to Clare's own critical-creative position in relation to the original text. With that authoritative sounding 'critical bibliography', Bate might even be inferring a claim to a position close to Clare's authorial authority, but with the added benefit of serious, professionalised scholarly technique. Deftly, Bate confers a vantage point for his editing that might be even *better* than Clare's own. If that were not enough to make us rely on the text he constructs, he then claims that his authoritative position means that any changes he makes will be unlikely to 'go against [Clare's] spirit'. Such talk of 'spirit' elevates an editorial methodology to a plane of communication with a long-dead poet, and suggests there is an 'essence of Clareness', known only to Bate. As Clare's biographer it is perhaps inevitable that in his supporting edition, Bate reconstructs Clare's 'spirit' as a guide for his editing. In case we had not quite got that point, the editor continues:

> This anthology is accordingly the first substantial selection from Clare's entire oeuvre to be prepared according to the principles that the poet himself wished to be applied to his work: the errors and unapproved alterations of earlier editors are removed, but light punctuation is provided and spelling is regularized without diluting the dialect voice.[12]

A 'principle' is an origin, a source; a source of action; a beginning, commencement; fountainhead; a fundamental source from which something proceeds; a primary element, force, or law which produces or determines particular results. It is a fundamental truth (all *OED*). If Bate is right, if Clare's principles can be located in a clear fashion and if, as he says in his biography, reading Clare's rejection of punctuation as a 'political gesture' is a 'mistaken modern assumption',[13] then clearly the Oxford editors have got it wrong, in point of fact and in point of fundamental principle. In a sense, Bate returns us to an original principle of standard editing, printing and publishing practice. He is therefore as much of a fundamentalist as the Oxford team. We might even say that his return to manuscripts to then edit with his 'new-found' fundamental principle is also a species of 'textual primitivism'. For all this, Bate still includes what he calls '"raw" or "unedited"' texts when the problems of regularising – and the resulting distance between 'raw' and 'cooked' text – seem too great. Perhaps he is not quite as certain about Clare's linguistic 'principles' as his argument asserts.[14]

Fundamentally, the Oxford editors' claimed intention is to transcribe from Clare's manuscripts exactly as the poet wrote them. Now of course, what I have just paraphrased is not, cannot, be true. In editorial terms, the action of 'transcription' carries a transformative, a transitional and a translatory effect; transcription is activity, not passivity. Also, we might say that manuscripts do not look like books, they do not read like books, materially they do not smell or feel like books. Equally, handwritten words do not look or read like printed text. You get the drift: the word 'transcribe' actually contains an enormous amount of intention and transformative activity on the editors' and subsequently on the printers' parts. The transition from handwritten text to printed regular type is a huge leap, and there is always a unbridgeable distance between manuscript and printed text, not only in what the two look like, but in what the reading process will involve and require. The Oxford text only provides room, for the majority of poems, for one manuscript-based transcription. And it is on this front that the word 'transcription' seems full of latent critical value judgement or, more politely put, editorial 'discernment'. Take, for example, the following quotation from the introduction to a *Middle Poems* volume (my italicised emphases):

> In most cases MS A54 supplies the copy-text. The exceptions to this are where the MS A54 text *seems* to represent a self-censoring of earlier versions, where we have *preferred* the earlier text; or where the transcription into Pforzheimer Library, Misc. MS 196, allowed him the opportunity substantially to revise a poem, where we have *preferred* the later text.[15]

My point here lies in those words 'seems' and 'preferred'. Inevitably, the editors' choices govern our reading, through a plain system of what they think is 'best' or rather what they think Clare would have thought 'best'. While this team of editors might not insert punctuation, regularise Clare's spelling or indent his rhymed lines, while they claim to follow his own handwritten words to the letter, they also decide which version of the poem to include. When there is more than one version of a poem in manuscript, the choice of copy-text, I would argue, is as invasive and reconstructive as any editorial intervention. Unless Clare was to get a truly complete edition, with all textual variants transcribed in full (not just fully footnoted), such choices are a necessary responsibility in the editing of his work and they permanently lead the way readers access the work. But such editorial choice runs counter to the self-presentation of these editors as simply transcribing from manuscripts. As much as it would be true for any editor, the Oxford team become creative rewriters of Clare's textual life. As some critics have pointed out,[16] the Oxford team will silently reorder a poem or a piece of prose if they think they can make more sense of it than is apparent from Clare's original manuscript ordering. They admit too that they do not always follow extant manuscripts. Where the poems were copied out by an amanuensis, the team corrects, sometimes silently, led by their unwavering beliefs about Clare's original intentions, according to their understanding of his politicisation of language. For example, Clare spent the last years of his life (1841–1864) in Northampton General Lunatic Asylum. Many of the poems he wrote there were copied out by an attendant, William F. Knight, and only Knight's versions of most of these poems remain; instead of transcribing Knight's version exactly, the Oxford team create a new text, their supporting argument reading as follows:

> Like other editors Knight sometimes misreads a word and where our own familiarity with Clare's practice has enabled us to suggest alternative readings, we have placed these in the main text if we think they make better sense than Knight's.[17]

Their resultant published texts are therefore sometimes new formations which do not directly reflect the manuscript source. Their editorial principle seems more complex than plain, faithful transcription. It is in fact as modulated and nuanced as that of Jonathan Bate.

It is a simple truism, but one often ignored, that the editor, not the author, is the organising agent of editions of this sort, even where the edition claims to be complete, fully inclusive and faithful to the original. Clare's Oxford team are fundamentalists, in that they have and maintain 'a leading or primary principle, rule, law, which serves as the groundwork of a system' and in that they present their methodology and their text as 'primary, original; from which others are derived' (all *OED*). Because that approach was reinforced by a private copyright claim to the publicly owned manuscripts by the lead editor of the standard Oxford edition, the variety of editing methodologies has been curtailed, for as many as fifty years,[18] though the effects seem to have diminished of late.[19] The greatest irony for an editing team so committed to non-standard textual presentation is that copyright law is itself a construction of the publishing industry – a mechanism which guarantees 'standard' behaviour, adherence to a regulated conception of text as property, and which requires deference and submission to authority and laws of commercial interest.

One of the problems that no editor can overcome, and one that Clare himself ran up against, is that print culture is founded on standards, on regularity and on consistency. In the previous chapter we saw how text perpendicular to the horizontal has to be regulated into order in printed forms, but that is just the most obvious and simple form of standardisation (Clare did not write emblem poems, nor any other model where text might be set other than horizontally). A text will also be given a standard font, regular sizes of letter and spacing, standard symbols of punctuation and inflection, line indentation to indicate rhyme or paragraphing, justification, margins, page numbering and all the various regularities in formatting and text-page design. Along with printed textual regularities, most books have the same quality, texture and size of paper throughout: pages are bound together, made compact and the text consistent in terms of ink colour and quantity used on the homogenous paper. Proofing, editorial interventions and all the processes that go into the physical making of a book, down to the presses churning out the final 'copies', all lead to exactly similar versions of the same, regularised product. From the shape of the books to the shape of the letters, printed matter *always* tidies and reorders the originating typed, handwritten, spoken or word-processed language, and this is surely a core function of printing and of publishing. Standardising and regularising are precisely what we expect from the normalising practices of the publishing industry. In publishers' agreed standards readers find security and reliability, and so to some degree there must be comforting pleasure in our relationship to any book if we can predict its approximate shape and contents, even when the words inside are as yet unknown to us. Standards let us know what we want to know: that there will be no hurdle between us and direct, straightforward understanding; that we have ready passage to something reliable. In resisting this hugely pervasive and naturalised industry, the Oxford editors are doing something radical indeed; but they are not B. S. Johnson. The hardbound, expensive, profusely and self-avowedly scholarly nine-volume edition of the poetry forms a fundamentally conservative organ. The editors do not acknowledge a problem which works against the foundation of what they say they are trying to achieve: their edition is only partially resistant to print culture in not standardising Clare's texts. Their introductions and notes are all sophisticatedly Latinate, the spelling is standard, the dialect, inflections and syntactical structures are standard; their unwieldy, aesthetically intrusive, textual apparatus is similar to a dense mathematical equation, so tricky is it to use; their limited explanatory notes are founded in the gravid standard-bearing authority of scholarly discourse and research. As was inevitable, what might have been a radical methodology in the 1960s has become the established norm, has become the conservative safe ground, guarded and defended as being the morally correct territory to work within. Paradoxically, the standard edition maintains Clare's non-standard linguistic practice from within an establishment position, framed, managed and explained within a standard type of scholarly text. While these editors question standards of language practice on Clare's behalf, they never question the politics of the standard text they have created, the established and authorising press which published it, the standard language of their own scholarly writing and its possibly problematic relationship to Clare's non-standard language. The result is a self-contradictory paradox: a radical version of Clare's language delivered upon and defended by the most conservative and elite of platforms.

If it is now time to move beyond the delimitations, positions and counter-positions of existing editorial practices, if we are to rebuild Clare's texts in ways that enable engagement with textual complexity – while also ensuring wider access to audiences with diverse interests in Clare – then we need to reconsider Clare's own conception of textual making, to forge something new yet based on principles unique to his aesthetics and idiosyncratic politics. We first go back to Jonathan Bate's point about 'Clare's erratic orthography'.[20] Erratic shares the same route as 'error', both from the Latin *errare*, to wander. It is a word which suggests Clare's spelling was erroneous, mistaken, incorrect, uncontrolled, random – in some ways hinting at the opposite of linguistic and political agency. Because of its route, 'erratic' also signifies a 'wandering from place to place'; to be vagrant, nomadic. An erratic is someone 'who is eccentric in modes of action' (all *OED*). It is a word which suggests a destabilising inconsistency, an aimlessness. It is inconsistency which, if followed as the Oxford editors do, is alien to print culture. As an aesthetic mode, though, erratic and creative inconsistency could be reflective of orality, of spoken language. Like other labouring-class poets of the Romantic era, such as Mary Bryan, James Hogg, Robert Bloomfield and Allan Cunningham, Clare was steeped in oral culture, with its folk tales and songs, story-tellers, fiddle-players and penny ballads – in other words, his primary cultural literacy was not in print, but in the spoken word, in voice, in speech acts, in tales, in music and in song. Clare's oral culture and his social class are the primary sources of his 'erratic', wandering, nomadic and social aesthetic. Here I am not referring to material geography, but aesthetic model. For someone supposedly so rooted to a place (as explored in the opening chapter), in fact Clare's idealised aesthetic is rambling and vagrant, itinerant and outside. Within this set of dynamic 'tactics' he explores his own resistance to humanity's authoritative governing subject position, 'that little personal pronoun "I"' which he condemns as a 'Deity over the rest of the alphabet'.[21] He resists the pastoral poet's formula for a delight in disorder, and through his modelling of nature he sometimes even attempts a levelling of human social hierarchy through a network of rural plurality. This all impinges upon his textual life, and should inform how his work is presented.

It might be that Clare will remain impossible to 'edit' in a satisfactory manner, as his manuscripts enact a wild, unmanageable inconsistency which is energised in many ways against the codification, stratification and careful organisation innate to any printed edition of his work. This could be a reason that neither the Clare created by the Oxford team nor that created by Bate or any other 'polishing' editor can be fully satisfactory or fully representative of what Clare was about. An edition cannot 'contain' Clare's manuscripts, because a book is too much of a standardising, organising, deadening, encapsulating machine, a machine of closure for the delivery of something which resists easy parcelling: Clare's unfinishable textual world. Bookish man though Clare was in life,[22] the legacy that is his textual world is shot through with shifting sands, with the erratic, the unstable, the inconsistent, the fluid, the indeterminate and the unfinished, because it is simultaneously reflective of nature in process. At the same time Clare's poeticity is always an oral world – sounded, heard, muttered,[23] spoken, sung, echoed, lost and recollected. Clare attempts to straddle the distance between vernacular or dialect orality and written language, between actual speech acts and the printed word – and all the sounds and silences in between. As poet Tom Leonard points out, words are not spelt when they are spoken.[24] Clare's aesthetic is partly generated by the active fault line between sound and print, but it is also always ecological, seeking and describing connections and conjunctions between humanity and nature, between the individual and the social.

Perhaps, then, we could begin to develop a more tentative, inclusive editing style out of the current, urgent environmental politics which is most directly linked to Clare's core aesthetic and which informs much of the current attention he is receiving. Perhaps instead of forcing Clare's texts into either red or blue extreme on the language-war spectrum, we might instead start looking to the colour green.[25] We might start to think of ways in which Clare's proto-ecology might help inform a contemporary editorial methodology which, instead of morally opposing 'raw' against 'cooked' texts (to use R. K. R. Thornton's useful terms[26]), could instead reach for interconnectedness between different branches of his textual legacy. This legacy includes all manner of species of textual variant, all of which interrelate, all of which can function independently, but which are most richly encountered with their bountiful multiplicity maintained. Tim Chilcott's edition of *The Shepherd's Calendar* – which places a transcription of Clare's 'raw' manuscript opposite the 'cooked' 1827 published version – takes us part of the way there[27]: it unfixes meaning, foregrounds, even *requires*, readerly choice, and defers much of the editorial determinism of previous editions. But even though it allows access to the inherent problem of editing Clare, and it laudably defers choices to the reader for the first time ever in the publishing of his work, the shape of the book-bound page means this is an edition physically limited still to those two opposing versions of Clare's text: for all Chilcott's diligent balance, his text remains limited by the shape of the book he presents. It embodies the same binary opposition this chapter has been describing – page against *opposing* page, left *versus* right, verso versus recto, Clare (pure, messy, original, raw) versus Taylor (corrupted, clean, secondary, cooked). Eco-editing might therefore have to free itself of the limitations of the book, not only because of the trees it costs, but also because the book is binary, constrains us to a two-dimensional reading space. It would be naive to think that online textual resources are carbon free, of course, or that they are not without their structural limitations, but it is to new technology that we should turn if we wish to fulfil, and fill out, Clare's potential textual resonance.

Now we will look at a famous instance of Clare's organicising model of the making of poetry. Through that analysis, we will be better positioned to consider further theoretical underpinnings for the ways in which Clare's texts might be edited in the future.

'THE BOOK I LOVE IS EVERYWHERE': THE MAKING OF CLARE'S TEXTUAL FUTURES

Having assessed the spectrum of versions of Clare's textual presentation, we now turn to Clare's own conceptions of how poetry is made, in order to forge a route through the current editorial landscape. The springboard is formed of two lines in Clare's work which have become famously talismanic. They have served as a catalyst for many critics, as they will do for this chapter. The first reference to the lines we visit is not the earliest and is perhaps the least analytical of all. But it is the one which confirms that, just thirteen years after the poet's death, these lines had become *the* signpost indicating that *Clareness* was close by. In 1876 Frederick Williams writes:

> Passing Helpstone, where John Clare, the Northamptonshire poet was born, in 1793, of parents even then receiving parish relief, and who tells us of his literary gifts, –
> 'I found the poems in the fields,
> And only wrote them down,' –
> we soon reach Peterborough, join the Great Northern Railway, enter its station, and then taking our way down to the Great Eastern, find there the end of our journey.

These lines alone form the signifier sufficient for passing local interest as Williams dashes past Helpston on the Syston and Peterborough line, in his extensive and detailed history of the 'mighty and beneficent revolution' and 'modern enterprise'[28] of the Midland railway network. Steamed up modernity has no time to ponder: on we must go.

The lines maintained their talismanic position way into the twentieth century, coming to stand for something inexpressibly Clare-like, for some vague and often unexplained essence of what Clare is about. Cecil Day Lewis uses the lines as evidence of Clare's 'hyperaesthesia' – he just cannot help himself: writing is urgently instinctual and uncontrollable.[29] Without much commentary to speak of, Harold Bloom slots the lines into his argument that Clare sought comfort – but ultimately withered – in Wordsworth's shadow.[30] Abruptly, Paul Chirico says the lines offer a 'conventionally naïve literary model', which amounts to a 'claim that has long been recognised as disingenuous'.[31] Most recently, in the bathetically entitled *Can Poetry Save the Earth?* John Felstiner deploys the two lines to affirm Clare's 'humbleness' before the natural world.[32] But of all uses by twentieth- and twenty-first-century commentators, most interesting is the role the lines play in John Ashbery's mystical version of Clare, which I will quote at length:

> What he sees, he is... The sudden, surprising lack of distance between poet and reader is in proportion to the lack of distance between the poet and the poem; he is the shortest distance between poem and reader. We are far from emotion recollected in tranquillity or even the gently shaping music of Keats's grasshopper sonnet. Clare's poems are dispatches from the front. 'I found the poems in the fields/and only wrote them down,' he wrote, and he tells us that a favorite method of composing was in the open, using his hat as a writing desk. The resulting *plein-air* effect is similar to the studies of John Constable, Clare's exact contemporary. In the case of both, the point is that there is no point. Clare is constantly wandering, in his circumscribed domain, but there is not much to see; the land is flat and fenny and devoid of 'prospects.' Unlike Wordsworth's exalted rambles in 'The Prelude,' there is no indication that all this is leading up to something.[33]

Ashbery revels in Clare's aimless, nomadic wandering, and does not condemn the poetry for being unaware of its own direction. The first clipped sentence of this passage is tersely summative of what follows. Ashbery's model of Clare squeezes out the Cartesian thought process: not 'I think, therefore I am' but 'What he sees, he is'. Seeing erases thought – and Ashbery's phrase even erases the Cartesian conjunction 'therefore' (or rather, 'donc' or 'ergo' in Descartes's original uses of the famous phrase in French and Latin, respectively). Ashbery elides the possibility of awareness of the relationship between seeing and being. He reads a process where the perception *of* something is immediately incorporated *with* it. Somehow, Clare successfully closes the gap between perception and existence, between subject and object, and frees himself of any overall design (for Ashbery this is squarely a positive aspect of his verse). This chapter will now interrogate the purpose and positioning of the closure of the gap between human subject and natural object to which Clare appears to lay a foundational claim (and over which Ashbery is so impressed), eventually to inform a prospective methodology for the presentation of Clare's texts.

None of the critics mentioned above quotes the poem from which each extracts the talismanic lines. 'Sighing for Retirement' was first published in an essay by Cyrus Redding in *The English Journal* of 15 May 1841.[34] There is no holograph copy of the poem, nor any manuscript version by an amanuensis known to Clare. The only version we have, therefore, has been through the textual mill of the recipient who was also *The English Journal*'s editor, Redding, an extensively experienced and well-connected man of letters (most notably editor of the *New Monthly Magazine* from 1821–1830); the title of the poem might be Redding's – we simply cannot know. We are therefore at a considerable remove from an 'original' textual source. How much editorial tidying and polishing of Clare's original text was carried out by Redding likewise we can never know. Having visited Clare in the High Beech Asylum in Essex where he acquired this and other unpublished poems, Redding reads the verse as a testament to the improvement of Clare's mental state since beginning his residence as a voluntary patient in 1837. For Redding, it was reassuring that the poet was still able to write well about the 'agreeable situation' of the asylum in Epping Forest: this is Redding's assessment of the place in which this poem was composed. After Clare's death, in a revised account of the meeting, Redding admits he was unsure as to why Clare was in the asylum at all, and so was the medic who ran the place, Matthew Allen: 'the Doctor said that Clare's mind was so slightly affected that he thought it might be as well if he were at home with his friends'.[35] The poems are offered to the readers of *The English Journal* in support of this assessment of Clare's condition. Here is the poem in full, as it appeared in 1841:

> O TAKE me from the busy crowd,
>   I cannot bear the noise!
> For Nature's voice is never loud;
>   I seek for quiet joys.
>
> The book I love is everywhere,
>   And not in idle words;
> The book I love is known to all,
>   And better lore affords.
>
> The book I love is everywhere,
>   And every place the same;
> GOD bade me make my dwelling there,
>   And look for better fame.
>
> I never feared the critic's pen,
>   To live by my renown;
> I found the poems in the fields,
>   And only wrote them down.

And quiet Epping pleases well,
  Where Nature's love delays;
I joy to see the quiet place,
  And wait for better days.

I love to see the brakes and fern,
  And rabbits up and down;
And then the pleasant Autumn comes,
  And turns them all to brown.

To common eyes they only seem
  A desert waste and drear;
To taste and love they always shine,
  A garden through the year.

LORD keep my love for quiet joys,
  Oh, keep me to thy will!
I know THY works, and always find
  THY mercies kinder still!

The first critical response to this poem appeared ten years later, written by Edwin Paxton Hood. Hood was a dissenting Congregationalist minister who promoted the cause, value and special cases of working-class poets in the middle of the nineteenth century. He was prolific in many other areas, publishing over fifty books between 1846 and 1886[36] (including collections of sermons, self-help books, educational and ethical treatises, works theorising biography, one on the morality of laughter, a number of works on anecdotes, two on Englishness, one on Scottishness, two polemics on Jamaica, and separate biographical studies of Cromwell, Milton, Marvell, Watts, Wordsworth, Carlyle, Swedenbourg and Queens Mary and Elizabeth). In the midst of this activity, Hood published three closely related works on the poor and art, entitled *The Literature of Labour* and *Genius and Industry* (both of 1851) and a revision, compendium and expansion of these two books in *The Peerage of Poverty; or, Learners and Workers in Fields, Farms, and Factories* (first edition 1859, repeatedly revised and expanded until its final, celebrated fifth edition of 1870). One of the founding voices of modern Clare criticism and editing, Mark Storey, considers Hood's response to be 'one of the best contemporary appraisals of Clare's work as a whole'.[37]

Hood's *The Literature of Labour* – with its resolute subtitle *Illustrious Instances of the Education of Poetry in Poverty* – provides the first major critical essay on Clare which is not hampered by a patronising set of class-based excuses and pity for the poet's impecunious lot. In so doing, it effectively clears the ground for all confident Clare criticism to come. Though it does romanticise the poet's peculiar sensitivities and physical frailty, Hood's critique lacks the latent anxiety over Clare's status that we can readily track through nineteenth- and twentieth-century critics. With all the didactic, polemical assertiveness of a committed liberal working against the conventional Victorian equation of economic power with moral worth, Hood claims that 'we may call Clare the Wordsworth of Labour', and is detailed, and convincing, as to why. Introducing Clare's 'Sighing for Retirement' and the talismanic lines in question, Hood writes:

> The following lines are very touching, when it is remembered that they are the pensive utterance of a soul ill at ease from the very frailty of the tabernacle in which it is confined – a house too fragile for the strong spirit within it – the cause at once of every poet's madness. His organic sensibility, his nervous nature responding to every varying tone and intimation, and his strong soul desiring to overleap the material pales and boundaries, and live entirely in the land, visiting it in his poetic dreamings.[38]

The expression of Hood's upon which I wish to focus is 'desiring to overleap the material pales and boundaries and live entirely in the land'. Pales could simply refer to wooden stakes or poles used as part of a fence – or fences in their entirety; Hood could also mean plots, territories, marked out by boundaries; or, more abstractly, pale could signify a 'realm or sphere of activity, influence, knowledge, etc.; a domain, a field' (all *OED*). Clare's poetic leap for Hood is into a process of desiring, a process of boundary-breaking, an ongoing project of desire to 'live ... *in* the land' (my emphasis), to go beyond demarcated territories, to break with an accustomed situation in order to write – we could borrow from Deleuze and Guattari and say that Hood sees deterritorialisation in writing, or rather finding, poetry. He is not on the land, or with the land, or a few miles above it, but *in* it. Hood sees Clare as the mole, rather than the eagle – surrounded by earth, encapsulated by fields. For Hood, as for Ashbery, Clare poeticises a 'desiring' to close the gap between himself and the land; in other words, as a poet he works against the physical, conceptual and subjective separation of himself from the natural world, against the normative separation of his subject position from nature as object. Clare's might have been an impossible dream, but I would maintain that 'in' is the direction in which his most significant work and commentary point: *in* is set against both anthropocentrism and the outward exhalations of Romantic egotism, as discussed in Chapter 2. The two lines themselves work against the accustomed practices and purposeful poise of the conventions of poetic composition, of deliberative, egotistical poetic agency.

For Clare in the two talismanic lines of 'Sighing for Retirement', text is the issue of something prior: poetry exists somewhere and sometime before text. Text is remnant, partial record, echo and trace. The field of this experience of discovery renders the writing subject of little or no significance. The writer becomes scribe, passive conduit, lightning conductor for something so powerful it courses through him to the page, with a sweeping dismissal of the writer's input. This is not just a model of organic authorship, it is also a model of the natural world, which communicates blankly – and communicates before man wanders accidentally upon the offerings of its meaning system, continuing to express long after man has quit the scene. In this model, it is man, rather than nature, who is vacancy, who is blank amanuensis. Shelley's 'human mind's imaginings' which seem to offer the only expression of, and meaning for, the void of nature's 'vacancy' are of no consequence here; actually Clare's lines invert Shelley's troubled interrogative which ends, and effectively reopens, 'Mont Blanc'.[39] Clare's God-fearing poet lies prostrate at the temple of a nature which cares not a jot for him and the poet loves it – the poet lives off the discovery and his passivity in the reception of it. Crucially, impossibly, perhaps foolishly, Clare's model claims to close the subject/object gap by denying subjectivity and agency to what we should no longer call the writing subject, and by providing communicative, artistic purpose to a living entity, object no more. The poet is little more than a delivery boy of exchange in fields of meaning, and is part of a project which he claims (and Ashbery believes) is beyond his understanding. The poet denies much active function to himself, but this is not necessarily evidence of social humility or self-effacing modesty. There is a long tradition behind Clare's faux-naive self-presentation, of course: he places himself squarely in the earliest 'troubadour' line as creative *finder* and discoverer, rather than the poesis model of creative *maker*, Romantic originator or Coleridgean fountain.[40]

Clare, as nature's delivery boy and troubadour, bidden by God, turns up the location of the strands of text which need picking up, copying down and redelivering: any social 'humbleness' Felstiner reads actually masks the implication that this poet is ethically superior to the aesthete, to the plotter, the schemer, the botaniser, the scholar or the documenter. Clare is emphatic about the ways in which his own special 'taste and love' see things 'common eyes' ignore. This poem is one of a number of instances where he claims to be part of an elite who see and understand in ways and modes the common order cannot manage – the self-important snobbery[41] expressed by Clare jars with prevalent assumptions about his archetypally supposedly 'down-to-earth' socially sympathetic simplicity.

Clare conceals his knowledge of his routes of access to this supersensory situation, because he has *become* her, if we can allow nature as woman for the purposes of this analysis. 'It' does not fully signify what Clare is conceiving here, whereas to address nature with the pronoun 'her' is to empower 'her' with a subject position of her own (though one admittedly of a man's making). Closing the distance between man and nature – 'the unbridgeable gap between the beautiful soul and the world', as Timothy Morton calls it[42] – has not only meant the poet is implicit in the natural world, but also suggests a rare achievement: the distinctions between man and nature, between nature and culture, have dissolved. The poet has abrogated these man-made categories. He *is* the natural world: he is becoming nature – and embodying nature, as she disembodies him through textual exchange. Effectively, he undermines the necessity of an ontological category called 'nature'. The poet is entwined so much with nature that he cannot distinguish his own subject position from hers, nor does he want to. The field of meaning of his own experience segues into her physical fields – at least, such unification is clearly implicated. Thought and ground, text and texture, are in a process of becoming one. In this poem, nature does not give him a voice: she instructs. Clare cleanses the problems, the compromises, the iterations, alterations and altercations of socialised authorship here too – erasing as he does so the significance of the 'critic's pen'. It is important to note that, in this poem, Clare does not compensate for his disdain of literary sociability by putting his poet in a familial structure of relation with the natural world. She is not a cosy retreat, and not Mother Nature, but Lover Nature. The power of the mother is denied; the anthropomorphism of the natural field is disavowed; the imposing hierarchies of relation with editor, with audience, with other poets, with critics, are erased. The poet *is* nature, so is beyond criticism. But logically and mutually, nature has wiped out the role of the poet too. He is reinscribed as fields of semiotic multiplicity; on acres of passive, flat, as-yet-unwritten paper. The poetry itself is not inspired, it is perspired. In this model, the poetic text becomes the emanation of a bodily congregation, of an assemblage, to use Deleuze and Guattari's terminology. The poet's disembodiment, his unimportance, his eradication, is proof of the power of green fecundity. This is poet as the Christ: the conduit, the purposeful, polemical, lonely self-sacrificer, embodying another ontological field. The instability of this position resolves itself conventionally, safely, though – as with 'I Am' – not entirely convincingly, in a closing recourse to God.

In 'Sighing for Retirement', poetry is not the sublime expansion of the ego, but the orgasm of its death, of its annihilation at the moment it renders itself into the levelling body of nature, at the moment it becomes a text, marking its own passivity and diminution in submission to a non-human other, Lover Nature. Actually the poet does not 'listen' conventionally to nature; she does not communicate with him either (the third line reads 'Nature's voice is never loud', after all). But loving, listening and communicating require dialectic distance to be defined between the existence of interlocutors, between bodies gazing, hearing, sniffing or entwining. In this model, such distance is closed: writing subject becomes natural object, and so there is no body. Subjectivity is thought *and* materiality; materiality unproblematically produces text; subjectivity is also becoming the state and status of the object. The object is trace, is textuality; subject/object positions, individuality and locality, all are absorbed as delimiting categories of separation and position into a limitless and multiplying unification of intersubstantiating process – an ongoing, decentred activation, prospecting beyond subject/object dualism.

If this reading of 'Sighing for Retirement' is characteristic of Clare's radical take on the relationship between his poetic art and the natural world, we might consider what implications such a conceptualisation could have for textual criticism. In the context of Clare studies, it might seem antithetical to introduce here a strand of thought which suggests that ecological thinking should not be static or rooted to one place or locality. In *The Three Ecologies,* originally published in 1989, Félix Guattari writes, provocatively:

> Environmental ecology, as it exists today, has barely begun to prefigure the generalized ecology that I advocate here, the aim of which will be to radically decentre social struggles and ways of coming to one's own psyche. Current ecological movements certainly have merit, but in truth I think that

the overall ecosophical question is too important to be left to some of its usual archaizers and folklorists... Ecology must stop being associated with the image of a small nature-loving minority or with qualified specialists. Ecology in my sense questions the whole of subjectivity and capitalistic power formations, whose sweeping progress cannot be guaranteed to continue as it has for the past decade.[43]

As well as being expansive beyond the *oikos*, the home and the local, ecological thinking has to admit that 'nature' is mind-made, that the 'environment's' troubled ground is human subjectivity, as Timothy Morton similarly contends:

We are treading a path between saying that something called nature exists, and saying that nothing exists at all. We are not claiming that some entity lies between these views. We are dealing with the raw materials of ideology, the stuff that generates seductive images of 'nature'. That is why it is important to go as 'far in' to the notion of nature in ecomimesis as possible.[44]

This chapter extends Guattari's urgency, to argue that ecological literary criticism needs to interrogate the construction of the raw materials of its work: needs to turn from its construction of nature to the making of text. As we saw through the example of 'The shepherds almost wonder...' in the previous chapter, and as we shall see in the following chapter in which we look at some paratextual materials, making printed 'coherent' textual matter out of Clare's manuscripts can be tricky, while making 'final' decisions over copy-texts can be problematic. Unexplored possibilities for that process of textual making, which might chime with unique features of Clare's work, deserve further consideration.

Michael P. Branch maintains that 'scholars of environmental literature have been slow to recognize the need for and importance of textual editing'.[45] The object of his argument is to stimulate ecocritics to make accessible the forgotten texts of 'nature writing'. No ecocritic has as yet taken the next logical step to explore the potential for ecological theory to inform an editorial methodology which might support the creation of 'green' text. In a discussion of genetic criticism, Louis Hay points out that 'editing has always embodied the main ideological and cultural concerns of its day'.[46] Because the context of editing Clare has always been determinedly political and ideological, as I suggest above, and because it has been such fiercely contested ground in the recent past, I think it would be healthiest and methodologically most sound to be explicit about the political colours and agendas of future editorial projects, and to ensure that a methodology is as aware of its own historical and political prejudices as possible (partly the concern of Chapter 5). What follows is an idealistic consideration of what might be possible in the future of editing and presenting Clare's texts.

The 'language-war' model of textual presentation of Clare results from a demonstrably oppositional politics which informs both camps of editorial methodologies. It has rendered the presentation of texts monological for the most part: to summarise the discussion above, this has seen the dominant 'primitivist' mode of transcription take a politicised stance against 'polishing' editorial interventionism. The primary, foundational editorial choice over whether to leave texts 'raw' or to 'cook' them informs all subsequent editorial choices. In contrast, an editorial methodology which is green in its political foundation will necessarily promote inclusive interconnectedness between and among manuscript and editorial variants, as a salve to the exclusive nature of Clare editing across the last fifty or so years. Where ecological theory tries to remove man from the top of an assumed hierarchy and to level and merge his subject position with the network of other parts of the natural world, so we might use a decentred and levelling hypertextual frame for the presentation of Clare's texts; here an editor would become a facilitator for user interactivity rather than a prescriptive determiner of the sort of text a reader would encounter. This editorial model would deploy an enriching interconnectedness, a branching 'rhizome', as explored above, of relation *between*, which is evocative of how mutual interdependence is a dominant motif for understanding (and for idealising) human relations with nature. A green editorial presentation would maintain the provisional nature of textual experience, would defer any 'final' decisions about what sort of text or texts should be central to the reader.

Such an editing project would maintain and foreground the provisional nature of text and so follow Félix Guattari's key assertion in *The Three Ecologies* that 'eco-logic no longer imposes a "resolution" of opposites'.[47] Stuart Moulthrop has demonstrated the potential of understanding hypertextual networks as rhizomes[48] and, more broadly, hypertextual theory has repeatedly concerned itself with the decentred, multi-vocal and provisional possibilities of internet textuality – deftly summarised by George P. Landow[49] – yet no work has been carried out on the ways in which ecological theory might forge a methodological and ethical bridge between the limitations of print-based media and new electronic textual technologies.

Thorough work has been carried out, however, on the benefits of 'genetic' hypertextual editing, which frames textuality and textual provenance in much the same way as I am suggesting 'green' editing could do. In the long quotation which follows, Daniel Ferrer summarises the potential advantages of hypertextual genetic editing:

> The traditional model of apparatus, presenting one text with a plurality of variants, is totally inadequate to the task: it involves a linearization of something that is not linear; it introduces an artificial hierarchy between elements that are only retrospectively hierarchized; and it causes not only a loss of the energy that nobody who enters into contact with drafts can ignore, but also a sheer loss of information.
>
> Genetic work clearly requires facsimiles of the documents, but it is not enough to deliver to the reader a bundle of rough material. It is often necessary to provide a transcription, and in some cases, alternative transcriptions, since any transcription is an interpretation. But the inclusion of transcriptions in the sequence of facsimiles only makes more difficult the insoluble problem of ordering the documents. Genetic files are multidimensional objects, and linear representations, such as books can offer, are necessarily mutilating. There is always a multiplicity of possible genetic orders, and each of them tells a different story. The mere juxtaposition of the manuscripts introduces, under the guise of total neutrality, an unacknowledged bias. The only way of bypassing this sly form of control is to provide a multiplicity of solutions.
>
> Undoubtedly, hypertextual presentation gives the best chance to do justice to the diversity of the material and the multiplicity of the relationships. It offers an unlimited number of paths through the documents; it allows instant juxtaposition of facsimiles, transcriptions, and commentaries (which can be as long as necessary, in various depths of accessibility, so as not to stifle the manuscripts themselves); and it welcomes dialogic readings, with unlimited possibilities of reordering, additions of new documents, and changes of readings (which are inevitable for most complex manuscripts).[50]

Ferrer is idealistic, provocative and liberating. He is also censorious. He rails against the 'sly form of control' of many editing projects, but at one point he claims genetic editing has a bedrock of 'common sense' – which looks too much like the recourse of a rationale refusing to account for itself. He then asserts that the genetic editor's resistance to 'absolute editorial decisions' does not emerge 'out of poststructural theoretical prejudice, but as the result of our daily experience with writers' manuscripts'.[51] Availing himself of defensive 'common sense', Ferrer then resists and rejects theory, claiming for his own editorial ideals the firm, empirical ground of hard-won experience at the manuscript coalface. Unlike Louis Hay, Ferrer does not allow for any ideological basis for the claimed superiority of the genetic critical approach: 'common sense', he implies, is its raison d'être and is justification enough.

Even with these reservations, Ferrer's discussion of the destabilising multiplicity of the genetic text, of the provisional nature of textual source and of deferred decisions over editing, is editorially liberating. From here, I would like to extend Hay's ideological understanding of editorial methodologies to questions of subjectivity. If Jonathan Maskit is right to claim that '[q]uestions about subjectivity often either are absent from environmental philosophy or tend to offer an account of some "natural" form of subjectivity that is somehow being violated',[52] a parallel absence of discussions of subjectivity in editorial projects is even more acute. I would like to suggest that the political positioning inherent in the production of any edition of a single author's texts determines that a version of that individual authorial subjectivity maintains a sort of 'consciousness' of the textual life of the edition. We might say that any edition – in having standards and coherent practices that inform the decisions constructing the transcription and rendition of the manuscript holograph (should there be one) into typewritten text – always attempts to dress itself as a coherent mechanism for the safe, linear delivery of a set of writings. Even in ostensibly all-inclusive *variorum* editions, the methods construct a certain *version* of the author, of a period, of a genre and so on; in other words, an individualised, fixed position, a rationalised, codified and standardised sense made out of the chaos of archives and manuscripts – but made despite that chaos, not because of it. Genetic editing prefers the term 'avant-texte' to 'variant',[53] because the latter determines, naturalises and finalises the choice made over what the central text is to be: all other texts are variations from this mainstay, which will become the 'copy-text'. For practical considerations in book printing – but for ideological reasons too – the journey to the choice over copy-text often remains latent. In genetic criticism, choice is permanently deferred. Even with the relatively straightforward manuscript problems of 'The shepherds almost wonder...' as outlined above, the openness to provisionality so central to genetic editing seems enticing.

A 'standard' scholarly edition has that editor's hard-won univocal intentionality, and a particularising version of the author's subjectivity, latent in the 'genetic code', if you will, of the editing methodology.

I would argue that this has been the case in the editing of Clare. It might be that the presentation of texts can be no other way, and there is not necessarily anything wrong with this: an edition will always enhance access to something, and in so doing must channel, guide and make clear, centred and coherent what is otherwise messy and dispersed – dispersed across manuscripts, fascicles, archives, institutions, even countries. But what could also be the case is that the construction of a coherent textual subjectivity through the deliberate – if not always explicit – choices of an editorial methodology represses exactly the sort of multiplying variety and manuscript faithfulness to which a variant edition is designed to adhere. Such an edition might reify a certain version of the author's intentionality, might codify and authorise something which is more to do with the considered subject position of the editor than the original author, who is, after all, nowhere, other than in the texts being edited. Texts reproduced under the aegis of such a book project therefore become mutually confirming, in the construction of an over-arching singular authorial subjectivity. We edit, therefore Clare is. The text is egocentric. The destabilising contradictions, vacillations, paradoxes, fluidities, declarations and immolations of a varied textual life are whittled away in the construction of an edition which seeks uniformity and consistency for its singular subject – *even where it commits to include notations of all textual variants*. In an edition like the Oxford Clare, there is a crucial temporal disjunction between the time-span of the poet's writing life which produced the work diachronically, and the presentationally and editorially synchronous delivery of all the poems according to a set method which shapes all the texts included. The following quotation from the Oxford Clare editors' introduction is illustrative of the problems arising from their determination to present Clare according to a set methodology:

> As Clare matured and became more confident he tended to reduce punctuation to a minimum both in prose and verse. In some of his early poems, in the versions submitted to Drury, however, he fell into the opposite extreme, probably in response to suggestions coming from several quarters that he ought to be more 'correct'. When he did this the punctuation became so excessive that it seriously interfered with the reader's enjoyment of the poetry. We have therefore removed the punctuation when it was clearly wrong but have provided the evidence of exactly what we have done.[54]

The early Clare does not match an ideal version of a later – and by implication, better – Clare, so the editors are compelled to intervene by the force of logic of their own method. Across all nine volumes, the fifty years or so of Clare's varied writing life are channelled through a homogenising editorial process which will try to produce poetry 'in the raw', sometimes despite the original source material. In seeking to deliver an overall similitude across texts produced by the wide varieties of Clare's language strategies, this edition tries to resolve problems which I contend are irresolvable and ongoing. They are problems of expression, orthography and presentation that Clare, like many other writers, raises and then writes through, but never finally answers, because such problems remain unanswerable, *unfinalisable*. The creative responses to each instance of a moment of language in practice will be inherently varied and inconsistent.

A green hypertextual edition of Clare would not have to try to resolve any of the problems sketched here, and would not try to clamp down or delineate a predetermined version of Clare's subjectivity (through a static over-arching version of his position on the politics of linguistic standardisation, for example); it would maintain instead his peculiar problems, seek them out, foreground them and editorially project the chaos. It could present the manuscript versions (in facsimile and a variety of transcription styles) *and* the lifetime-published texts. It would deliver texts variously, and provisionally, projecting possible editorial judgements, but never reaching or isolating them conclusively. It would enable a reader (can we bibliophiles ever be happy with 'user'?) to determine the sort of textual experience desired. Its purpose would be to promote the excitement and trouble produced by clashes, by the instabilities of the 'avant-texte', by contradictions of editorial transcription choices, by inconsistencies of representation, by multi-vocalities, by pluralities – those both at manuscript source and at the editorial 'end' of transcription style. It would see a singular authorial subject turned into a decentred textual rhizome of networks and nodes. This green editorial methodology would question the reification of a particular editorial subjectivity and would instead deliver something unmanaged, untrammelled, uncompromised, wild, rough and smooth, spiky and unsettling. The user would read in spaces of interlocking planes of textual fields, open and green for the discovery and manipulation of poems presented in order that they could be ceaselessly, freely remade according to whatever sort of textual experiences the reader might wish to pursue. Unlike Clare's poet discovering texts in the fields, the reader would be made fully aware of the agency necessary to reading and of the choices available – choice being a foundational and readerly role in the process of engagement with explicitly greened hypertexts.

NOTES

1. First quotation: Letter to James Augustus Hessey, 2 April 1822. Second quotation: Letter to John Taylor, 19 December 1825. *Letters*, p. 235 and 351.
2. The editor was Alaric Watts. For details see *Letters*, p. 350n2.
3. For comprehensive yet contrasting accounts of the development of *The Shepherd's Calendar*, see Tim Chilcott's 'Introduction' to *The Shepherd's Calendar: Manuscript and Published Version* (Manchester: Carcanet, 2006), pp. i–xxxi; Bate, *Biography*, pp. 303–17; and Eric Robinson's 'Introduction' and 'Note on the Text' in Eric Robinson, Geoffrey Summerfield and David Powell (eds), *The Shepherd's Calendar* (Oxford: Oxford University Press, 1993), pp. ix–xxv.
4. For the red corner's argument, see Tony Crowley, *The Politics of Discourse: The Standard Language Question in British Cultural Debates* (Basingstoke: MacMillan, 1989); for the blue corner's response, see John Honey, *Language Is Power: The Story of Standard English and Its Enemies* (London: Faber and Faber, 1997).
5. The essays by R. K. R. Thornton weigh up, among other pertinent things, the 'evidence' for either case in Clare's own words: 'What John Clare Do We Read?', *PN Review*, 31.4 (March–April 2005), 54–6; 'The Raw and the Cooked', *JCSJ*, 24 (2005), 78–86.
6. For an early discussion of this editorial method, see Jack Stillinger, 'Textual Primitivism and the Editing of Wordsworth', *Studies in Romanticism*, 28.1 (Spring 1989), 3–28.
7. MPV, pp. xii–xiii.
8. See Erick Kelemen, *Textual Editing and Criticism: An Introduction* (New York and London: W. W. Norton, 2009), pp. 15–16 and 567. Kelemen defines an 'accidental' as an 'element in a text that is not substantive, that is, whose variation does not affect meaning; traditionally includes spelling, punctuation, and capitalization' (p. 567). See also D. C. Greetham, *Textual Scholarship: An Introduction* (New York and London: Garland Publishing, 1994).
9. Bate, *Biography*, p. 351.
10. Clare to Taylor, 21 February 1822, *Letters*, p. 231.
11. Jonathan Bate (ed.), *John Clare: Selected Poems* (London: Faber and Faber, 2004), pp. xxxi–xxxii.

12. Bate (ed.), *Selected Poems*, p. xxxii.
13. Bate, *Biography*, p. 566.
14. Bate (ed.), *Selected Poems*, p. xxxiii.
15. MPIV, p. ix.
16. See, for example, Valerie Pedlar, '"Written by Himself" – Edited by Others: The Autobiographical Writings of John Clare', in John Goodridge and Simon Kövesi (eds), *John Clare: New Approaches* (Helpston: John Clare Society, 2000), pp. 17–31; John Goodridge, Review of John Clare, *Poems of the Middle Period V, Romanticism* 9.2 (2003), 215–19.
17. LPI, p. xii.
18. For Clare and copyright, see Hugh Haughton, 'Revision and Romantic Authorship: The Case of Clare', *JCSJ*, 17 (1998), pp. 65–73; Simon Kövesi, 'The John Clare Copyright: 1820–2000', *Wordsworth Circle*, 31 (Summer 2000), 112–19; Jonathan Bate, 'John Clare's Copyright, 1854–1893', *JCSJ*, 19 (2000), 19–32; Eric Robinson, 'John Clare Scholarship and Copyright' [letter], *Times Literary Supplement*, 1 September 2000, p. 17; Eric Robinson, 'Clare's Rights' [letter], *Guardian*, 1 February 2003.
19. Other than the withdrawn selection of Merryn and Raymond Williams published by Methuen in 1986, Bate's Farrar, Straus and Giroux selection of 2003, reissued by Faber and Faber in 2004, was the first from a major publisher to ignore Eric Robinson's private claim to copyright ownership since it was established in 1965. Bate's Picador biography pays no heed to the copyright in quoting from manuscripts and includes a rich discussion of editing and copyright issues in Clare (Bate, *Biography*, pp. 563–75). Since then, Tim Chilcott's edition with Carcanet, and Paul Farley's selection with Faber and Faber (which draws on Bate's), both ignored the claim. For all this diverse activity, the public institutions which own Clare's manuscripts do still refer those seeking reproduction rights to the agents of the private claimant. See Merryn and Raymond Williams (eds), *John Clare: Selected Poetry and Prose* (London and New York: Methuen, 1986); Jonathan Bate (ed.) *'I Am': The Selected Poetry of John Clare* (New York: Farrar, Straus and Giroux, 2003) and *John Clare: Selected Poems* (London: Faber and Faber, 2004); Tim Chilcott (ed.), *The Shepherd's Calendar: Manuscript and Published Version* (Manchester: Carcanet, 2006); Paul Farley (ed.), *John Clare: Poet to Poet* (Faber and Faber, 2007).
20. Bate, *Biography*, p. xviii. See also Jonathan Bate (ed.), *John Clare: Selected Poems* (London: Faber and Faber, 2004), p. xxxi, discussed above.
21. See discussion above of Clare's letter to Emmerson, March–April 1830, and the text in *Letters*, p. 504.
22. A point made by Richard Cronin, 'In Place and Out of Place: Clare in *The Midsummer Cushion*', in John Goodridge and Simon Kövesi (eds), *John Clare: New Approaches* (Helpston: John Clare Society, 2000), pp. 133–48 (p. 136).

23. For an acute analysis of the significance of hearing, being overheard and muttering, see Erin Lafford, 'Clare's Mutterings, Murmurings, and Ramblings: The Sounds of Health', *JCSJ*, 33 (2014), 24–40.
24. 'Least, they never say it the way it's spelt. Coz it izny spelt, when they say it, is it?', Tom Leonard, 'Honest', *Three Glasgow Writers: A Collection of Writing by Alex.Hamilton, James Kelman, Tom Leonard* (Glasgow: Molendinar Press, 1976), p. 47.
25. For an accessible table of the political philosophies informing a variety of environmentalisms, see David Pepper, *Eco-Socialism: From Deep Ecology to Social Justice* (London: Routledge, 1993), p. 47. See also Greg Garrard, *Ecocriticism* (London: Routledge, 2004), pp. 16–32.
26. Thornton, 'The Raw and the Cooked'.
27. Tim Chilcott (ed.), *The Shepherd's Calendar: Manuscript and Published Version* (Manchester: Carcanet, 2006).
28. Frederick S. Williams, *The Midland Railway: its Rise and Progress. A Narrative of Modern Enterprise* (London: Strahan, 1876), pp. vii and viii. The reference to Clare is on p. 597.
29. C. Day Lewis, *The Lyric Impulse* (London: Chatto & Windus, 1965), p. 111.
30. Harold Bloom, *The Visionary Company: A Reading of English Romantic Poetry*, rev. edn (Ithaca, NY: Cornell University Press 1971), p. 448.
31. Paul Chirico, *John Clare and the Imagination of the Reader* (Basingstoke: Palgrave, 2007), pp. 138–9.
32. John Felstiner, *Can Poetry Save the Earth? A Field Guide to Nature Poems* (New Haven: Yale University Press, 2009), p. 58.
33. John Ashbery, 'John Clare: "Grey Openings Where the Light Looks Through"', in *Other Traditions* (Cambridge, MA: Harvard University Press, 2000), pp. 1–22 (pp. 16–17). For an extended account of Clare's significance both to Ashbery and to the future of American environmental poetry, see Angus Fletcher, *A New Theory for American Poetry: Democracy, the Environment and the Future of the Imagination* (Cambridge, MA: Harvard University Press, 2004). For critical accounts of Clare and Ashbery, see Ben Hickman, *John Ashbery and English Poetry* (Edinburgh: Edinburgh University Press, 2012) and Stephanie Kuduk Weiner, *Clare's Lyric: John Clare and Three Modern Poets* (Oxford: Oxford University Press, 2014).
34. Cyrus Redding, 'Clare, the Poet', *The English Journal*, 20 (15 May 1841), 305–9. The essay continues in the same publication, 22 (29 May 1841), 340–3. For an extracted text, see *Critical Heritage*, pp. 247–56.
35. Cyrus Redding, *Past Celebrities Whom I Have Known* (London, 1866), p. 135.
36. Brian Maidment, 'Popular Exemplary Biography in the Nineteenth Century: Edwin Paxton Hood and His Books', *Prose Studies*, 7.2 (September 1984), 148–67.

37. Mark Storey, 'Edwin Paxton Hood (Not the Reverend Romeo Elton) and John Clare', *Notes and Queries*, 18.10 (October 1971), 386–7 (386).
38. Edwin Paxton Hood, *The Literature of Labour: Illustrious Instances of the Education of Poetry in Poverty*, 2nd edn (London: Partridge and Oakey, 1852), p. 123.
39. Percy Bysshe Shelley, 'Mont Blanc', in Neville Rogers (ed.), *The Complete Poetical Works of Percy Bysshe Shelley*, 2 vols (Oxford: Oxford University Press, 1975), 2, pp. 75–80 (p. 80).
40. Samuel Taylor Coleridge defensively maintains himself as an originating 'fountain' in the prose preface to *Christabel*, in anticipation of criticisms that it had derived from celebrated poems upon which it had wielded some influence, through pre-publication readings and circulation. Kathleen Coburn (ed.), *The Collected Works of Samuel Taylor Coleridge*: J. C. C. Mays (ed.), *Poetical Works*, 16 vols (Princeton: Princeton University Press, 2001), 16, p. 482.
41. For accounts of Clare toying with kinds of elitist dismissal of others, see *Natural History*, p. xlv; M. M. Mahood, *The Poet as Botanist* (Cambridge: Cambridge University Press, 2008), pp. 112–46; Adam White, 'John Clare: "The Man of Taste"', *JCSJ*, 28 (2009), 38–54.
42. Timothy Morton, *Ecology Without Nature: Rethinking Environmental Aesthetics* (Cambridge, MA: Harvard University Press, 2007), p. 170. In this book, Morton's premise seems to be that the word 'nature' – and all of the ideological forces the word incorporates – prevents humanity from being in real proximity to 'natural' or ecological experience; the terminology, the language of the way we encounter nature as object, effects an ideological and experiential rupture where there need be none. The word itself separates us from that which it describes.
43. Félix Guattari, *The Three Ecologies*, trans. Ian Pindar and Paul Sutton (London and New York: Continuum, 2000), p. 52.
44. Morton, *Ecology Without Nature*, p. 68.
45. Michael P. Branch, 'Saving All the Pieces: The Place of Textual Editing in Ecocriticism', in Steven Rossendale (ed.), *The Greening of Literary Scholarship: Literature, Theory, and the Environment* (Iowa City: University of Iowa Press, 2002), pp. 3–25 (p. 5).
46. Louis Hay, 'Genetic Editing, Past and Future: A Few Reflections by a User', trans. J. M. Luccioni and Hans Walter Gabler, *Text: Transactions of the Society for Textual Scholarship*, 3 (1987), 117–33 (117).
47. Félix Guattari, *The Three Ecologies*, p. 52.
48. Stuart Moulthrop, 'Rhizome and Resistance: Hypertext and the Dreams of a New Culture', in George P. Landow (ed.), *Hyper/Text/Theory* (Baltimore: Johns Hopkins University Press, 1994), pp. 299–319.
49. George P. Landow, *Hypertext 3.0* (Baltimore: Johns Hopkins University Press, 2006), pp. 56–65.

50. Daniel Ferrer, 'Production, Invention, and Reproduction: Genetic vs. Textual Criticism', in Elizabeth Bergmann Loizeaux and Neil Fraistat (eds), *Reimagining Textuality: Textual Studies in the Late Age of Print* (Madison: University of Wisconsin Press, 2002), pp. 48–59 (pp. 55–56).
51. Ferrer, 'Production, Invention, and Reproduction: Genetic vs. Textual Criticism', pp. 56–7.
52. Jonathan Maskit, 'Subjectivity, Desire, and the Problem of Consumption', in Bernd Herzogenrath (ed.), *Deleuze|Guattari & Ecology* (Basingstoke: Palgrave Macmillan, 2009), pp. 129–44 (p. 130).
53. For a full account, see Daniel Ferrer and Michael Groden, 'Introduction: A Genesis of French Genetic Criticism' in Jed Deppman, Daniel Ferrer and Michael Groden (eds and trans), *Genetic Criticism: Texts and Avant-textes* (Philadelphia: University of Pennsylvania Press, 2004), pp. 1–16.
54. EPI, p. xxiii.

CHAPTER 4

Looking, Painting, Listing, Noting: Clare, Women and Nature

THE LOVE POET

Introducing Clare's first collection in 1820, publisher and editor John Taylor has no doubts as to what thematic commitments predominate in the work of his new poet:

> He is most thoroughly the Poet as well as the Child of Nature; and, according to his opportunities, no poet has more completely devoted himself to her service, studied her more closely, or exhibited so many sketches of her under new and interesting appearances... He loves the fields, the flowers, 'the common air, the sun, the skies;' and, therefore, he writes about them. He is happier in the presence of Nature than elsewhere. He looks as anxiously on her face as if she were a living friend, whom he might lose; and hence he has learnt to notice every change in her countenance, and to delineate all the delicate varieties of her character.[1]

Though standard and idiomatic to conceive it so at the time (as it remains today), it is nevertheless indicative that 'Nature' is female; that Clare is said to exhibit the obsessive and exclusive devotions to her that we might expect of a lover; and that 'her countenance' and 'her character' are the things noted by the rare observational capacities of the poet. Nature is a woman, Clare is cast as the male 'nature lover', and the flirting, courting and conjoining between active, gazing, longing male poet with passive female partner are set in train. Yet actual human women and human-to-human love – as a thematic commitment or a subject of interest in the poems that follow this introduction – are not alluded to at all by Taylor.

This is a pattern of interest in the study of Clare that continues to some extent to this day: Clare as a love poet remains a fairly marginalised area in critical work, even when amatory lyrics (especially later works often described as 'visionary') are among his most celebrated and anthologised pieces today, and even when the opening love poem of *Poems Descriptive* – 'The Meeting', as discussed in the opening chapter – became so prominent in Clare's nineteenth-century legacy. It has not been consistently the case that Clare's love poetry has been overlooked, however. In 1910 Edward Thomas saw love poetry as the super-genre, including all others in its glories, when closing his effusion over Clare's late poems with a bracing idealism:

> Hence the strangeness and thrill and painful delight of poetry at all times, and the deep response to it of youth and of love; and because love is wild, strange, and full of astonishment, is one reason why poetry deals so much in love, and why all poetry is in a sense love-poetry.[2]

For Thomas, Clare's late song 'Love lives beyond' 'is remarkable for nothing so much as for its eloquent but inexplicable expression of this harmony of nature and love'.[3] While it might be dissonance and despair that Clare locates in 'nature and love', as much as it is Thomas's 'harmony', it is nevertheless the argument of this chapter that considerations of woman are as important to Clare's conceptualising of the rural natural world as flowers, grass and trees, and vice versa. If critical work is to determine the kind of vision that drives Clare's poetry – to green ends or red or any colour – then it cannot skip over a broad swathe of work that seems so foundational, and so persistent, across the whole of this poet's career. To simplify: if Clare can be described as a 'nature poet', then he is so because he was simultaneously a practised love poet. The features that Thomas reads in the later love poetry can readily be located in the early and middle periods of the works too. The figuration of women is central to Clare's sophisticated work on that commonly unproblematic division of human from non-human, and more broadly of culture from nature.

As we saw in the account of the musical flight of 'The Meeting', by no means everything Clare wrote could be said to be driven or designed by a primarily ecopolitical conscience. For all of his constant attentions to the non-human inhabitants and elements of the natural world, for all of his various attempts to secure a space on his own and 'green delight' in a place of his own, far from the busy 'hustling world'[4] of responsibility and orthodox quotidian pressures, Clare's 'Looking... Painting... Listing... Noting...'[5] eye still tracks the movements and diurnal habits of women as carefully and persistently as it does any animal, or any plant. So any critique seeking to trace overall patterns in his work has to engage with representations of women. This chapter aims to consider what happens when Clare's 'botanising' lyrical eye is trained on women. This is necessary because, firstly, the area remains contentious across assessments of his work precisely because it tends to disrupt critical truisms about him; and, secondly, because this area has been relegated by an understandable focus upon Clare's nature poetry. In its explorations of the representation of women in Clare, this chapter will consider some 'paratextual' work – namely, lists and letters in manuscripts. Wherever we look in Clare, complex textual and interpretative issues arise, and his representation of women is no exception.

Clare's poetic work on women, and on love and lust *for* women, does not suddenly emerge as a product of his committal to an asylum which compounds a general depletion or narrowing of the capacity of his poetic vision. Even if love poems seem to predominate in the later years, in fact Clare had always written poems about, to or in dialogue with women figures – both the real and the imagined; both the up-close and present and the distant and long absent. As he tries on various models for his early poetic experimentations, Clare inevitably follows in style and subject a heterosexual male tradition of writing about women: in Northampton manuscript 1, which contains poems conceived between 1808 and 1819, as transcribed in the Oxford edition,[6] Clare wrote acrostics to named women; epistle exchanges between lovers; sexist aphoristic stanza-long epigrams; patronising, dramatised moral mini-tales of women's foibles; a comic poem presenting a 'real' woman 'form'd by nature hard & tuff'[7]; pastoral ballads about maids called Chloe or Myra or Flora living near Helicon in a muted neo-classical pastoral setting; songs of desire and broken hearts; and long narratives about lovers and couples in the traditional ballad 'eight and six' metre.[8] As if to confirm his love-drunk yellow trouser-wearing status as a man of 'rare sensibility' and capacious affection, Clare even ventriloquises Goethe's suicidal protagonist in a sixteen-line couplet entitled 'Supposd to be utterd by Werter at the conclusion of his last interview with Charlotte'.[9] On my count in this early notebook more than a third of the poems and fragments are centrally about love, women and adult relationships between the sexes.[10] Clare is learning his craft here, growing through various literary models and modes of engagement with love, grafting himself in a sometimes ungainly fashion onto a well-trodden male tradition – though with a lot of variance and diversity in the attempt – flitting from tones and attitudes that are youthfully and happily innocent, through to the suicidally futile and lustfully cynical. To reiterate, then, at this formative stage of his writing, it is a fact that more than a third of his poetic practice is taken up in staging encounters with femininity. Clare shows himself to be a committed love poet, tussling actively with a broad, albeit narrowly male and masculinised, literary tradition. If the themes engaged with here will come to predominate once he is 'shut up' in the urban Northampton Asylum – his horizons and freedom to roam limited more than ever – it is hardly surprising. The truth is that Clare had always nursed an interest in various modes of writing love poems and poems of sexual desire: the love and lust poems of the asylum are the culmination of a career-long commitment to the genre.

For this supposed organically 'born not made' devotee of nature, it is worth remembering that in his early years, when Clare talks about a 'rose' it is often a woman he is addressing and not a flower in and of itself (though of course a 'cultivated' rose would never grow to be the type of Clare's favoured flower, botanically or politically speaking).[11] The 'problem' of woman for the fledgling poet is addressed from many angles, sometimes clumsily and crudely, yet replete with the promise of the subtlety, style and voice to come. Arguably, in his earliest extant manuscript, poems of love and women predominate over any other singular preoccupation, just as they will come to do in his later years. It is also worth noting that the process of collecting and refining these poems into his first collection *Poems Descriptive* in 1820 effectively reduced the significance of such poems of love and relationship: of the seventy-three poems published, twenty could be said to be about love and women (just above a quarter of the published poems). Although the editing process of making this first published book effected a drop in the number of love poems relative to the commitments of the early manuscript (*Poems Descriptive* drew on materials other than this manuscript too), still it means that Clare's published interest in these themes is important at the outset of his public career, no matter how much Taylor opted to ignore that fact in his introduction. Others have followed Taylor in overlooking this genre of Clare's work.

As in 'The Meeting', Clare rarely writes a poem about a lover's tryst that is set indoors: love, courtship, loving companionship, invitations to link arm in arm – all are pursued outdoors, promenades always framed by natural fecundity, or wintry or drought-driven asperity, the frames dependent entirely on the emotional weather being charted. Perhaps squeezed outside by the tiny, cramped homes of the poor, the presentation of lovers in Clare maintains a relation of natural setting to emotional state that is much more than mere pathetic fallacy: nature is not just providing a set of symbolic motifs to help us read his version of a love affair (though Clare certainly does do that too, as we shall see). Nature is often the means by which the male speaker loves a woman, and understands his affection and her responses: nature provides his language both of seduction, of loving confirmation and mutuality, and of disconnection and loss. Nature seems to be the channel through which he negotiates an understanding of his love object and his loving feelings, though of course for the reading process, nature is only text – and we will see that, even with the tools that nature offers the poet, the urgency of the envisioning of a lover quickly pushes the speakers to the edge of what they feel able to express. Dumbfounded, stunned isolation often threatens at the moment of reaching out, of expression. As for poems featuring a more immediately solitary speaker, as the putative couple pulls away from the society of humans, it immerses itself in the sociability of nature – a social access mostly granted only by the male speaker's leading botanical and geographical knowledge. In Clare's love poems, nature offers him a palette, a range of textures and perspectives on amatory feelings. Sometimes this naturally sourced palette curtails his range of options as a love poet, and to an extent the general critical view that Clare's love poems are less original or conceptually precise than much of his other work is supportable. In more than one poem, nature provides 'love's bed' (a phrase which appears most notably in 'First Love'[12]) in which mutual affection will either grow in intimate privacy or wither in exposure to the elements; but it is clear that 'love's bed' does not always offer a multitude of options for the poet, just as it is not always fertile for the lover. It is no coincidence that in many of Clare's love poems, 'that little personal pronoun "I"' which – as discussed earlier – he declaims in 1830 to be 'such a presumption ambitious swaggering little fellow'[13] is dominant, asserting itself as the lead of the self-reflective confessional aspects expected in a traditional, lyrical mode, propelling the voicing of affection. In some ways, then, some of these love poems would seem to resist the lines of argument this book has been building thus far, about the ecocentric levelling and mutualising relationships of Clare's best and most original nature poetry.

There is a clear division in Clare's love poems about women in how they construct womanhood: his narrative poems see working women trick and nurse, flirt, labour and play with men, children and one another. This sort of presentation could be said to be community-confirming, locally rooted, socially healthful and, broadly speaking, narratologically and ethically content, with women often serving as the social glue holding relations together. Clare's more lyrical studies of women tend to have them function as little more than types, while the male speakers are far more prone to be debilitated by loneliness, misanthropy and a distracted displacement – which is anything but healthy for the first-person speaker of such poems; certainly they do not build towards any sense of confirming community. As in 'The Meeting' – with its wish that words could 'unseal' and that language was stronger for his purposes – such poems are often painfully aware of the limitations of language to express, or to engender, or to conjure or inspirit, love. Adam White is right to observe that 'a persistent theme in Clare's imitations of Burns [is] the inability of language to express affection for a beautiful woman' and 'The Meeting' is a case in point.[14] Yet the issue of the limitations on expression and understanding that underpin Clare's speakers' apprehension of love is in fact a much broader one than Clare's following Burns. It is a recurrent feature of male Romantic poetry in general. 'Woe is me!' writes Shelley as the love vision of 'Epipsychidion' dissipates after its crushing climax:

> The winged words on which my soul would pierce
> Into the height of love's rare Universe,
> Are chains of lead around its flight of fire[15]

In Clare, language can not only feel weighty and obstructive, it can seem redundant entirely – dangerous even, to the likelihood that love will live – such as in the intensely fragile world of 'Silent Love'.[16] Clare's visions of love frequently remain remote and leave his speakers with a cold closure of poetic and amatory failure.

In the most intensely effective of Clare's lyrical love poems, women are on remote pedestals, god objects of idealising yearning who produce itchy, lusty, febrile discontent in the serenading male troubadour. Such irritated discontent in the doubtful speaker pushes dynamically against the otherwise clear guiding lines of the traditional shape of the male love lyric.

In between the socially cohesive narratives (mostly third-person tales of others' loves) and heart-wrenched lovelorn lyrics, there are more song-like cavalier balladeering forms which, though voiced from a first-person perspective, conjoin the male speaker with his lover – and often cajole her directly into coming with him hand in hand on walks to off-piste trysts situated on the blanket of a vernal fecund undergrowth of ever-deepening sexual intimacy, entwined by woodbine and bedded on grass. And then there are the peculiar, exposed Byronic poems of the summer of 1841 – Clare's 'Don Juan' and 'Child Harold'. These combine to form a study of poetic emasculation, amatory fracture and middle-aged, masculine, highly sexualised, misogynist rage; these poems have been studied in depth by many critics,[17] but somewhat in isolation from the rest of his love and lust poetry, perhaps because they are such unique creations (and so tantalisingly intertextual and dialogic for the literary scholar). This chapter will instead read an array of symptomatic love and lust poems which will, in succession, typify Clare's main modes in his presentations of woman.

April Fools and Lovers in May

An untitled narrative poem of 280 lines of ballad metre, with the first line 'Up crows the cock with bouncing brawl', drafted across the mature Northborough period, presents a farm and village community on April Fool's Day.[18] Sarah Houghton offers a keen reading of the 'scapegoating' in the poem, which features a duped male split into two: the awkward rhyme pair of Roger and Hodge.[19] Quite a few women repeatedly and cruelly trick this hapless, love-lusty young man. Hodge is the diminutive form of Roger, and his haplessness confirms that Clare writes doubly in pursuit of a long-standing tradition of stereotypes – Hodge having been crudely and widely used to denounce a type of degeneracy and stupidity in male agricultural labourers across the midlands and the south of England in the eighteenth and nineteenth centuries.[20] Hodge is a fairly regular occurrence in Clare's poetry – in narrative poems, love lyrics and even Northborough-period sonnets.[21] Problematically, nothing in this poem seeks to contest that blunt stereotyping; in fact, if it offers a relatively powerful and canny characterisation of rural women, of the male labourer it rather seeks to confirm stereotypes of gullibility and naivety at some length. If Simon Dentith is right in saying that Clare's even more frequent use of the word 'clown' shows he had adopted 'rather too much of the downward glance of his betters', then the persistence of 'Hodge' across his verse similarly disrupts notions of Clare's supposedly inclusive social politics (of course, he could come close to being a social snob over issues, for example, of taste or natural history).[22] As Dentith suggests, perhaps such usage illustrates the dangers inherent in 'drawing on the idiom of the elite'.[23] But to assume so is to deny a knowing linguistic playfulness in Clare; is to ignore the inverting, potentially empowering frisson in 'linguistic reappropriation' of stereotyping terms with which other social groups have stigmatised your own kind. Or else, in characterising 'Hodge' as a clown the way he does, Clare puts some distance between himself and other kinds of rural masculinity – a separation determined by cultured intelligence rather than class difference.[24]

With this specific poem in mind, Sarah Houghton offers a nuanced reading of the play at its heart:

> Clare explicitly altered his text to render it less serious and further to make Hodge a figure of fun, and the reader is led to value the tricks played as entertaining aspects of the exuberance of rural culture... Hodge is no innocent victim in this poem... [and] within the traditions of his own community, he is a fair target for the tricks played upon him... Nor is Hodge's love in 'Up crows the cock' to be understood as rarefied devotion, cruelly spurned: the apparently wretched account of thwarted adoration (which is 'Roger's') actually appears on second glance to be a teasing courtship, a Beatrice and Benedick flirtation-game in which both participants know the rules.[25]

In this poem, Roger starts the April foolery early: he 'mocks his masters call' (l. 3) to send the milkmaids scurrying and then revels in their disarray. He is to be victimised for the rest of the poem, and seems haplessly prone to teasing, largely due to his affection for one of the women. He is said to be 'rather small in wit' (l. 22), and 'easy catched & bit' (l. 24). This gullible man falls for every trick and jape proffered: errands to fetch 'a somthing from a shop' (l. 27), to buy 'stirrup oil' (l. 43), to locate 'pigeons milk' (l. 53 – an eighteenth-century staple of April Fool's Day tricks);[26] to get 'needles with glass eyes' (l. 111); 'to get a whool rake' (l. 159); he is tricked by a weaver and covers his face in soot, 'A blackamore out right' (l. 80); and straw on his back is set alight by the girl he loves – Kate – which pushes him into a animalistic rage (ll. 204–16). This is a lively, populous tale: raucous, rancorous and flirtatious. At the heart of it is Hodge's/Roger's heart. Here he is described after discovering the fire on his back:

> But when the straw began to smoke
> In terror for his cloaths
> He tore from off his back the joke
> & swore all sorts of oaths
> He wished her oer & oer as dead
> Oaths which she never heard
> The fire had been so near his head
> To rob him of his beard
> In weeding time of blades of wheat
> He plaited true love knots
> He wished her both to hear and see't
> Though seeming as if not
> 'If they love me as I love them'
> & turned his back to say't
> These links will lap & named a name
> All seemed to hear but kate (ll. 209–24)

The sufferings of Roger are not just to be found in the tricks and jokes of the woman he has fallen for. He is suffering because he is enduring an unreciprocated, and seemingly lengthy, love for a woman whom we know – through delicious dramatic irony presented just before the fire is set – felt as follows: 'no such love had kitty sparks/That dwelt in rogers mind' (ll. 199–200). Roger is April's fool, but he is more permanently love's fool: ardent and deluded; impassioned and lost. The intertwining imagery of the 'sparks' of love with the 'crackling flaze' (l. 205) of the fire she sets on his back becomes a moving symbol of the lusty heat he carries. His love is mocked – and it would burn him alive. After she then manages to douse 'Rogers skull' (l. 244) with a bucket of water, Roger swears to get his revenge on Kate and attempts to lock her in a barn. She sneaks out easily, sets a trap of 'Milk bucket stool & thrall' (l. 266 – a thrall being the frame for barrels or milk pans) and, sure enough, he 'tumbled over all' (l. 268). The poem concludes with a thoroughly battered Roger giving up on a rotten April Fool's Day and his misplaced love:

> No april fool was so deep in
> The wet dropt in his track
> & now he'd sorely bruised his shins
> & nearly broke his back

> Ill never more for such sweet hearts
> Hide apples in the hay
> Nor save brown shelly nuts by quarts
> For her to give away
> Says he & tried to wring his slop
> & slove unseen away
> To bed as wet as any mop
> So ended april day (ll. 269–80)

The social power in this world resides mostly with the women – though also with the weaver, cobbler and grocer who add to Roger's humiliations. April Fool's Day allows a Bakhtinian carnival of reversals of power – and in this case it is women using the play of the spring custom to invert the usual dynamics of the farmyard's patriarchy and its concomitant sexual politics. Such a festive inversion of social norms would be plainly the case were it not for the fact that Clare frequently presents the fact of a man feeling love for a woman as placing all the power of choice in the woman's hands: the clear implication is that it is not just on the first of April that men in unreciprocated love are made fools. In this poem, it is not only that the men are made to do foolish things, but that they are already prone to be disempowered because they are said to be either 'rather small in wit' (l. 22) or 'easy catched & bit' (l. 24). Their foolishness, their gullibility, is not festively temporary, it is sadly permanent because it is generated by male desire. Roger's natural gullibility is exacerbated by his being in love, so that overall the male situation here is utterly hopeless. The bizarre activities of the spring custom merely reveal, and revel in, what is already the case: Roger is hapless and witless and presumes a power he should not have, and does not deserve. His humiliation in this poem is absolute – and speaks of social as well as amatory failure – though the poem does not steer us towards sympathy for men at all; and in Houghton's reading it is a poem celebrating the social success of the April fool custom.

If this April fool poem successfully presents a community cohering over the ritualistic ridiculing of a love-drunk hapless man, 'The Enthusiast: A day-dream in summer' explores the intensity of the beginnings of a more serious relationship. The poem also offers a superlative example of how Clare puts nature to work both around, and to some extent in the minds of, the lovers. This is a long, 236-line poem of terse, sometimes pacy tetrameter couplets, first written in 1823[27] and rewritten many times after that, but which missed out on inclusion in *The Rural*

Muse (1835) and so was never published in Clare's lifetime. Drawing on a one-line epigraph from the poet Henry Kirke White – a son of a butcher who, like Robert Bloomfield, had Capel Lofft as a patron and who, like Chatterton, died tragically young[28] – placed to lead us into a world of melancholic daytime nostalgia, the poem starts out with a third-person account of a 'lone enthusiast' (l. 9). Any enthusiasms appear to have been worn down into his thoroughly depressed and isolated state by the commencement of the time-frame of the poem. He is embedded in the landscape like a silent, vagrant, unemployed Wordsworthian figure – '[o]f wood & heath in brambles clad' (l. 6) – and within a few lines has settled in shade 'by a stream' (l. 11) to dream on a hot summer day. With its 'fairy light' (l. 18), the dream transforms – yet is contiguous with – the natural world around him, which is now brighter, more dynamic, more populous. Quickly, the newly refreshed surroundings start to affect his identity and he becomes a child once more:

> & mid the sweet enchanting view
> Created every minute new
> He swooned at once from care & strife
> Into the poesy of life
> A stranger to the thoughts of men
> He felt his boyish limbs again
> Revelling in all the glee
> Of lifes first fairy infancy
> Chasing by the rippling spring
> Dragon flyes of purple wing
> Or setting mushroom-tops afloat
> Mimmicing the sailing boat (ll. 23–34)

That dreaming in this way without the 'thoughts of men' is described as the 'poesy of life' means that the process of poetic composition is organic and subconscious, childlike and not artfully or deliberately conceived. It might also suggest that the closest we can come to describing the forging of poetry is that it reveals itself like a dream unbidden, untutored, ungoverned. The 'poesy of life' describes immaterial moments of intensity which are extra-textual, yet still dense and multiplying in terms of significance and depth of field – a contrivance rather undermined by the fact of Clare's writing the experience into poetry. Our 'enthusiast' is a character who is 'sickened at the sight/Of lifes realitys' (ll. 4–5), after all.

The characterisation also means that 'poesy' is an idealised space, necessarily and sharply separable from the ordinary cares of human life – and in this poem that is the framing device used (though this is not characteristic of all of Clare's versions of how poetry works). The conventional conflation of dream with 'poesy' suggests here that both offer a retreat – an intellectually private nesting space of freedom from the quotidian, a kind of thinking which allows for the safe conceptualising of ideals and the avoidance of material realities. A perfect space, then, for idealisations of childhood and first love.

Raptured thoughts about youth continue for another fifty lines, running in lively fashion through all manner of outdoor games where the child plays with tactile toys of natural dispensation – 'butter flyes' (l. 36), 'red & purple flowers' (l. 40), 'pootys' (l. 44), trees (l. 44) and birds' eggs (l. 46). As if they were in a William Blake song, the free play for these children is cut short by the 'old church clock... [i]n its dull drumming drowsy way' (ll. 55, 57) and they are now in a rush to school. Unlike Blake, Clare revels in childish delight in learning and, without irony, celebrates the school's situation next to a graveyard – not least because the stones offer uncannily inflected reading opportunities for the children (l. 81). The account of frenetic youthfulness now steps ever so gracefully into puberty, and so the young man's thoughts turn to femininity. Technically, at the transition point, Clare allows the narratological perspective to step just outside the dream, perhaps to remind us who is doing the dreaming. The graveyard's stillness is the fulcrum:

> All all was blest & peace & plays
> Brought back the enthusiasts fairy days
> & leaving childhood unpercieved
> Scenes sweeter still his dream relieved
> Lifes calmest spot that lingers green
> Manhood & infancy between
> When youths warm feelings have their birth
> Creating angels upon earth
> & fancying woman born for joy
> With nought to wither & destroy
> That picture of past youths delight
> Was swimming now before his sight
> & loves soft thrills of pleasant pain
> Was whispering its deciets again
> & Mary pride of pleasures gone
> Was at his side to lead him on (ll. 87–102)

The teenage years are the perennial spring whose effects are permanently refreshing in the recollection – and whose status as the originary site of the first rush of confusing love can be recursively turned to again and again by the wizened adult. The fissure of the word 'destroy' effects another rupture in the dream and the perspective moves once more to a place slightly outside of the dreamscape, and so the experience becomes a 'picture' again – a two-dimensional representation of the past only. This poem successfully manages to create a visual field of considerable depth when retreating into a deep, remembered past, only to flick a switch and return to a flatter present – at the moment we return to a narratological awareness of the fact of dreaming. This fluctuating technique gives the poem a temporal dynamic whereby we move inwards (in space) and backwards (in time), deeper (in memories) and more intensely (in emotional, psychological significance). The range of this movement is enhanced by the fact of its being recursive: the poem's 'dream' is intermittently interrupted by a return to narratological awareness of its status as a dream. This staging lends the 'dream' a psychologically interiorising dynamic. The return to the frame repeatedly reminds us of the contrast between the bottomless riches of the enthusiast's past and his reduced and flattened present.

In the lines quoted above, Mary appears as the zenith of the enthusiast's departed loves: the turning away from 'lifes realitys' (l. 5) has met its apotheosis. What follows is a tender account of his intimate time spent with Mary – 'through field & lane' (l. 103), her 'small hand pressed within his own' (l. 119). Outdoors, walking together, the dream of this contentment returns the sensation 'as love had just begun' (l. 122); the hawthorn 'blooming still' (l. 128) suggests the time recalled is May (or even late April) – and indeed the 'enthusiast' gathers in this 'may' (hawthorn) for Mary. Here, a rhyme pair which is to become a feature of the late lust lyrics as discussed above – 'rest' and 'breast' – appears in a way which is controlled in a more mutual and sympathetic understanding of the woman's body:

& pleased he clumb the thorny grain
To crop its firstling buds again
& claimed in eager extacys
Loves favours as he reached the prize
Marking her hearts uneasy rest
The while he placed them on her breast

&felt warm loves oer bounding thrill
That it could beat so tender still
& all her artless winning ways
Where with her as of other days
Her fears such fondness to reveal
Her wishes struggling to consceal
Her cheeks loves same warm blushes burned
& smiled when he its warmth returned (ll. 131–44)

The male here takes on a hunter-gatherer task, risking the scratch of the thorn bush in his pursuit of the award for his lover. The passage is replete with a slight awkwardness in the young lovers' play – there is 'unease' in the 'struggle' between indulgence in expression and the continuing concealment of desire, as public appearances give in to private thoughts. But happily the 'struggle' is one against convention, against orthodox mores, rather than of the man's desire against the woman's resistance (examples of which we will see below). There is here a clear sense of the love being 'returned': tentatively celebrated, but nevertheless fondly grasped and reciprocated. Yet still, we can see how the male uses a natural abundance as a tool – the 'prize' – for the emblematic seduction of the woman he pursues; though Clare is at pains to stress the innocence in both parties. This is 'firstling' love, symbolically captured in the 'firstling' blooms heralding summer – the diminutive suffix '-ling' carrying with it a lively yet infantilising effect similar to the 'duckling', the 'gosling' or the 'stripling'. A word functioning as an adjective but ending with '-ing' contains an active adverbial inflection – in much the same way that Keats's speaker is an active child of the night in the line 'Darkling I listen...' ('Ode to a Nightingale'). The enthusiast's flowering hawthorn is an infant creature of the spring, though 'firstling' implies more of a nascent, growing process, a becoming of primariness, than it does a fixed state. 'Firstling' is itself a primary word of the English language, appearing in print for the first time in William Tyndale's Bible in 1530 (*OED*). It is perhaps not at all coincidental that the word 'firstling' appears in Clare's own copy of *Selection from the Poetical Works of Thomas Carew*. In Carew's poem 'The Primrose', the early flower of spring – the 'firstling of the infant year' – is said to have a weak, garish yet resolute frame which here is set to embody 'What doubts and fears are in a lover'.[29] The other poet Clare certainly will have read using the word for similar purposes is Robert Burns. In his poem 'The Posie', the lead flower in his arrangement for his lover, the conveniently monikered 'May', is 'The primrose... the firstling o' the year', while the hawthorn nestles amongst the other flowers in this posy of seduction:

> The hawthorn I will pu', wi' its locks o' siller grey,
> Where, like an aged man, it stands at break o' day.
> But the songster's nest within the bush I winna tak away;
> And a' to be a posie to my ain dear May.[30]

Burns is always ready to dust off his caring credentials as he constructs this lovers' nest of a floriferous posy for his love: he will take some hawthorn, but will not wreck the songbird's home in the process. This performance of animal consideration and environmental delicacy is another feature Clare will go on to develop substantially.

Clare's own 'firstling' plant of choice is less fraught than Carew's, yet no less complicated than either his or Burns's, symbolically speaking. Richard Mabey details so many associations with the hawthorn or may tree that it might be a risk to consider whether there is any specific symbolic import to its appearance here – other than in confirming the promise of spring, in the future of this early, 'firstling' love. But the separate associations of the plant – on the one hand with another Mary, albeit the Catholic Virgin one, and on the other hand with an exclusively outdoors set of May rituals celebrating fertility – should not be ignored. The latter association is perfectly apposite, in the words of Jack Goody, as quoted by Mabey:

> The hawthorn or may was the special object of attention at May Day ceremonies that centred on the woods, the maypole and the May queen... In contrast to Christmastide greenery and Easter willow, it is a plant kept outdoors, associated with unregulated love in the fields rather than conjugal love in the bed.[31]

The account of their 'unregulated love in the fields', as Goody puts it, carries on for many more lines to form what is one of the greatest – yet one of the least celebrated – presentations of a young couple in love in the whole of Clare's work. At its core, this part of the poem is a celebration of the connection of the lovers with the natural world; more than that, it is an assertion of the necessity of a munificent natural world in the enabling of this human mutuality. The natural world as it is presented across forty or so couplets (ll. 103–226, starting just before the hawthorn is gathered) is not a mere 'backdrop' or framing device or simple 'setting': it is the meaning system through which the lovers understand each other. It affords their principal channel of communicative exchange which, in this early stage, is purposed on the building of trust. This passage of rapturous love is extended and sustained. Though there are understated reminders that this is a dream experience – such as when Mary's voice is described as the 'self-same...which met his youthful ear' (ll. 106–7), her 'bloom' is also the 'self-same', her 'eye' as blue as it was 'thirteen summers bye' (ll. 113–14) and his 'heart beat as it once it had done' (l. 121) – these moments when the dream experience of the present is weighed up against the reality of the past are confirmatory and so do not quite manage to fracture the relating of the action. But still they are comparative hesitations which – even while primarily serving to reinforce the quality and detail of the recollected similitude of the dreamscape – still act to build a layer of dissonance, a subtle reminder that this bubble will have to pop soon. Stating that our enthusiast 'felt as love had just begun' (l. 122), the speaker ensures he refers to both time-frames simultaneously: the younger dreamed self is realising what the new sensation is; the older dreaming self is aware that the sensation is the same as first love, but possibly that it offers similitude to a past reality, not reality itself. In that direct and simple-seeming pluperfect phrase 'felt as love had just begun', the emergence of the 'firstling' love is already captured as a past moment. The recollection of the memory relies on an act of dreamy historical imagination: a personal history of feeling, rather than of fact. Another implication of this temporally compound presentation is that the love ineluctably would have been beginning to be over from the outset. This is a lyrical spin on the immediately mutable decline of love, to which Clare often has recourse.

Yet for a long while in this poem, the love is as committed to, as sustained, as anywhere in Clare's verse. Indeed, this is possibly the most sustained account of 'firstling' and mutual love in all of his work. Many other love poems might not seem to have an ecopolitical heart to them at all, being reduced as they are to a reductive binary and entirely centred desire. But there are qualities about the way love is described in this poem that make it participative within a network of ecological relations and affections. Seth T. Reno is right to find a distinction between love of nature and love between humans as he seeks to define the ideal shape of 'ecological love' in Clare:

> The major distinction between 'ecological love' and 'human love' is the former's inclusivity and the latter's exclusivity; while human love refers to an

affectionate or passionate relationship between two individuals, ecophilia refers to a love of all things.³²

The 'excluding' and binary nature of the affection driving love poetry is the main reason the resultant poems are not always of an aesthetic piece with Clare's great nature poetry: the relational diversity, the 'rural plural' as I described it earlier in this book, which has such deep structural implications in Clare's response to the natural world, is reduced to a narrowed, singular, centred intensity in much of the love poetry. At its worst, the effect of such narrowing is to generate reductive versions of femininity; to reduce love to physicality, lust and little else, and the poetry to clunky doggerel. But poems such as the one under consideration seem to rest somewhere between an inclusive ecopoetics and an excluding amorousness, and so incorporate potent elements of both forms of attentive affection. Gary Harrison's identification of particular characteristics of Clare's ecopoetics can assist here. Harrison convincingly details Clare's particularising 'acknowledgement' of his environment's 'otherness and mystery':

> Clare has recorded a humble testimonial to the power of acknowledgement to displace knowledge, for a kind of intuitive intimacy to displace violent possession, in our quest for coming to terms with the natural world³³

This acute assessment is perfectly in tune with the mode at play in this love poem: the feelings on display here are detailing a personal history of affection, but this is not done to build 'knowledge'; it is an account of the passions of love, but (as it is in so many of Clare's love poems) the purpose is not to delimit 'violent possession'; the 'acknowledgement' of the lover is mutualising and built upon 'intuitive intimacy' – albeit an intimacy that is delicate, fragile and uncertain. It is a great strength of Harrison's modelling of 'acknowledgement' of the natural world that it is transferable to Clare's best love poetry. It is also indicative that we have a poem as much about the structures of relation with, and within, the natural world as it is about a pair of human lovers. In this poem, the natural world as explored and detailed by the speaker operates as both fecund symbol and catalyst of the loving relations between the two, and as the language of the process of their growing mutual understanding. The kind of love being presented here is expressed, felt and comprehended by the rich array of elements of the natural world.

In the following passage, for example, a rhizome of complex relations operates between all constituents of the scene, as they seem to become one another through rhymed density. There is a focalised male gaze, but there is a female one too, which leads the trajectory of the poem in its exploration:

> He loved to watch her wistful look
> Following white moths down the brook
> & thrilled to mark her beaming eyes
> Brightening in pleasure & supprise
> To meet the wild mysterious things
> That evenings soothing presence brings
> & stepping [on] with gentle feet
> She strove to shun the larks retreat
> & as he near the bushes prest
> & scared the linnet from its nest
> Fond chidings from her bosom fell
> Then blest the bird & wished it well
> His heart was into rapture stirred
> His very soul was with the bird
> He felt that blessing by her side
> As only to himself applied (ll. 179–94)

As in the classic 'The Nightingales Nest', a naturalist's attentiveness to the birds nesting reminds us of man's unintentional intrusiveness. Here the woman is more delicate in her alertness to step and to sound, and in her awareness of the fragility of the bird. She leads the man's environmental consideration and, while he follows clumsily (Hodge-like?) yet deferentially, he also wants her blessings of the birds to be directed only at him – his selfishness grasping for a love that has not yet been stated, even if it has been demonstrated. The male wishes to tilt all of her affection his way, but it is only a semi-serious wish and in the following lines 'she neer denied' (l. 199) that the blessings count for him as much as the birds. For all the self-centredness of his desire, that '[h]is very soul was with the bird' means that his growing love for the woman enhances – rather than detracts from – his love for the natural.

Just a few lines later, however, almost immediately the love has been confirmed, surety seems to be dissolving: we now move towards the closure of the poem and the awakening from the layers of dream that the poem has structured. Fear (l. 201), doubt (l. 203) and pain (l. 205) suddenly surface as the man worries at the reality of all before him (ll. 213–16) even through her voiced reassurances (l. 208). As the poem works to its close, the slipperiness between wish, desire, dream and reality lubricates a flood of voiced assertions from both man and Mary that they will be permanent even as evidence crashes in to the contrary. The more the assertions come, the less linked we seem to be to any reality, any material or bodily surfaces offering security. Sanctuary derived from mutuality in relations with other bodies is disappearing, as so often happens in Clare's more sophisticated love poems. Here are the closing lines, worth quoting at length:

> Yet he did feel as like a child
> & sighed in fondness till she smiled
> Vowing they neer would part no more
> & act so foolish as before
> She nestled closer by his side
> & vowed 'we never will' & sighed
> He grasped her hand it seemed to thrill
> & whispered 'no we never will'
> & thought in raptures mad extream
> To hold her though it proved a dream
> & instant as that thought begun
> Her presence seemed his love to shun
> & deaf to all he had to say
> Quick turned her [tender] face away
> When her small waist he strove to clasp
> She shrunk like water from his grasp
> He woke – all lonely as before
> He sat beside the rilling streams
> & felt that aching joy once more
> Akin to thought & pleasant dreams (ll. 217–36)

To conclude, it is worth briefly considering that Clare made many revisions to this poem. Most significantly, the figure of the dreaming 'enthusiast' was a late introduction; earlier versions do not feature this third-person position at all – instead they maintain a first-person lyrical subject. This means that few of the tensions between the dream of the past and the intruding knowledge of the present are in place early on in the poem's development. The shift of the poem from an extended lyrical account into a more complex structure indicates just how deliberate – and carefully planned – were the effects of the narratological layering in the version of the poem that the Oxford editors rightly choose as their copy-text. The end result is evidence that Clare could do some of his most subtle and studied work on the subject of lovers: the subject did not always make his vision crudely simplistic, nor his composition impulsive. At the close, the framing return to the time of the opening of the poem is an obvious enough trick, but an effective one. The conjoining of the lovers has been so intimately developed that the bleak loneliness of the male lover – back to dreams of the past – has considerable impact. This is one of Clare's most effective love poems, but, like many more lyrical works, it characteristically ends with a male completely alone, living with only his own thoughts and dreams, memories and fading visions. The late poem 'To Mary' (first line 'I sleep with thee and wake with thee') sees a lonely man tortured by constant natural reminders of a woman's absence; in the untitled 'My spirit lives in silent sighs', the male speaker silently loves the 'fairy form' of a woman who seems only half present; while in 'First Love' – perhaps the greatest of all Clare's late love lyrics – the effect of falling in love leaves the speaker transformed into a visionary poet who 'could not see a single thing' and can instead only see plurality, connection, dizzying relations of meaning, but still the poem ends abruptly with the speaker cold, lost and alone, the lover long gone.[34]

Assertive Lust, Silenced Women

Sometimes in Clare's poetry, however, men are much more confident and capable in their pursuit of women than either Hodge or the enthusiast, in their vastly differing contexts. Clare's reading in English poets he called 'those beautiful minstrels of Elizabeth'[35] – of what we now call the Early Modern period – provided models of confident, assertive male seduction.[36] He respectfully adopted a version of this kind of voice, while being careful to avoid aping its equally prevalent pastoral simplicity (though in early work he did that too). By comparison, Clare's speaking voices are never quite as confidently or stridently sexual as those to be found in John Donne, Robert Herrick or Andrew Marvell or, more pertinently in Clare's case, in the Cavalier 'amatory' verse of Thomas Carew and John Suckling. Clare's own copy of *Selection from the Poetical Works of Thomas Carew*, mentioned above, is dominated by the opening section of verse labelled 'Amatory', the majority of which are addressed to the love object 'Celia' – a classically derived model woman who is for Carew what Beatrice was for Dante, Julia for Herrick and Laura for Petrarch, and what Mary was to become for Clare.[37] Such a weight of 'amatory' interest is replicated in Clare's verse throughout his writing career, but is never labelled as such in any collections of his work.

In poems such as 'Morning Walk', 'Come come my love the bush is growing' and 'Song' (first line 'We'll walk my love at eve unseen'),[38] a male speaker enjoins a woman to be alone with him, on an exploration of known places, in a contemplation of populous nature on the fringes of agricultural activity, but pulling away from other human eyes. In the early, unfinished 'Morning Walk' of tetrameter couplets (written 1819–1820), the speaker leads Lucy on a nature trail to 'mark each object as we pass' (l. 6). As he displays like an unfurling peacock his knowledge of both natural phenomena and his study of natural history of Erasmus Darwin[39] and John Ray[40] (ll. 17–18), and draws a grim, momentary conclusion that, like an ever-running stream, man 'does no rest or pleasure know' (l. 33), he worries that such studied piety risks losing his audience, and uses a quite cloying presentation of the scene to win her back:

> ...Lucy why so wan and pale
> Dost thou dislike my moral tale
> Or does some wrankling thought molest
> The peaceful harbour of thy breast
> If so the lurking fiend disarm
> Drive away this magic charm
> All thy meek beauties reasume
> Let the soft flush thy face illume
> Let all be gentle all be gay
> Like yon skipping lambs at play (ll. 35–44)

The male is not subtle in his steering of Lucy's vision here (it is the motivational equivalent of 'don't be sad – look at this fluffy thing'), but it is important to note how the young poet is ready to deploy his poetry manipulatively: to charm, to dissemble, to win the woman's affections and continuing, hopefully growing, trust. The vision alights on the lambs here in highly ornate poeticising style ('dost', 'thy', 'illume', 'yon') with a primary intention of governing the female mind, to construct a tableau suitably and comfortably cushioned for a loving relationship. The lambs are tactically manoeuvred to effect seduction; the female eye is directed to dynamic flocculence through a mellifluous stream of lines about the archetypal 'joyful' spring lambs in a display of male mastery and control. He piles it on, fluffing it up, summarising that 'None but the foolish dream of harm' (l. 56) to counteract (and utterly contradict) the earlier intrusion of the transitory mutable life of man. He then moves to a highly condensed account of birds and their songs: nine different birds in as many lines (ll. 63–72). In this poem, nature is only coerced into verse to enable the inspiriting of trust, dependency, love and – the speaker implicitly hopes, further down the line – lust, for the talented male lead. The walk, on passing 'every nymph and goddess slim' (l. 87), fades through a 'leafy maze' (l. 94) and into the beckoning incompletion of an ellipsis marker (Clare deploying punctuation there with knowing deliberation).

The Northborough-period untitled poem 'Come come my love the bush is growing'[41] features a ballad-like metre, alternating lines of nine and eight syllables – the longer lines carrying an extra unstressed syllable in a feminine closing rhyme – lending the eight-line stanzas an awkwardly hesitant yet simultaneously breezy balance. The poem starts with a speaker's call to a woman to enter the natural scene with him, but immediately offers memories of a former talk the couple enjoyed. This recollection is then framed by a return to the present tense and a closing call – in the tenth and final stanza – for the woman to 'hither come' (l. 78). The poem retains 'thy' and 'thee', though this form of address is meant to be redolent of a regional tongue, rather than anything formal. The usage is instead local and intimate. For the most part, by the early 1830s Clare had let go of the ornate, rather strained poetic diction which is so much a feature of the early 'Morning Walk' above. Also characteristic of this period – of *The Rural Muse* book and the fatter *Midsummer Cushion* manuscript – is a plaintive air which draws in the long experience and perspective of a more mature male voice. The urgent imperative of the repeated 'come' opening the poem is quickly moderated by a wistful sense of a rich past – collocated in space if not in time by the sound of a common bird, the linnet:

> Come come my love the bush is growing
> The linnet sings the tune again
> He sung when thou with garments flowing
> Went talking with me down the lane
> Dreaming of beauty ere I found thee
> & musing by the bushes green
> The wind enarmoured streaming round thee
> Painted the visions I had seen (ll. 1–8)

In the past, the woman stepped into the speaker's pre-existing 'dreaming', which internally rhymes with the 'streaming' wind. So dense is the movement of this stanza that it is hard to untwine the relations between the moving forces, or to work out which came first: the bush grows, the linnet sings, the garments flow, the lovers talk, the speaker dreams and muses, the wind streams, and all entwine into the speaker's 'Painted visions'. The visions are ongoing, because this is all happening 'again'.

After describing from various angles the sensation of falling in love, the speaker tracks through a forlorn period of extended absence – a common enough feature of Clare's mature love poems – yet, given that the opening addressee is the returned lover, in this poem the sadness never overwhelms. A rare moment of domestically situated reconnection appears as the reunited lovers warm themselves against long winters of being parted:

> But winters gone & spring is going
> & by thy own fire side Ive been
> & told thee how with garments flowing
> I saw thee by the bushes green
> I told [thee] & with rapture glowing
> I heard thee more then once declare
> That down the lane with garments flowing
> Thou with the spring wouldst wander there (ll. 41–8)

The repetition of those 'garments flowing' of the first two stanzas ensures a close and cosy continuity, and echoes the rejoining of the lovers and the retelling of their first encounter. After the anaphora of the opening ampersands in the second and third lines, the three successive first-person singular pronouns construct a more breathless anaphora – and the speaker's excitement is repaid with the promise of the lover's return 'down the lane'. In the eighth stanza the 'bush is growing' (l. 57) again: the same location, in spring, is seeing the lovers 'plighted' (l. 61). In the ninth stanza as the same bird sings, the speaker returns to the encouraging imperative of the first line, but with an enriched, calm sense of genuine mutuality. The lover is here, and now:

> The linnet shining like the bushes
> With bits of yellow on its wings
> Is singing & the speckled th[r]ushes
> A most delightful ballad sings

They sung when I thy journey greeting
Heard thee to praise in whispered words
Then come love promised me the meeting
& be as happy as the birds (ll. 65–72)

The final stanza, inevitably, reconnects with the 'garments flowing' (l. 77) and leaves the lovers alone at last in the 'green lane... the dearest place in song' (ll. 79–80). The tight parallels, repetitions and echoes, the centrally rehearsed image of the unnamed woman's clothes moving in the natural power of the wind, combined with the poem's broader movement from a particular place, up and away in memory and through dream, fancy, art and song, across absence and then finally back to the same fecund locale, make this unsung love lyric particularly effective in its safe delivery of contentment and happy, matured union. And this level of resolute loving and domesticated communion following a haunted period of separation is a rare commodity in Clare's love poetry.

What becomes a more dominant version of lusty confidence in his late poetry is exemplified by 'Song', the first line of which is 'We'll walk my love at eve unseen'.[42] This poem will be used here to unlock a whole series of late poems in which confident, unbridled lust is presented in a similar manner. Written during the first decade of his committal to Northampton Asylum, this particular poem is available to us – along with 800 or so of his late poems – only in a transcription by the asylum steward W. F. Knight, who was in post from 1845–1850.[43] In comparison to the texts discussed just above, this poem is more relaxed about predicting a future for a meeting between speaker and his lover, and far more detailed about the bodily qualities of their intimacy. Yet it still embeds the relationship in a welcoming natural world – albeit painted sometimes in broad brush strokes relative to the intricate portrayals of botanical features we might otherwise expect of a Clare poem. Lust in this late period seems to make the poetic vision rather hazy over things other than the woman's body.

This poem is slightly fragmentary, with a few words missing and with the first two eight-line stanzas of octosyllabic tetrameter couplets being rounded off in rather incomplete fashion by a six-line third stanza. In attitude and subject matter, and structurally, there are many poems like this in the Northampton Asylum period; like this one, they often name the female object, and intended recipient, of the address. Perhaps surprisingly, in frequency Mary does not dominate across these poems in terms of named women: there are in fact over eighty different female names addressed in such lust-lyric songs in the two Oxford *Later Poems* volumes. In this poem the name happens to be Anna. The male speaker is assertively direct over his descriptions of what they will do together or – more accurately – over what he will do to her:

> A kiss without thy leave I'll take
> With one arm lapped round thy white neck
> While curls by thy white earings [shake]
> Like so many coal black rings
> And loll upon thy heaving breast
> And in my secret wishes rest
> My arm around thy shoulder thrown
> Thy hand in mine I^d. hold my own (ll. 9–16)

The boldness, the sexual confidence, the assertion that intimacy will happen – such characteristics are strikingly different to most earlier poems about women, and broadly (though not entirely) characteristic of a whole raft of late poems. The sense that he will be sexually physical with the woman without her permission is disturbing, even if the subsequent relaxation he claims will follow suggests a remote fantasy of mutuality; but unquestionably this is dangerous territory. And territory she is: many of the female figures in such poems seem to be peeled away at, layer by layer, from the clothes to the face, down the neck, to shoulders, to a broad back, through the locks of the hair, to the breasts, arms, hands, ankles.[44] As the male speaker gazes at her she develops into little more than a detailed object for the poet's fantasy – and to call this kind of fantasy masturbatory would not be an exaggeration. The women are not characterised or personalised at all, but instead are reduced, as a general construction of a set of images brought together by the territorial wanderings of the male gaze. The characterisation Anne K. Mellor gives of Wordsworth's poetic women applies here: 'Rarely allowed to speak for themselves, the female figures in Wordsworth's early poems... do not exist as independent, self-conscious human beings with minds as capable as the poet's'.[45] Broadly speaking, in such late Clare poems the women are of a physical type – always healthily (to quote from various poems) big or even fat, buxom, with thick ankles, calves and arms, strong backs, ruddy cheeks either red with hot blood or tanned by the sun.[46] These are working women – the 'red and rosey' farmers' daughters Clare bemoans the loss of in *The Parish*.[47]

In 'We'll walk my love at eve unseen', the 'breast' offers a place of 'rest' – a predictable enough rhyming pair Clare deploys elsewhere;[48] similarly, in other late lyrics breasts are called 'pillows' for the poet to sleep upon, or 'clouds' for him to float upon. Sometimes breasts embody the transcendent, raising through ardent contemplation the thoughts of the male into a relaxed state: in the late lust lyric 'Angels of earth', for example (which is framed devotionally by praise for 'Gods own masterpiece', woman[49]), the essence of womanhood is embedded in her 'bosoms white all full o' joy/Wafting our thoughts above'.[50] Breasts represent or house a cloyingly relayed angelic and Edenic natural purity, as they are invariably said to be like 'milk', 'cloud', 'swan', 'lily' or 'snow'. They are the source and seat of female passion and the main initialising stimulant of male desire. The emotional and lusty heat they are said to contain sometimes contrasts with their external coolness, as in the first stanza of the poem 'In beauty there is joy':

> In beauty there is joy for ever
>   That fadeth not and never will
> It changeth not to sorrow never
>   Its smiles are balm for every ill
> It burns in love from its own bosom
>   Yet never melts those hills of snow[51]

It is not unfair to say that Clare's concentration on breasts is obsessive. Breasts heave, swell, beat, bud, ripen, nest; they can be bare, fat, big, soft as silk or eider down; purple or blue veins map them and moles adorn them. They are leant on, slept on, handled, kissed and, most dominantly, gazed at.[52] The speaker, we are always reminded, is watching, waiting: alert to the body of the woman upon whom he is focused, and always sexually predatory. He delights in the stolen glimpse of an exposed bosom in 'Oh whither fair maiden':

> Neath ribb'd maple stovens sweet lies the blue bell
> And Harrietts bosom bent low to the ground
> To crop two or three as she liked them so well[53]

Like Harriett here, a woman will often be surrounded by flowers, situated in a fecund spring or summer scene, with colours and light dazzling the narrator and enhancing his portrayal of her. Clare uses some of the width of his 'natural' palette to cope with the over-abundance a woman's body has to 'offer' him – but in truth this is a tightly narrowed application of any botanical knowledge he might claim. Just as frequently as the 'breast' and 'rest' rhyme pair mentioned above, these late lust lyrics feature the half-rhyme pair of 'bosom' and 'blossom' which will dominate the way the woman is represented. Not only is she in a flowery scene, with the 'wild flowers spread round at her feet' in 'O sweet is the sound',[54] for example, she might also be called the most beautiful flower herself, or a flower might evoke a memory of a woman, for example in the line 'wild flowers are the image of Susan' in 'Of thee I keep dreaming still thee'.[55] Parts of the woman's anatomy might also be likened to a flower: lily-white necks,[56] rosy cheeks, budding breasts, or she might have 'breath...like the violets bed'.[57] Flowers can also have the anatomical characteristics of a woman: 'the bosom of a flower'[58] is one of Clare's stock images, as is 'lily bosom' as mentioned above.[59] The words and images of the bosom and the blossom are almost interchangeable, and this feminised personification of flora is added to by the repeated appearance of bees. Predictably enough perhaps, the male speaker is often positioned as a bee, penetrating the female flower, of which simple model the following untitled poem offers a clear example (first line 'Honey words make charms of blisses'):

> 2
> The busy bee will kiss the flower
> As often as he pleases
> The butterfly in sunny hour
> Will kiss but never teazes
> The skylark mounts to kiss the sun
> That o'er the green corn glitters
> Then like a stone he drops when done
> And in the meadow twitters
>
> 3
> The twilight kisses mornings blush
> In coal black night's retreating
> And midday breezes kiss the bush
> Its pleasant shadows meeting
> Grass, corn and leaves in windy days
> Are stirred by mighty putther
> The flowers are ravished by the bees
> The rest kiss one another

> 4
> But Mary fairest of thy kind
> No woman ne'er was fairer
> Nature's a puzzle to my mind
> A flirt I cannot bear her
> For me and love she only cheats
> Days sunshine and eve's dew
> She kisses everything she meets
> And I've not once kissed you[60]

If the bee is the male speaker and the flower is Mary, then it is clear that the poet is positioning himself as a ravisher, who wishes to kiss 'as often as he pleases' – though kisses in themselves are not only a prelude to sexual penetration – they are also half a euphemism for it. Bees, after all, might have tongues but they do not kiss, and neither do flowers or skylarks. The orgy of kissing here is entirely euphemistic; a baroque tableau of excess, worthy of the more gaudy cockney sensuality of Leigh Hunt (though the style of language is less ornate or poised than Hunt's). Nature offers a model of highly active, blatant sexuality, all of which is designed to load pressure on that final line and its final word: the 'you' here just has to participate in kissing the speaker. The poem has mounted evidence that kissing is – to use an idiom which excuses rather than explains – 'only natural'. The conflation of woman with the natural world works both ways, however: here, nature is a 'puzzle' and a 'flirt', teasing the poet for his inactivity through its blatant, varied displays of play – all entirely sexualised in his inflamed mind and by his engorged libido.

In the late lust lyric, the activity and power rest squarely with the active, leading man, while the woman is passive and accepting. If she is not, the speaker will say that she should be – or that he will be physical with her without her permission. In 'Honey words make charms of blisses...', the dreamy sexuality of accommodating flowers is extended to an image akin to a lesbian harem of flowers kissing one another; those flowers, that is, not about to be ravished by the bee. It is perhaps typical of Clare's poetry as a whole that the prurient speaker of 'Honey words make charms of blisses...' remains at the close an outsider to all this kissing, a peeping Tom; the poem ends with a whinge of familiar sexual frustration. Keen, penetrative, obsessive, unreciprocated though the speaker's male gaze might be, nevertheless it remains clear that observation is dominant all the way through the trajectory of such late lust lyrics: as root cause of initial attraction; as the overall mode of discourse; and finally as outcome – if there is one – of the attention. Nature offers rich examples of how abundant is its sexual play and accounts of that profusion are directed to the male's cause – and focused on the woman, to press her into acquiescence. Predominantly, looking leads to nowhere but more looking, more recycled images of a nature which seems to offer fertile ground, but only for sexual play. Oftentimes in such poems that same sexual energy of natural bodies serves to confirm its absence in the speaker's life. Consummation might be implied by penetrative bees – by skylarks kissing the sun – and the male orientation might well be entirely determined by a desire for bodily access to the woman – to whatever woman he plucks from his fantasy roster and names and shapes and chisels into two-dimensional, voiceless embodiment – but nature serves as a source of symbols of a wished-for sexual outcome rather than tokens, mementoes, of a completed cycle of looking, lusting and sexual coition.

It seems obvious that sexual frustration was one private source of all of these asylum lust lyrics, but to say so is not to excuse their evident reduction of woman to sexual meat. Nature, in these poems, is much reduced too, to a thin veil over the base intentions of the speaker. Nature is not so much the successful tool of seduction or the language of mutual understanding, as we have seen in earlier poems. Instead, in these poems nature offers a source of a set of deceptive and often stale tropes which Clare would have heard in songs and pub ballads all his life. If we expect consistency of moral design from our poets, this will amount to a pitiful neglect of Clare's integrity of focus on a natural world in and of itself, and on a folk culture and rural society with rich personality, ritual and hard-working endurance. Only faint and fragmentary echoes of those earlier commitments and explorations remain here in the asylum verse.

The late lust lyrics might even leave us wishing for the honesty and crass comedy of the bawdy songs that Clare would also have heard through all of his adult life. Why does he hesitate to be actually bawdy or even pornographic, or to have fun with these images as he surely would have done in hearing (and playing) songs in pubs and London clubs – and, no doubt, in places closer to home too?[61] Radical printers captured for posterity many bawdy songs of the Romantic period: they can be characterised both by their explicit language and imagery and by their constantly comedic nature, from a male perspective, written and sung for men. Yet Clare's lyrics are not sexually explicit and they are almost never humorous. The question is: what was it that restrained Clare from allowing these poems to reach the climax of consummation they so persistently seek?

Clare wrote these poems as a committed, private patient in an asylum – and mostly that is how they have been presented by twentieth-century editors and critics, seemingly keen to delineate a distinct marker between such poems and the rest of Clare's more acceptable oeuvre. In Northampton, Clare's behaviours were policed and regimented as never before; whether it was less or more liberal than Matthew Allen's institution is a moot point. What we do know is that little of what Clare thought of Northampton remains, while Allen will always be known, thanks to Clare, as having been 'Dr Bottle Imp ... who deals in urine' and who ran a 'buggershop'.[62] It might not be a balanced opinion, but it is an expression repeatedly copied out nonetheless.

About Northampton, considering the length of his stay, the blunt truth is that we know little of Clare's responses to the conditions, though when he does speak up he is almost always negative about his life there. Certainly by the late 1840s he was calling the asylum 'the purgatoriall hell & French Bastile of English liberty', his 'Prison', his 'Captivity', a place where 'there is neither room nor time for pleasure or commonsense', while he called himself

> a prisoner under a bad government so bad in fact that its no government at all but prison disapline where every body is forced to act contrary to their own wishes ... this is the English Bastile a government where harmless people are trapped & tortured till they die[63]

A similar lack of contextual knowledge pertains for the poetry written in the asylum. While Clare seems to have been encouraged to continue to write in Northampton, and while he was 'assisted' by an amanuensis in steward W. F. Knight, it is impossible to know whether more sexually explicit or politically toxic work was censored: ignored, then quietly disposed of. If not for reasons of changing contexts, it is certainly odd that there is such a change of direction and focus, intensity and style once Clare is resident in the Northampton General Lunatic Asylum. What did Knight and the asylum authorities do with the manuscripts if, as we might assume, Clare was writing on his own too? Knight's own brief, unsigned introduction to his two volumes of transcriptions does not give much away at all:

> Poetry by John Clare
>   written by him while an
>   Inmate of the Northampton
>   General Lunatic Asylum

> Copied from the Manuscripts as presented to me by Clare – and favoured with others by some ladies and Gentlemen, that Clare had presented them to – the whole of them faithfully transcribed to the best of my knowledge from the pencil originals many of which were so obliterated that without refering to the Author I could not decipher, some pieces will be found unfinished, for Clare will seldom turn his attention to pieces he has been interrupted in, while writing – and in no instance has he ever rewritten a single line – and whenever I have wished him to correct a single stanza he has ever shewn the greatest disinclination to take [^ in hand] what to him seems a great task.[64]

By this time, it appears Clare was not so particular as to the presentation of poems he could not have imagined would see the light of print publication. Whatever the historical truth might be of the Northampton poems' provenance, it is simply not true that his work's 'quality' descends precipitously in one direction after Clare's admittance to Northampton. Some of the late love poems – better described as love lyrics or love songs than 'lust lyrics' – are as sophisticated as anything Clare had ever written, and happily, while still concerned with women, they are not distended by the hollow dance of an unfulfilled old man's lust. But it is to the sexist aspects of that same lust that we now turn.

Lust and Lists: Sex in the Paratexts

It is now a quarter of a century since Lynne Pearce wrote what remains the only significant feminist assessment of Clare's later poetry. Her response is personally inscribed with a profound resentment of her experience of a patriarchal British academia, as much as it is written with an openly embittered distaste for Clare:

> My clearest response to John Clare today is that he took up five years of my life that could have been much better spent doing something else... I do, indeed, perceive my 'involvement' with John Clare to have been pre-determined by institutional forces. Clare was made my academic destiny when I was just 20 years old and submitting my applications for postgraduate research. John Clare, my tutor suggested, was a 'safe bet': on the margins, but respectable. He told me that a 'good book on Clare' had yet to be written. Not knowing what I really wanted to do, the subject of my doctoral thesis was thus decided for me.[65]

Although these comments are interesting in their own right as a short history of mid-1980s female experience in male-dominated literary studies, they are relevant because they inform Pearce's comments on Clare's 'profound misogyny'.[66] She is admirably open and self-reflexive about her agenda and its origins, admitting that 'the reading which follows is inscribed in resentment: that its resentment is the site of its feminism'.[67]

Pearce's rejection of Clare opens up a wide set of problems in the study of the poet, but is also a challenge to the way we practise postgraduate academic study. Few critical works on Romantic writers are theoretically explicit about their agendas in the way that Pearce is. She poses serious questions of literary worth, reader exclusion and the sexual politics of academia, most of which have gone unanswered by Clare scholars, or by literary criticism more broadly for that matter. So why does Clare scholarship not attract feminist criticism? Helen Boden makes a rare comment about feminism and Clare studies:

> Feminist critics seem to have avoided Clare, perhaps following the example of Janet Todd who after writing an early book on Clare, moved away from the subject to write principally on early women's writing. Similarly Lynne Pearce in a recent 'reluctant' and 'resenting' essay regrets the time she spent on Clare. Pearce argues that Clare's expressions of desire, loss, etc., refuse access to a female readership, because they are derived from an exclusively male tradition.[68]

That two feminist critics 'moved away' from Clare does not in itself constitute a pattern. Nevertheless, while many critics and editors of Clare have no doubt personally been committed feminists, it is probably true that there remains a dearth of purposefully and expressly feminist criticism of Clare.

Pearce suggests that because of Clare's misogyny, displayed with such alacrity in his 'Don Juan' and 'Child Harold', feminists have a moral obligation, as it were, to avoid him and writers like him, because his texts exclude women as readers and because his 'obsessional eye', as she calls it, objectifies women. Thus Pearce offers a reason not to read Clare poems whose principal object is the representation of women, because they belong 'to literary traditions that constitute the female merely as object'.[69] Helen Boden seeks to moderate that position somewhat:

> it is important and necessary that feminist critiques of the canon continue to take place. After all, the mixture of false modesty and fear often in evidence rarely actually deters men from engaging critically with *women's* writing. Clare will continue to be a man speaking to men unless women listen and

respond to him... There may be an important role for women critics of those male writers who have never quite made it into the canon.[70]

Pearce makes a well-argued case for reassessing Clare's sexual politics, while her Bakhtinian doctoral study of his later poetry gives her a range of insights into Clare's textual life too; she is an expert in the asylum-period notebooks and in literary theory.[71] The reason for her eventual rejection of Clare is all the more shocking and impressive for this proven expertise and the level of commitment it required.

At the core of her argument was a reading of 'catalogues of names and addresses found in Northampton MS 19... as disturbing as those sometimes found amongst the documents of sex-murderers'.[72] Because it is so contentious and inflammatory, this albeit momentary statement at the core of Pearce's departure from Clare studies has been largely ignored by Clare critics, where it has not been dismissed out of hand as extreme. Yet, given the seriousness of the scholarship and theoretical understanding which inform Pearce's closing rationale as she leaves Clare behind her, this chapter will take the accusation levelled at Clare head-on, at some length. To do so, we have to assess the kinds of 'paratexts' – texts that are neither poem nor prose – in Clare's manuscripts that would never end up in any standardising edition.

Northampton manuscript 19 is not the only place Clare wrote lists of women's names,[73] but it is a major location of them and will be the focus of the following consideration, as the central source of Pearce's disgust. To look at these lists in situ is also to respond positively to Tim Fulford's recent complaint that 'far too little attention has been paid to the manuscript notebooks that Clare compiled in Northampton asylum'.[74] Fulford problematises seemingly 'coherent' genre-based editions of Clare – whether of letter, prose or poems. In doing so, he complements a line of critique in Clare studies (discussed in detail above) pointing to the impossibility for a standard edition to fully capture the variety of the kinds of texts and paratexts a Clare notebook might contain. This is especially the case when an original manuscript contains more than simply poems, prose or letter drafts, as is the case with Northampton manuscript 19. Yet even as the most significant editing project was getting underway in 1962, the leads Eric Robinson and Geoffrey Summerfield held sincere doubts about the efficacy of standard editions for Clare's work:

> A John Clare manuscript may tell the reader more of the poet and the pattern of his creation than any number of printed volumes of his work.

Letters and poems there follow close upon each other so that their relationship can be seen at once and where a letter to a young woman is followed in the manuscript by a poem to her, it is clear that they both arise from the same burst of feeling; narrative verse may be interspersed with lyrics, and the handwriting may reveal that both were written together in the same moment of inspiration; fragments of essays may intermingle with scraps of biography and make reciprocal comment; a poem telling of Clare's isolation and abandonment may have interwoven among its stanzas a verse paraphrase of the Book of Job... But his editors are usually obliged to unravel the skein and to publish each poem teazed out from the letters and notes with which, in Clare's notebooks, it may be united, and sometimes they have taken the disentangling process further than is artistically justifiable... Naturally these editorial problems become most critical in the notebooks of the High Beech and the Northampton Asylum periods, and no editor is ever likely to arrive at a completely satisfactory solution.[75]

Following this early concern, Robinson of course went on to lead the nine-volume Oxford edition which – while meticulously inclusive of any and all textual variants of poems in footnote form – was, with good reason, committed only to the transcription of a primary poetic text in each case. Mark Storey's *Letters*, and Margaret Grainger's *Natural History*, likewise offer little of the textual context that falls outside of their remits – though as a thematic edition Grainger's does aim to include all manner of lists and fragments, and lists Clare's drawings too.[76] So, again, we are led back to the original manuscripts in pursuit of the context not of poems, but of those 'catalogues' Pearce finds so disturbing.

The particular manuscript Pearce refers to, Northampton manuscript 19, is a green leather-bound notebook, of roughly *sextodecimo* (16mo) size (measuring 172 mm × 113 mm, or 6¾ inches × 4½ inches). It is dated and addressed, yet misleadingly so, in the inside front cover and at the head of the first page proper, in ink, thus:

> John Clare
> Northborough
> Northamptonshire
> Novr 1845[77]

Pearce is disturbed by 'catalogues of names and addresses' in this manuscript; while 'names' do appear – as we shall see – sometimes appended to a village or parish name, this is the only item set out as an 'address' (such as it is) in the notebook; the implication that Clare has listed a name against an address to which the named person could be tracked is therefore Pearce's exaggeration. The dating and place of the inscription are mutually exclusive: Clare was resident in Northampton General Lunatic Asylum from December 1841 onwards. This twice-repeated inscription might indicate where the poet wanted the book to have been written, and insistently so, but not where he did in fact write in its pages. He had not been a Northborough resident for four years. This means the notebook is led by a displaced fantasy – inscribed to a combination of place and date which is impossibly unreal, if ostensibly perfectly humdrum; the book writes itself to a long-lost but not forgotten home. Let us not forget that this is the same place that Clare is supposed to have found so alienating on moving there in 1832; clearly, by the end of 1845 Northborough was the family home he wrote himself towards.

Given this addressing of the notebook – of its desired direction of travel – we have to consider that the contents might be doing a similar act of reaching out to a place long lost, a situation out of physical reach, but textualised and captured here into some sort of handwritten reality. While the address inscriptions are in ink, the poems and notes, lists, tables and doodles – in fact, all else that the book contains other than some seemingly random exceptions[78] – are written in pencil. Ballad-metre poems to various women predominate, often with the title 'Song'. Tim Fulford describes the notebook thus:

> It comprises 133 pages, all covered in Clare's pencilled handwriting, and written from both ends (Clare having turned the book upside down and made entries from the back as well as having proceeded from the front). Verse predominates: there are first drafts, revised drafts and fair copies of poems. There are prose transcriptions of the Book of Revelation and versifications of these; there are letter drafts and lists. Many entries are placed consecutively; some appear to have been grouped thematically; in a few instances Clare has squeezed a poem onto the remaining white space before and after one previously entered even if this involves working backwards, leaving the new poem dispersed across several pages[79]

This notebook contains the lists of women's names that Pearce censures: the question is, is it a disturbing 'hit list' of women – evidence of rapacious, threatening, dangerous male desire – a set of predatory, planned sexual conquests? Are the lists in any way 'murderous' in intent? In a rich account of the late lusty songs in conjunction with the lists as they appear in manuscript form, Jonathan Bate thinks that the songs to women proliferated at this stage because they were a form of work, while the lists were a functional tool in getting the work done:

> The lists of girls' names in his notebooks may have begun as an *aide mémoire* in relation to these commissions. Increasingly, though, he mingled the names of Northampton girls with those of villagers from Helpston, Maxey, Barnack and Glinton... One possibility is that the [late love songs] were simply commissions from boyfriends, fathers, brothers or husbands, undertaken in return for tobacco or beer. Another is that Clare saw, took a fancy to, then fantasised about these girls... A third is that he actually presented the girls with their poems, perhaps in a vain attempt to seduce them... There is firm evidence of Clare's interest in a number of local girls[80]

In his analysis of the continuing late tendency of Clare to list women's names, Bate writes further:

> He was also filling up an old pocket diary with more names. It was as if, having begun by listing the local girls for whom he wrote poems in return for tobacco, he felt compelled to go on and write down the names of every female he had ever met. We cannot know what drove the compulsion: sexual frustration must have played a part, but there was a deeper sense in which he was recording names in order to hold on to his past, his identity.[81]

Bate authoritatively traces a mixture of such names 'from almost every phase of John Clare's life'[82] in one manuscript instance. He goes on to push away the accusation of Pearce:

> For some female readers today, the asylum notebooks make Clare a repellent figure – one critic compares the lists of girls' names to the documents of a 'sex-murderer' – yet his respect for the work of Laetitia Landon and the spirit of shared poetic enterprise that animates his long correspondence with Eliza Emmerson tell a more sympathetic story about his dealings with women.[83]

To use Clare's enthusiasm for contemporary women poets to counter the lists which Bate presents at some length remains too simple a tactic – and cannot on its own amount to a convincing riposte to mollify Pearce's

LUST AND LISTS: SEX IN THE PARATEXTS   197

revulsion at the sexism she reads in the lists. Extremes of engagement – from the politely, publicly friendly through to the malevolently objectifying – can of course co-exist within a supportive patriarchy, which will neither test nor expose the contradictions and paradoxes in such manifestations of male desire. By the account of Bate, and of other critics too, Clare's late poetry manifests precisely this sort of paradoxical and simultaneous adulation of and revulsion towards women – real and imagined, angel and whore, hand in hand (though only explicitly so in 'Don Juan'). The lists deserve further consideration.

If the lists, or catalogues, are paratextual at best, or mere accidentals in textual interstices at least, they remain important facets of Clare's textual engagement with women and femininity – even if only for repulsing a modern feminist critic. Unlike a lot of asylum texts which come to us only via the transcription of other hands, Clare wrote these texts himself, with some sort of intention. Beneath a poem's end, we might, for example, read a list like this:

> Mary Hobbs
> Fanny Broughton
> Eliza Jones
> Susan Harris
> Mary Ann [?]Sweeby
> Jane Hobbs[84]

This list appears right beneath the last lines of 'Song: O beautifull Sorrow', which starts on the preceding page.[85] Similarly, beneath the continuation of the part of a song entitled 'Sally Jo – Song continued', we find:

> Duchess Bridgewater
> Eye on Weed ⎫   Weeding Pun
> Iron Weed   ⎬
> Emma Betts   ⎭
> Pro – Pen Sigh T
> Ann Pickering[86]

These lists are placed hard up against songs and poems, yet clearly divided from them with solid, often double, pencil lines. These are not poems and they cannot be read as such. The question remains: what are they? Are they notes of ideas for future reference? Is Clare squirrelling these nuts away for later consideration? Are they lists of subjects about which the poet will write? Are they a writer's shorthand for an idea which pops up, to be accessed at a later date (never to come in most of these cases)? Or is this instead evidence of a male marking his sexual domain over a harem of fantasy sexual slaves? Are the names of real women that he hoards for later fantasies? Measuring any degree of 'reality' in these lists is the most obvious problem. It is possibly indicative of the sort of games Clare is playing that in 1845 there was no living 'Duchess Bridgewater': Francis Egerton, the third and last Duke of Bridgewater, died in 1803, without wife or issue (*ODNB*). Thus the textual trace is redolent of someone socially elevated who simply did not exist, for Clare or anyone else. This non-existent Duchess appears again, on her own, on another page of the same notebook, right above a list which features 'Cartwrights Poems/Mary Popple Maxey/Ann Hatherley Glinton'.[87]

Is such a 'catalogue' evidence of a disturbed sexually obsessive mind as Pearce contends? She accuses Clare of the most malign intention imaginable: rape and murder. If this is a list of targets designed to guide future sexual prowling – or a historical record of victims – what then do we make of the terrible puns, which hark directly back to the word sport of the dining culture Clare enjoyed in London in the 1820s? What do we make of the odd, created names, like 'Duchess Bridgewater', of people who did not exist? It would be an understatement to say that without context the puns are just as odd as the women's names are without referents. What does 'Pro – Pen Sigh T' mean – the 'propensity' to do what? How is it comedic? Clare is notorious as always having his 'Eye on Weed' (by which I mean that he looks at plants usually considered only with intolerance by gardeners), but what is the pun form 'Iron Weed', other than a popular name in Bedfordshire at the time for the purple-headed plant viper's bugloss (*Echium vulgare*)?[88] Is this pun a jotted-down fragment of a far wittier conversation he had? Or is it instead just a pure sound game – almost meaningless other than in the joy of word play? At a stretch, it might take us back to a pun in an 1841 notebook, where – facing Jack Randall's challenge to the world, and beneath a prose recollection of Easter Sunday in 1841 when at Buckhurst Church (about three miles walk from High Beech) he encountered a nine-year-old boy 'Just Like My Son Billy' – Clare plays with Byron and boxing, and locates both in punning conjunction, in one of the fields of the High Beech asylum:

> Boxer Byron
>   made of Iron, alias
>   Box-iron
>   at Spring-Fields[89]

A word-play doodle, perhaps, and one he crossed through. Still, it is not necessarily a completely idle word sketch, given the significance of Byron and boxing at this particular time, and a general sense Clare had of being 'boxed' in, and flattened out, by the rules and pressed social smartness of the asylum, all signified by that weighty domestic ironing implement, the 'Box-iron'. His poetry, his masculinity, the rules of his asylum life making mockery of domesticity – all of these facets of other creative responses Clare was writing through at the time could well be at play here.

The overall 'propensity' to note and store and list is evidently more complex in this manuscript than being purely or only sexually aggressive: something artistic might even be going on here. At the foot of 'There is a vision in my eye'[90] in Northampton manuscript 19 appears a notice:

> Preparing for Publication
> A New Vol: of Poems
> By Eliza Cook

Here is yet another woman's name, but this is a real woman, a celebrated London-born working-class poet and someone who – by 1849 – was an influential woman of letters, producing an eponymous weekly miscellany which sold 40,000–50,000 copies a week in its first year.[91] Two Cook collections Clare might have been referring to, entitled simply *Poems*, appeared in 1845 and 1848. She published her own essay about Clare in *Eliza Cook's Journal* on the front page of an issue in 1851.[92] To William Knight, former steward at Northampton and Clare's amanuensis, Clare wrote in 1850 that he knew Cook, and in 1851 that he liked her *Journal*.[93] As Jonathan Bate speculates, Cook might well have visited Clare in Northampton.[94] Even without such first-hand experience, she might have found in him an inspiring example for her democratic, reformist and levelling politics.[95] Cook is precisely one of those neglected women writers to whom Pearce advocates a turn, rendered even more marginal by her social status and by her Chartist political commitments (and still she remains relatively neglected). In his notebook, Clare testifies somehow to her significance – and perhaps anticipates a book he should buy, in copying out or rehearsing a notice of a forthcoming issue of her poetry. For Cook, recovering Clare from a socially elitist neglect, the peasant poet was proof that it 'is not necessary to graduate at a University to see Nature with a poetic eye'.[96] The note of her name in Clare's hand is so curt that we can only speculate about what she or her work might have meant to him. Because of Pearce, though, we have to ask if that 'poetic eye' is turned obsessive over Cook. Did he meet her, objectify her and want her sexually? Or is this a note to remember a wish to see more of her poems, rather than more of her? Does Clare adopt her massive success – her *Journal* purposefully designed to educate and ameliorate the condition of the working classes – to his own ends, fantasy-hitching her name to his own long desire to get another book out, just as he does with Byron and Burns in the early 1840s?

This manuscript also contains lists of books – school books rather than literary ones; pathetic, for this old and learned man, perhaps. It is as if Clare is setting out an inventory of an old library he wants to sell. Such lists of books and chapbooks – sometimes priced up (as items he wishes to buy or sell?) – abound across the extant manuscripts.[97] And lists proliferate in this notebook. Following the last stanza of 'Song: Sweet Susan' appears the following:

>   Bess [?]Gimbie
>   Queen Adelaide
>   Mary Ann Collingwood
>   Wild Roses
>   Harriet Turner
>   Harriet Clare
>   'Harriett'[98]

We might ask what it means if the lists of names turn to women in Clare's family, or else to female members of the royal family. In this list, it is notable that Queen Adelaide, King William IV's widow, died in December 1849. As the Queen Dowager in 1841, Adelaide had been a lead respondent to Matthew Allen's call for subscribers to support Clare's welfare, pledging fifty pounds.[99] There are two doodling instances on the number '49' in this notebook (the same number that appears to an obsessive level in another manuscript),[100] indicating that 1845 might not have been the only year Clare wrote in it; the reference to Cook suggests that he might have been writing when her journal was in print, from 1849 onwards. Adelaide of Saxe-Meiningen might be included here to mark the passing of a benefactor Clare felt warmly towards; perhaps he even mourned her death? Following the Queen Dowager comes Mary Ann Collingwood who, without the 'Ann', is the putative recipient of two extant letters – one of which was written in code.[101] The list turns through the capitalised 'Wild Roses' (which could be a collective, reductive noun for the women, as much as an individual item in itself) and then on to three 'Harriets': one has the surname of Clare's wife, Martha; one has his own surname; while the last is placed in quotation marks, on its own, with a closing double 'tt'. Was this a ghost daughter – or an imaginary lover he fantasised about marrying, somehow incorporating his real wife too? This might be a ripple of the pattern of conflating Clare makes of his wife with Mary, or a bigamist fantasy of having – even becoming – two wives, that appears in 1841 in a draft letter to Mary Joyce, and in the misogynistic 'Don Juan' and the plaintive 'Child Harold'.[102]

If any of Clare's lists is poignant, it might be the one that follows a quotation about adultery from the Book of Revelation (2.22). Below that quotation appears a grid-like doodle, and then a list of seven names:

> Anna Maria
> Eliza Louisa
> Frederick
> John
> William Parker
> Sophia
> Charles[103]

This is a list of the Clare children who survived birth, in precise order of their birth.[104] Perhaps the saddest aspect is that by 1845 when this notebook was seemingly started, Anna Maria and Frederick were dead; Frederick died in his nineteenth year in 1843 and Anna Maria in her twenty-fourth in 1844 – both dying years after Clare moved from home to the Northampton Asylum in late 1841. Following the list of his children there appears a double ruled line, followed by three more women's names:

> Maria Coteman
> Ruth Coteman
> Ruth Rebecca

There is a redundant sound pattern here as he splices the names together, toying with them, combining them. On the facing page we see yet another list of women's names, seemingly evolving in a distinct fashion:

> Kate Pollard Stamford
> Kate Pollard St Martins
> Pollard St Martins
> Hannah Birdsall
> Betsey Crump[105]

Kate Pollard and Hannah Birdsall are both identified as living women by Robinson and Summerfield,[106] but what we are to do with that historical fact is hard to fathom. In the same run of pages, just before the list of his children's names, appears a pencilled letter draft:

> My dear Childern
> I wrote to you sometime ago & have had no answer at present but I should suppose you got my Letter I should hope you think of & behave well to your poor Mother for I myself am rendered incapable of assisting or behaving well to anyone even of my nearest relations – I am in a Prison on all hands that ever numbs Common sense – I can be civil to none but enemies here as friends are not alowed to see me at all[107]

The textual situation of the lists of names, their partnering in collocation with different types of texts, and the fact that they seem to carry with them dimensions of change and patterning, of the poetic and the personal, altogether mean that the lists in this dialogic, multi-dimensional and textually autographed situation become more complex – in the round, and in the absence of so much explanatory support from the author or any of his observers in this period – than being simply evidence of a murderously sexual intent. This draft letter shows that Clare believes himself to be not 'behaving well', to 'be civil to none'. The isolation – from 'enemies . . . as friends' – is total. Whether it was real or constant or not is of little consequence. Clare's purpose in each instance of the listing of women's names will never be known and, for sure, there is a disturbing pressure of masculine sexual control laced through them when considered overall. But that grasping for masculine power – the sheer urgency of its need set in motion most acerbically in 1841's 'Don Juan' – is set up to counter a quite hostile and curtailed environment, as described in the same notebook in a letter never sent, to children never seen, two of whom were dead. Whatever the actual regime at Northampton, the attempt to reconnect with gendered, patriarchal power – the urge to collect the names, to 'botanise' these women – comes from a place of disempowerment and alienated disaffection. Lynne Pearce's hyperbole rather undermines her legitimate point about both academic hierarchies benefitting men and the study of men, and Clare's late tendency to riddle some writing with misogynist rage; nevertheless, Clare the man was not actually collecting women as if he were a lepidopterist, like John Fowles's protagonist in the novel *The Collector*. Clare was capturing, imagining or recollecting names, rolling their sounds around the tongue, hearing other resonances the names excited and writing those down too – poetic, remembered, historical, contemporary, textual, familial – chewing them over again and again, perhaps readying them for future reworking, or a letter, and lining them up alongside lists of his children, of school books, of dates and doodles, and alongside his love songs. Much of the material in Northampton manuscript 19 is thin, desperate stuff and speaks of an etiolated life. As Clare says himself on 8 July 1850, in a letter to his youngest son Charles, 'I would write you a long Letter only I have nothing to write about for I see Nothing & hear nothing'.[108] The absence of stimulation is not presented here to excuse Clare's obsessions at all; but it might go some way to account for their seeming relentlessness, their circularity, their diminishing scope, their limited horizons. This is not to say that Clare is not treating the women as objects to lust over: the late lust lyrics written in and around the same period confirm this is precisely what he was doing creatively. But for all of Pearce's justification, frustrated desire is not sex, and obsessive, reiterative, objectifying lust expressed in a notebook with no evidence of actions in response is not necessarily murderous in design, intention or outcome. The notebooks allowed Clare creative access to log any name he fancied, and in one sense he was following a pattern of recording and accounting that was habitual. As Ronald Blythe points out, as both folk historian, village geographer and natural observer, listing had always been core to Clare's method:

> A common question with Clare is why is so much of his work an inventory? Why did he feel compelled to list what everyone in Helpston, or in every other English village at that time, possessed?[109]

Margaret Grainger provides transcriptions of Clare's natural history lists – some of them written across the same period as that of manuscript 19, or in notebooks where he also listed women's names.[110] And she also includes transcriptions of much earlier lists, of types of hyacinths, or polyanthus or auriculas, or plants he has seen at specific locations; he listed birds too with rich annotations.[111] Clare was habitual in his desire to 'botanise'[112]: that is, to identify and to name, and to make note of, to capture in relation to a specific environment or locale, whatever natural feature of the natural world he might witness on an exploratory ramble; this process inevitably resulted in lists.

The lists might indicate that Clare is yearning for a return of 'his all-important sense of community' which, as John Goodridge puts it, 'is invariably edged with an unblinking awareness of its limits'.[113] Is it too generous to Clare to think that the lists of names operated for him as communitarian nodes – markers of inclusive connection no matter how tenuous; private confirmations of human relation no matter how distant the object of desire? What other way of understanding the list of names in the following late asylum letter to his son Charles is there, than to regard it as an eager grasping after a sociable set of connections – connections as shadowy and pencil thin in his confined situation at the time of his writing as the pencil traces in the asylum notebook are for us now:

> How are your Brothers & Sisters & your Grandfather & Neighbours – & 'Country Cousins'
> How is your Mother & Uncle & Aunt at Barnack I hope U send the young ones to School – besure not to forget that – how is your Grandfather – tell John I shall be glad to see him – Give my Love to all your Brothers & Sisters...
> ...but I can ask a few more Questions with my Pencil   how is Mary Buzley & is Miss Parkinson at Northborough still – How is John Woodward his Wife & Daughter   How is Peach Large Mary Large & her 4 or 5 sisters   how is Mary Burbadge & her Mother & Father & does your Brother Jhon ever see Jane Sisson & her Brother William or her Father or Mother   tell Jhon to remember me to Dame Porter & Ann & Thomas & also to Betsey Newbon & her Brother & Father & Mother[114]

In the end, we have to allow that the lists are not art even if they reside in notebooks alongside poems and prose. Sometimes they are blank, lacklustre reminders of what Clare could not have: safe, happy and independent control of the people he met, when and where. If the lists do commit violence towards women, it is of a remote and diluted form. The texts are facets of a controlling desire, the thinnest trace of an assertion of Clare's masculine, sexualised power long made redundant by the august and thoroughly male authority of medicalisation, and imprisonment as he labelled it. Clare was grasping at the world, in a manner he understood best, but towards people and figures he could only wave a pencil at, to gain some semblance of, to offer some witness to and to inscribe a private hold on the identifiable and the knowable.

NOTES

1. *PD*, pp. ix–x.
2. Edward Thomas, *Feminine Influence on the English Poets* (London, 1910), quoted in *Critical Heritage*, pp. 311–14 (p. 314).
3. Thomas, *Feminine Influence*, in *Critical Heritage*, p. 313. This Northampton Asylum poem exists as a Knight-only transcript; see LPI, pp. 406–7.
4. The phrases 'green delight' and 'hustling world' are taken from the following lines of an untitled late poem (first line 'There is a charm in Solitude that cheers'): 'A green delight the wounded mind endears/After the hustling world is broken off', LPI, p. 596, ll. 3–4.
5. These present-tense verbs structure stanza 96 of 'The Village Minstrel' (unpublished version), in which Clare offers as succinct an account of his investigative, ruminative activities in the natural world as anywhere else, through the world of Lubin:
Wi village merriments digressd awhile
We'll now resume his native joys again
& aptly find him bending oer a stile
Or stretchd in sabbath musings on the plain
Looking around & humming oer a strain
Painting the foliage of the woodland trees
Listing a bird thats lost its nest complain
Noting the hummings of the passing bees
& all the lovly things his musings hears & sees (EPII, p. 161, ll. 897–905)
'Listing' here most directly means 'listening', but of course it carries with it the image of a botaniser writing down lists of natural phenomena, which Clare certainly did, as if to confirm by conflation the importance of first-hand experience in developing understanding. 'Listing' is significant in the reading below of the asylum notebooks.
6. EPI, pp. 3–352.
7. 'My Mary', EPI, pp. 78–82 (p. 82, l. 94). See also the first edition of *Poems Descriptive* (1820), p. 88.
8. A list of examples from the first pages of Clare's earliest extant notebook of this kind of woman- and love-focused poetic experimentation would include 'Robin and Suke; or The Midnight Quarrel. A Ballad' (EPI, pp. 21–29); 'The Invocation' (EPI, pp. 30–2); 'Song' ('Since Flora disdains me – her once loving swain', EPI, pp. 36–7); 'A Maiden-Haid' (EPI, p. 38); 'Wonder!! If a Woman Keeps a Secret' (EPI, p. 39); 'Song' ('Fast by a

Brook beneath a bending willow', EPI, p. 41); 'Song' ('If Kittys rosy presence now', EPI, pp. 42–3); 'A Character' (EPI, pp. 59–60); 'The Powerful Smile' (EPI, pp. 60–1); 'Love Epistles Between Richard and Kate' (EPI, pp. 64–7) – and these are just from the opening pages of poems in Nor. 1.
9. EPI, p. 296.
10. Of the *c*. 209 poems and fragments transcribed from Nor. 1 (EPI, pp. 3–352), as many as 79 are thematically focused on women, love, lust and loving (and resentfully disappointed) relationships between men and women.
11. On the politics of Clare's favoured flowers, see Mina Gorji, 'John Clare's Weeds', in John Rignall, H. Gustav Klaus and Valentine Cunningham (eds), *Ecology and the Literature of the British Left: The Red and the Green* (Farnham, Surrey: Ashgate, 2012), pp. 61–74. See also Richard Mabey, *Weeds: The Story of Outlaw Plants* (London: Profile Books, 2012), and M. M. Mahood, *The Poet as Botanist* (Cambridge: Cambridge University Press, 2008), pp. 112–46.
12. LPII, p. 677, l. 18.
13. *Letters*, p. 504.
14. Adam White, 'The Love Songs and Love Lyrics of Robert Burns and John Clare', *Scottish Literary Review*, 5.2 (2013), 61–80 (66).
15. Percy Bysshe Shelley, 'Epipsychidion' in Donald H. Reiman and Neil Fraistat (eds), *Shelley's Poetry and Prose* (New York and London: W. W. Norton, 2002), pp. 392–407 (p. 407, ll. 587–90).
16. 'Silent Love', LPI, p. 499.
17. For example, Anne Barton, 'John Clare Reads Lord Byron', *Romanticism*, 2.2 (1996), 127–48; William D. Brewer, 'John Clare and Lord Byron', *JCSJ*, 11 (1992), 43–56; Tim Chilcott, 'Child Harold or Child Harolds: The Editing of Clare's Texts', *JCSJ*, 19 (2000), 5–17; Jason N. Goldsmith, 'The Promiscuity of Print: John Clare's "Don Juan" and the Culture of Romantic Celebrity', *Studies in English Literature, 1500–1900*, 46.4 (Autumn, 2006), 803–32; Gary Harrison, 'Hybridity, Mimicry and John Clare's "Child Harold"', *Wordsworth Circle*, 34.3 (Summer 2003), 149–55; Philip W. Martin, 'Authorial Identity and the Critical Act: John Clare and Lord Byron', in John Beer (ed.), *Questioning Romanticism* (Baltimore, MD: Johns Hopkins University Press, 1995), pp. 71–91; Lynne Pearce, 'John Clare's "Child Harold": A Polyphonic Reading', *Criticism*, 31.2 (Spring 1989), 139–57; Valerie Pedlar, 'John Clare's "Child Harold"', *JCSJ*, 8 (1989), 11–16; Margaret Russett, 'Like "Wedding Gowns or Money from the Mint": Clare's Borrowed Inheritance', *Romantic Circles* (February 1999) https://www.rc.umd.edu/praxis/law/russett/mruss.htm [accessed 13 July 2016]; Edward Strickland, 'Boxer Byron: A Clare

Obsession', *Byron Journal*, 17 (1989), 57–76; Adam White, 'Identity in Place: Lord Byron, John Clare and Lyric Poetry', *Byron Journal*, 40.2 (2012), 115–27.
18. MPV, pp. 145–54.
19. Sarah Houghton, '"Some Little Thing of Other Days/Saved from the Wreck of Time": John Clare and Festivity', *JCSJ*, 23 (2004), 21–43.
20. Mark Freeman, 'The Agricultural Labourer and the "Hodge" Stereotype, c. 1850–1914', *Agricultural History Review*, 49 (2001), 172–86. Freeman discusses Clare and quotes Dentith, 173.
21. Examples can be found in 'A Scene', EPI, p. 413; 'Hodges Confession', EPII, p. 110–11; 'The Lodge House: A Gossips Tale', EPII, pp. 233–47; 'Rural Morning', EPII, pp. 612–18; 'Going to the Fair', MPII, pp. 91–118; and 'St Martins Eve', MPIII, pp. 269–78; 'The merry children shout the herd is come', MPV, pp. 285–6; 'The ploughman are out before the cock crows', MPV, p. 311; 'The old hens cackle & begin the day', MPV, p. 315; 'Maids shout to breakfast in a merry strife', MPV, pp. 327–8.
22. For a study of Clare's complex response to issues of taste, see Adam White, 'John Clare: The Man of Taste', *JCSJ*, 28 (2009), 38–54. See also Jonathan Bate's account of Clare's laughter at urbanite amateur botanisers mistaking the song of a thrush for that of a nightingale: Bate, *Biography*, pp. 278–9, and M. M. Mahood's analysis of Clare's aloof botanical 'pretentiousness', in *The Poet as Botanist* (Cambridge: Cambridge University Press, 2008), pp. 119–22.
23. Simon Dentith, *Society and Cultural Forms in Nineteenth-Century England* (Basingstoke: Macmillan Press, 1998), p. 81.
24. A thorough account of debates over the forms and politics of 'linguistic reappropriation' in contemporary culture appears in Anne Curzan, *Fixing English: Prescriptivism and Language History* (Cambridge: Cambridge University Press, 2014), pp. 137–69. A key question that can be applied to Clare's use of 'clown' and 'Hodge' is '[d]oes a group respect itself by reappropriating a historically derogatory term and defuse its power through self-reference within the community?' (Curzan, p. 145). My thanks to Jon Herring for generous assistance on this front.
25. Sarah Houghton, '"Some little thing of other days/Saved from the wreck of time": John Clare and Festivity', 22–3.
26. Jacqueline Simpson and Steve Roud, *Oxford Dictionary of English Folklore* (Oxford: Oxford University Press, 2000), p. 7.
27. MPIII, note, pp. 617–18. The poem appears in MPIII, pp. 504–15.
28. *ODNB*. Originally from Nottingham, White died of tuberculosis in Cambridge in 1806, aged just twenty-one.

29. 'The Primrose', in John Fry (ed.), *Selection from the Poetical Works of Thomas Carew* (London: Longman, Hurst, Rees, and Orme, 1810), pp. 49–51 (pp. 49, 51).
30. 'The Posie', in *The Poems & Songs of Robert Burns* (Ayr: Wilson, McCormick and Carnie, 1819), pp. 264–5 (p. 265).
31. Jack Goody, *The Culture of Flowers* (Cambridge: Cambridge University Press, 1993), quoted in Richard Mabey, *Flora Britannica* (London: Sinclair-Stevenson, 1996), p. 212. As Mabey goes on to detail, the smell of the may also means it has suffered strong associations with death (which might be the main reason it is superstitiously kept out of the house), though that particular set of meanings is possibly not carried through by Clare here – much though this new spring love is doubtless doomed for the 'enthusiast' from the outset; after all, we know he is now utterly alone. See Mabey, pp. 209–15.
32. Seth T. Reno, 'John Clare and Ecological Love', *JCSJ*, 35 (2016), 59–76 (59).
33. Gary Harrison, 'John Clare's Poetics of Acknowledgement', *Romanticism*, 18.1 (2012), 41–54 (52).
34. 'To Mary' (first line 'I sleep with thee and wake with thee), LPI, pp. 294–5; 'My spirit lives in silent sighs', LPI, pp. 453–4; 'First Love', LPII, p. 677 (quotation, l. 13).
35. 'Journal' entry for 'Sunday 10 October 1824', *Natural History*, p. 189.
36. A list of typical examples would include Christopher Marlowe's 'The Passionate Shepherd to his Love' (famously countered by Walter Raleigh's 'Nymph's Reply to the Shepherd'); John Donne's 'The Bait'; Robert Herrick's 'Corinna's Going a Maying'; and Andrew Marvell's 'To His Coy Mistress'.
37. John Fry (ed.), *Selection from the Poetical Works of Thomas Carew* (London: Longman, Hurst, Rees, and Orme, 1810). Item 147 in [David Powell], *Catalogue of the John Clare Collection in the Northampton Public Library* (County Borough of Northampton: Public Libraries, Museums and Art Gallery Committee, 1964). Carew's 'Amatory' section takes up more than half of the book, with other sections devoted to poems 'Descriptive', 'Elegiac' and 'Epistolary'. It is perhaps indicative of the prudish tastes of the poetic Romantic times that the editor Fry, working out of Bristol in 1810, does not include Carew's most notorious 'amatory' poem 'A Rapture' (probably written in the 1620s, *ODNB*). This poem drools at length in heroic couplets over the prospective sexual conquest of the perennial love object Celia, who is the addressee of this – and many another – Carew poem, a classic of the 'come hither' poetic genre, neo-classically endowed yet more sexually direct and sustained in its imagery of coition than most.

38. 'Morning Walk', EPI, pp. 494–7; 'Come come my love the bush is growing', MPV, pp. 124–6; 'Song', first line 'We'll walk my love at eve unseen', LPII, pp. 901–2.
39. Clare owned copies of Erasmus Darwin's *The Botanic Garden* (London: Jones and Company, 1825) and *The Temple of Nature* (London: Jones & Company, 1825). See item 183 in [David Powell], *Catalogue of the John Clare Collection in the Northampton Public Library*.
40. As Margaret Grainger summarises, 'Clare lived through this period of natural history's greatest popularity... the great period of collecting, classifying, and arranging... Linnaeus's enormous contribution, the devising of a system of classification... had ousted the wordy charm of John Ray.' Grainger usefully lists all of the items in Clare's library 'relating to Natural and Garden History' (*Natural History*, p. xlii. 359–60), though Clare's reading in natural history was far wider than this list.
41. MPV, pp. 124–6.
42. LPII, pp. 901–2.
43. Arthur Foss and Kerith Trick, *St Andrew's Hospital Northampton: The First One Hundred and Fifty Years (1838–1988)* (Cambridge: Granta Editions, 1989), pp. 135–6.
44. Many examples could be given (perhaps over one hundred), but the following song [She is a sweet and bonny thing] seems as apposite as any:
I love to see her gown of green
Her breast of fairest clay
Her thoughts are purity within
Like th' pink inside o' may
And frae the ancle to the shin
She's like a bunch o' flowers
Lovely without & fair within
Like summer choices hours (LPII, p. 874, ll. 9–16).
45. Anne K. Mellor, *Romanticism and Gender* (New York and London: Routledge, 1993), p. 19.
46. Compare the following examples: LPI, pp. 192; LPII, pp. 770, 771, 831, 839, 860, 867, 906, 921, 1013.
47. E.g.:
Thus housed mid cocks and hens in idle state
Aping at fashions which their betters hate
Affecting high lifes airs to scorn the past
Trying to be somthing makes them nought at last
These are the shadows that supply the place
Of farmers daughters of the vanished race
And what are these rude names will do them harm
O rather call them 'Ladys of the Farm'

The Parish: A Satire, ed. Eric Robinson and David Powell (London: Penguin, 1986), p. 35, ll. 173–80. Also see Bram Dijkstra, *Idols of Perversity; Fantasies of Feminine Evil in Fin-de-Siècle Culture* (Oxford: Oxford University Press, 1986) for a cultural analysis of the middle-class late nineteenth-century fashion for female pallor and thinness, and the male fetishising of female illness. Perhaps in *The Parish* Clare is decrying early signs of a change in female body fashion.

48. 'Song' (first line 'We'll walk my love at eve unseen'), LPII, pp. 901–2, ll. 13–14.
49. 'Angels of earth', LPII, p. 969–70. The exclamations 'Gods own masterpiece/ Woman!' and 'Creations masterpiece is woman!' appear in ll. 6–7 and 25.
50. 'Angels of earth', ll. 11–12.
51. 'In beauty there is joy', LPII, p. 983–4.
52. Examples can be found in poems in LPII, pp. 703, 719, 721, 722, 756, 764, 767, 768, 770, 771, 772, 779, 782, 789, 790, 793, 804, 817, 830, 831, 842, 860 and 861.
53. 'Oh whither fair maiden', LPII, p. 991–2, ll. 25–7.
54. 'O sweet is the sound', LPII, p. 791, l. 22.
55. Untitled; first line 'Of thee I keep dreaming still thee', LPII, p. 873–4, l. 16.
56. Untitled; first line 'The corn craiks rispy song', LPII, p. 788, l. 7.
57. Untitled; first line 'She is a sweet and bonny thing', LPII, pp. 874–5. See l. 3 of variant text in footnote, p. 875.
58. 'The corn craiks rispy song', LPII, p. 788, l. 11.
59. 'Good e'enin to ye lassie', LPII, pp. 1028–30, l. 44.
60. Untitled; first line 'Honey words make charms of blisses', LPI, p. 595–6, ll. 9–32.
61. For a collection of over 1,100 such songs – some of which Clare would surely have heard – see Patrick Spedding and Paul West (eds), *Bawdy Songbooks of the Romantic Period*, 4 vols (London: Pickering & Chatto, 2011). Although it captures poems published surreptitiously in the early 1840s, this edition is full of songs which were circulating in London and beyond for decades before; they are far more explicit and lewd than anything Clare wrote, other than the few explicit lines in 'Don Juan'. To compare these sociable men's-club songs with Clare's late lust lyrics is to reveal just how restrained and inexplicit the latter really are.
62. 'Don Juan', Nor. 6, p. 41 [my transcription]:
Theres Doctor Bottle imp who deals in urine
A keeper of state prisons for the queen
As great a man as is the Doge of Turin
& save in London is but seldom seen
Yclep'd old A – ll – n – mad brained ladies coming...
And the following stanza on the same manuscript page begins:

>   Earth hells or b – gg – r sh – ps or what you please
>   Where men close prisoners are & women ravished
>   I've often seen such dirty sights as these
>   I've often seen good money spent & lavished
>   To keep bad houses up for doctors fees…

63. All quotations from letters written across, approximately, 1849–1850. *Letters*, pp. 657, 661, 666, 669.
64. Nor. 20, p. [iii]. Knight's deletion and insertion.
65. Lynne Pearce, 'John Clare's *Child Harold:* The Road Not Taken', in Susan Sellers (ed.), *Feminist Criticism: Theory and Practice* (Hemel Hempstead: Harvester Wheatsheaf, 1991) pp. 143–56 (pp. 143–4).
66. Pearce, 'John Clare's *Child Harold:* The Road Not Taken', p. 145.
67. Pearce, 'John Clare's *Child Harold:* The Road Not Taken', p. 144.
68. Helen Boden, 'Clare, Gender and Art', in John Goodridge (ed.), *The Independent Spirit: John Clare and the Self-Taught Tradition* (Helpston: The John Clare Society and The Margaret Grainger Memorial Trust, 1994), pp. 198–208.
69. Pearce, 'John Clare's *Child Harold:* The Road Not Taken', p. 145.
70. Helen Boden, 'Clare, gender and art', pp. 198–9.
71. Lynne Pearce, *John Clare and Mikhail Bakhtin: The Dialogic Principle. Readings from John Clare's Manuscripts 1832–1845* (University of Birmingham: PhD thesis, 1987) and 'John Clare's "Child Harold": A Polyphonic Reading', *Criticism*, 31.2 (1991), 139–57.
72. Pearce, 'John Clare's *Child Harold:* The Road Not Taken', p. 147.
73. For an account of Clare's lists of names and his asylum-period letters to various women, see Eric Robinson and Geoffrey Summerfield, 'John Clare: An Interpretation of Certain Asylum Letters', *Review of English Studies*, n.s., 13.50 (May 1962), 135–46.
74. Tim Fulford, 'Personating Poets on the Page: John Clare in his Asylum Notebooks', *JCSJ*, 32 (2013), 27–48 (27). See also his *Romantic Poetry and Literary Coteries* (New York: Palgrave Macmillan, 2015), pp. 165–88.
75. Robinson and Summerfield, 'John Clare: An Interpretation of Certain Asylum Letters', 135.
76. 'Appendix IV: Clare's Sketches of Scenes and Natural Phenomena', *Natural History*, pp. 357–8.
77. This is the name, address and year as they appear on the inside front cover (dark brown paper); on the first page proper the inscription is the same, other than that the county name 'Northamptonshire' is dropped.
78. Items written in ink in this notebook, in total, are as follows:
    p. 8: Mary Roddis – Crow & Horse Shoe Inn (which appears in pencil on the line just above);
    p. 18: arithmetical doodle diagrams of circles and triangles;

p. 57: last item on the list 'Ann Hatherley Glinton' is in ink;
p. 58: last four lines of the poem 'The thunder mutters loudest' are in ink;
p. 61: last two-and-a-half lines of 'O woman lovely woman how beguiing' are in ink (see LPI, p. 196), plus the name 'Ann Preston' which is inserted in ink between ll. 7 and 8 of this poem;
p. 63: first four list items, plus a '49'crossed-out doodle, are all in ink. Ink items are:
Bess Gimbie
Queen Adelaide
Mary Ann Collingwood
Wild Roses [see discussion of this list in its entirety, below];
p. 151: [this list is predominantly in the ink of the first five items]
Arabella Seymour
Sally Seymour
Jane Seymour
Ann Pickering
Mary Pickering
[while in pencil follows] De La Martin's Travels to the Holy Land – Jewish Maidens.

79. Fulford, 'Personating Poets on the Page: John Clare in his Asylum Notebooks', 27.
80. Bate, *Biography*, pp. 486, 496 and 497.
81. Bate, *Biography*, p. 500.
82. Bate, *Biography*, p. 500.
83. Bate, *Biography*, p. 509.
84. Nor. 19, p. 55.
85. Nor. 19, p. 54.
86. Nor. 19, p. 52.
87. Nor. 19, p. 57.
88. Thomas Batchelor, *General View of The Agriculture of the County Of Bedford* (Board of Agriculture) (London: Richard Phillips, 1808), p. 321.
89. Nor. 8, p. 43.
90. Nor. 19, pp. 23–24.
91. *ODNB*.
92. Eliza Cook, 'John Clare, The Northamptonshire Poet', *Eliza Cook's Journal*, 94 (15 February 1851), 241–3. Discussed in detail in Bate, *Biography*, pp. 408–9.
93. See *Letters*, pp. 678 and 679.
94. Bate, *Biography*, p. 508.
95. On Cook's politics, see Solveig C. Robinson, 'Of "Haymakers" and "City Artisans": The Chartist Poetics of Eliza Cook's "Songs of Labor"', *Victorian Poetry*, 39.2 (Summer 2001), 229–54. Robinson quotes an

1854 essay by Cook: 'The levelling of this day is all of the *levelling-up* character...The number of self-risen men, sprung up from the ranks, is increasing, and must increase. They are growing up to the highest standards. And the mass too is advancing with education and knowledge, and they must too become levelled up'. See also Florence S. Boos, 'The Poetics of the Working Classes', *Victorian Poetry*, 39.2 (Summer 2001), 103–10.

96. Cook, 'John Clare, The Northamptonshire Poet', 243.
97. George Deacon provides transcriptions of Clare's lists of chapbooks (Deacon, p. 43). An example of book lists appearing across some seemingly randomly collected fragments (literally back-of-an-envelope jottings) can be found in and amongst a primary collection point of the Northborough-period sonnets, in Pet. A61, pp. 2, 3, 9, 14, 15, 16 and 17. Here is one such list from just one page (p. 3) of this manuscript collection:

    Carlisles One Vol Edit of Paines Works &+
    Culpeppers Herbal by Parkins Col. Cuts Baldwins Edit: 8/.
    Bingleys Botany by Frost Col. Plts 7/.
    Burders Oriental Customs 1 Vol. Longmans Edit 8/6
    Harris's Natural History of the Bible plates 8/.
    Peter Nicholson's (of Yorkshire) Poems–Head 6/.
    Jones's Attempts in Verse 10/6
    Album Verses by Charles Lamb h
    Hazlitt's Liber Amoris a New Pygmalion 7/6

98. Nor. 19. The poem starts on p. 62; the list appears at the poem's end on p. 63.
99. The Dowager Queen Adelaide is listed, along with Earl Fitzwilliam and the Marquis of Northampton, as a subscriber in a letter from Matthew Allen to Cyrus Redding in May 1841 (Nor. 51, no. 2). See also Bate, *Biography*, p. 431.
100. There are two doodles on the number 49: pp. 115 and 52. No other year, apart from 1845 in the opening inscriptions, appears in the notebook. But in Nor. 110, '49'occurs sixteen times. Eric Robinson and Geoffrey Summerfield speculate that this might have been to mark Mary Joyce's forty-ninth birthday, 'which would have fallen in January 1846, had she lived'. Eric Robinson and Geoffrey Summerfield (eds), *The Later Poems of John Clare* (Manchester: Manchester University Press, 1964), pp. 16–17 (p. 17).
101. *Letters*, pp. 666 and 672–3.
102. In *Living Year, 1841*, cf. references to 'two wives' in 'Don Juan', p. 53, ll. 255–9; two letters to Mary, pp. 143–5; 'Reccolections &c of journey from Essex', p. 151. In 'Child Harold', however, the references are more subtle and foreground the messianic resonance ('Mary & Martha once my daily guests/& still as mine both wedded loved & blest', p. 26, ll. 237–8) or healthful maternal qualities ('Babes of two

mothers...', p. 46, ll. 478), or else one wife is replaced bluntly by another ('They took me from my wife & to save trouble/I wed again & made the error double', p. 42, ll. 443–4).
103. Nor. 19, p. 83.
104. Martha and John Clare's children who survived childbirth were Anna Maria (1820–1844), Eliza Louisa (1822–1906), Frederick (1824–1843), John (1826–1911), William Parker (1828–1887), Sophia (1830–1863) and Charles (1833–1855). They had two children who died at birth, in 1821 and 1827. See Mary Moyse, 'John Clare's Family Tree', *JCSJ*, 8 (1989), 24–30 (28, 27).
105. Nor. 19, p. 84.
106. Kate Pollard is listed as having lived at Stamford Baron (St Martin) and being either daughter or wife to a grocer called Joseph Pollard, in 1849, in Robinson and Summerfield, 'John Clare: An Interpretation of Certain Asylum Letters', 146.
107. Nor. 19, p. 81. This is my transcription, but it also appears in *Letters*, p. 661.
108. *Letters*, p. 677.
109. Ronald Blythe, 'Common Pleasures', in *Talking About John Clare* (Nottingham: Trent Books, 1999), pp. 135–41 (p. 138).
110. *Natural History*, pp. 343–4.
111. *Natural History*, pp. 347–55.
112. See Grainger's account of his 'botanising', in *Natural History*, p. xlv. e.
113. John Goodridge, *John Clare and Community* (Cambridge: Cambridge University Press, 2013), p. 190.
114. To Charles Clare, 25 July 1851, *Letters*, p. 681.

CHAPTER 5

Conclusion: Clare as Our Contemporary; Clare as History

Clare operated, like all great poets, in an active present, in which deep images from the past continued to assault him. Time is plural, form a convenience.[1]

'TIME IS PLURAL'

John Clare seems more present than ever in contemporary literary culture. Across the United States, Canada and United Kingdom especially, there have been memorable engagements with Clare from contemporary poets such as John Ashbery, Ken Babstock, David Baker, William Bedford, Alison Brackenbury, Wendy Cope, Sarah Corbett, Patrick James Dunagan, Paul Farley, Anthony Hecht, Edward Hirsch, Jeanette Lynes, Michael Longley, Glyn Maxwell, David Morley, Wendy Mulford, Alice Oswald, Tom Paulin, Michael Symmons Roberts, Derek Walcott, Sam Willetts and David Wojahn[2] – to name just a few. These poets join a long tradition of poems to or about Clare, which started in the 1820s when his name first became known. Many of the early works are forgettable encomiums, from writers like Charles Elton, Eton-educated heir to a baronetcy. In 1824 in the waning *London Magazine*, he published the moderately patronising half-comic poem 'The Idler's Epistle to John Clare'. The poem worries about Clare's 'church-yard cough' and urges him to let go the fading charms of the *London* and London, and to return to the relative safety of his native 'rural air'.³ If he stimulated chummy confectionery among gentleman poets, Clare could also be a beacon to aspiring working-class poets. They saw in the peasant poet's example a route to literary culture and also, eventually, a warning of its dangers.⁴ The first book-length poem ever published about and for Clare, however, is *Go to Epping!* by the reforming, Chartist shoemaker James Dacres Devlin. It calls on the public of 1841 to save Clare from poverty, neglect and the asylum, though there is no evidence that Clare knew it existed and no extant copy has yet been found.⁵ Between then and now, many more creative writers across all manner of genres, and from all kinds of social and political positions, have threaded Clare into their work.⁶ Such attention looks set to grow and, though Jonathan Bate and Mary Jacobus are right to think of him primarily as 'the poets' poet',⁷ Clare's presence in other literary genres is burgeoning too.

In our own era, we could follow Clare across the contemporary stage: Edward Bond's 1975 play *The Fool*⁸ places the poet in a world of violent class war; he is the lead of Simon Rae's play *Grass*,⁹ which deposits an ecowarrior, insane Clare amidst the horror of the bovine pyres of the 2001 foot-and-mouth pandemic in the United Kingdom; and his life story haunts D. C. Moore's 2010 play *Town*,¹⁰ which features a terse Clare-like figure called John, caught between two lovers, recently fled from London (and Epping Forest), now seeking sanctuary in the working-class world of Northampton. Staying in Northampton but moving to prose, in a novel devoted to the town transfigured through stages of human history, Clare's autobiographical intensities of 1841 may be heard, refracted, by the magic and visionary anarchism of Alan Moore in his *Voice of the Fire*.¹¹ Moore also writes Clare into his epic novel *Jerusalem* (discussed below).¹² Staying in prose, Clare plays the fiddle, goes courting and bird-nesting, and sets fences while mourning the 'new order' of enclosure, in folklorist and story-teller Hugh Lupton's novel *The Ballad of John Clare*.¹³ The intimacy of his loves and fraught family relationships is rendered in a more lyrical fashion in John MacKenna's innovative *Clare: A Novel*¹⁴ – narrated by women in Clare's life (sister, wife, patron, daughter), with Clare himself speaking only for a brief coda. And, though it might be wise to steer clear of the Clare in Adam Foulds's Booker Prize–shortlisted novel *The Quickening Maze*,¹⁵ which builds the asylum-bound poet vividly into a rapine, freedom-fighting, feral, green man, he is nevertheless found among the feminist sympathies of Judith Allnatt's poignant novel *The Poet's Wife*, voiced (in a technique similar to that of MacKenna) by the poet's historically silenced and long-suffering Patty.[16] Clare may offer a private 'use' as an edgily therapeutic 'companion, an urgent, troubled part of me, dodging from bush to bush', as leading nature writer Richard Mabey suggests when chronicling his recovery from depression in the memoir *Nature Cure* (just one of many places he writes of Clare).[17] And finally, Clare's footsteps may be charted using Iain Sinclair's layered psycho-maps, iteratively tracing the contours of his – and the poet's – situated mind in *Edge of the Orison*.[18] Perhaps unsurprisingly, many of these writers are interested in Clare's understanding of nature, his proto-environmentalism and his botanising eye; many of them are just as interested in his madness, his voice, his escape from High Beech, his class position, his solitude, and his lyrical paeans and elegies to landscapes and lovers long lost. In his essay comparing Bond's play with MacKenna's novel, Christopher Innes surmises that 'both contemporary authors identify themselves with Clare and use him as a projection of their own views of art'.[19] While there is no doubt that Clare's profile continues to benefit from such acts of personal identification, the creative purposes to which his life and work are put range far beyond commentary on art and the artist, and deserve more critical attention than they currently receive as serious interventions into ways in which we might understand Clare.

Yet is it possible to pursue such 'contemporary Clares' while still practising serious literary criticism? Do our current critical orthodoxies make such works of recent and contemporary writing irrelevant to an understanding of Clare? Should we not instead be trying to read Clare in the context of his times – avoiding the facile 'presentism' involved in treating recent creative works as if they were critically relevant? If the idea of a 'contemporary Clare' does not sit well with our dominant historical critical mode, then does the problem lie in the lingering assumptions of 'historicism' itself? Rita Felski locates a widespread 'restiveness with historicism...[which is] beginning to make itself felt across the spectrum of literary studies'. She continues:

> the literary object remains trapped in the conditions that preside over the moment of its birth, its meaning determined in relation to texts and objects of the same moment...phenomena are related only to phenomena in the

same slice of time. We are inculcated, in the name of history, into a remarkably static model of meaning, where texts are corralled amidst long-gone contexts and obsolete intertexts, incarcerated in the past, with no hope of parole.[20]

Felski argues that the problems and theorisations of interpretation, hermeneutics and historical methods which originally inspired New Historicism have increasingly been submerged: the orthodoxy of historical context now goes largely unquestioned across various modes of inquiry into literature. Introducing their 2011 collection *The Limits of Literary Historicism*, Allen Dunn and Thomas F. Haddox offer a similar criticism:

> Since the heyday of methodological debates over the New Historicism, it has become unfashionable to worry about historicism's methodology or its theoretical foundations... unlike the old New Historicists, contemporary practitioners of the historical method no longer spend much time worrying about the fact that their work may be nothing more than a reflection of the unacknowledged prejudices of their own time.[21]

Elsewhere, Eric Hayot portrays a hollowed-out kind of New Historicism, one so dominant that its self-awareness has all but disappeared:

> the norms of New Historicist approaches to literary criticism have become fully ideological and substructural, rather than being, as they were throughout the 1980s and early 1990s, subjects of intense critical debate. This victory of New Historicism is, like the victory of theory itself, a tragic one: the measure of its triumph rests on the paradoxical disappearance of its force as a trajectory or a school, the loss of institutional memory regarding the contexts of its initial emergence, and hence a loss of urgency, specificity, and deep engagement with the basic questions and challenges it initially posed (to deconstruction, for instance). Almost everyone now thinks 'new historically,' but no one is really a New Historicist anymore.[22]

A recent piece by one of New Historicism's founding voices in the Romantic period might be taken as symptomatic of historicism's changing fortunes. It appears in *The Cambridge History of English Romantic Literature* of 2009, in the introduction to which editor James Chandler clarifies his book's mission: 'A central task for any history of British literature in this period, therefore, is to chart the impact both of this perception [of Wordsworth's, that the period was one of unprecedented revolutionary change] and the facts that lay behind it on the practices of writing and reading.'[23] To envisage an unproblematic 'history' which sets out 'facts' might seem to characterise the unreflective hegemony of historicist assumptions in current Romantic literary study. But the Cambridge volume's opening commitment is intriguingly complicated by the chapter which closes the collection, 'Is Romanticism Finished?', in which Jerome McGann sets out a new interpretation of Byron through the creative lens of J. M. Coetzee's 1999 novel *Disgrace*. McGann describes this novel as a set of 'running meditations on Byron and the ethos of Romanticism', one 'organised around the Twin Towers [of Wordsworth and Byron] – the ultimate dialectic – of the Romantic Movement in England'.[24] Assertively canonical but also piquant and ironically postmodern, McGann reads Coetzee's take on Romanticism as an argument strung between two male poles: 'Coetzee's book is thus in great measure a satiric investigation of a wide range of Romantic ideologies – from Wordsworthian sincerity, on one end, to Byronic intellectual flamboyance on the other.'[25] McGann deploys Coetzee's take on 'an extreme of the Romantic sceptical tradition' because it proves both that Romanticism is far from finished, far from being merely esoteric or of narrowly academic concern, and that it still requires active moral responses from its readers. For McGann, Romanticism stays relevant through the rewritings of later authors as well as in the work of scholars. The position is not simply good news, however: any positive purpose granted to such contemporary engagements is undermined to some extent by McGann's cutting suggestion that Romanticism might be limited to the 'public function' of 'purveying antiquities to an E-Bay world'.[26] He writes: 'In an age of "spin," hypocrisy and aggressive moral certitude – our dregs of early Romantic sincerity and imagination – we are arrested by art forms grounded, like Coetzee's, in what may appear to us a willing suspension of *belief* rather than disbelief.'[27] What might be valuable in Romantic writing is, for McGann, resisted by contemporary culture; and he secures a determined role for continuing critical scepticism. Romanticism is valuable in the raw, or cooked through a contemporary novelist, because it is critically self-reflexive and, as McGann portrays it, 'variously disgraceful, empty-headed, well-meaning, stupid and dull, comical and moving, wilful, determined, even often admirable'.[28]

McGann is encountering the history of Romanticism not as a direct 'interview', as Alan Liu once suggested,[29] but rather as mediated through the creative rewriting of Coetzee. As McGann characterises our own times in a self-consciously Byronic manner, he moves through Coetzee to reach a point from which he can determine Romanticism's usefulness, its necessary position within a satirical version of McGann's own context. Even though the contemporary situation of Romanticism is stylised and ironised through the downgrading of the role of the academic expert to that of a sort of shop security guard – watching and valuing the detritus of the consumerist tide as it washes in and out of an online storefront – yet still McGann folds academia, Byron, a contemporary South African novelist, all into one, all into *now*. And though only just surmounting his despair with postmodernity, McGann concludes with the possibility of Romanticism's relevance to the future.

That critical situation is far from the pseudo-objective historicising interviewer's glare sought by some early New Historicists, McGann included.[30] Here, we are no longer truffling for hard historical facts amidst the irritating mud and clutter of ideological art; we are no longer arguing that because a poet does not say something at all about history, his work is in fact dominated by that all the more present absence. Instead, in 2009, McGann purposefully suffuses his own times, and his reading of Coetzee, with all the personal historical prejudice and knowingness he can muster, to encounter a recent version of Byron who is not at all interested in being historicised or factual or even contextual. McGann's essay crumples histories all together – into a miasma where a version of the past constructs the critical present; where a present voice revels in an ironic, aping, slippery knowingness of a past it creatively toys with. The objective literary historian is no more: this critical subject is suffused with the ideology of the past, reached in part through the diffusion of the past through the work of a contemporary creative artist. McGann plays with the unholy trinity of 'sins' up with which a New Historicist should not put: namely – as Jeffrey Insko lists them – 'presentism', 'of being ahistorical' and 'of committing "anachronism"'.[31] McGann also answers Rita Felski's call to take up 'cross-temporal networks [which] mess up the tidiness of our periodizing schemes, forcing us to acknowledge affinity and proximity alongside difference, to grapple with the coevalness and connectedness of past and present'.[32]

Fusing Horizons

In complicating broad historicist tenets, McGann is effectively emulating what Hans-Georg Gadamer termed the 'fusion of horizons' in *Truth and Method*.[33] Gadamer offers a clear and positive way out of the sealed boxes of a narrow historicism. He complicates the idea of history as an object, or a thing possible to study as an object by a critic. For Gadamer, history is relational and dialogic: 'a truly historical consciousness always sees its own present in such a way that it sees itself, as well as the historically other, within the right relationships'. And, further:

> We are always affected, in hope and fear, by what is nearest to us, and hence we approach the testimony of the past under its influence...We start by saying that a hermeneutical situation is determined by the prejudices that we bring with us. They constitute, then, the horizon of a particular present, for they represent that beyond which it is impossible to see...the horizon of the present is continually in the process of being formed because we are continually having to test our prejudices. An important part of this testing occurs in encountering the past and in understanding the tradition from which we come. Hence the horizon of the present cannot be formed without the past. There is no more an isolated horizon of the present in itself than there are historical horizons which have to be acquired. Rather, understanding is always a fusion of these horizons supposedly existing by themselves[34]

Gadamer positively reclaims historical prejudice:

> Every encounter with tradition that takes place within historical consciousness involves the experience of a tension between the text and the present. The hermeneutic task consists in not covering up this tension by attempting a naïve assimilation of the two but in consciously bringing it out.[35]

The ideal critical effort is to expand an horizon sufficiently – by asking the right questions, by reading as many texts as possible – so that the prejudices brought about by historical situatedness are moderated, muted, qualified, adapted, but never erased or entirely surmounted. Gadamer's is a hopeful vision: truth can be found in that interplay of historical horizons. Truth-seeking becomes the declared purpose and possibility of historically self-conscious textual inquiry, but only if the critic admits honestly to his or her own historically determined prejudices. The ideal method should assess its attempts to express and understand its own prejudices even while reaching out to a past which it makes and with which it melds. As Robert Piercey puts it:

> Interpreter and interpreted must not be understood as a subject and an object, entities capable of being defined independently of one another. Instead, they must be understood as poles of a complex historical process – a process of *'thoughtful mediation with contemporary life'*...At one end of this process is

the 'past', but it might be better described as the *past for us* – the past as we understand it, a past that has been filtered through our biases and preoccupations. At the other end is the 'present', but a present affected by the past – a present that is itself the product of historical forces. The past and the present mutually shape each other... The humanities attain truth not when the present correctly mirrors the past, but when horizons fuse.[36]

Of the recent creative responses to Clare, that which enjoys fusing historical horizons most, and knowingly so, is *Jerusalem*, by Alan Moore. Moore writes Clare into a play within his gargantuan work, which is again, like his earlier *Voice of the Fire*, centred on Northampton. Observing an arguing husband and wife, the ghost of Clare leads a conversation with John Bunyan, Samuel Beckett and Thomas à Becket. Beckett reveals himself to be a hugely knowledgeable enthusiast for Clare's work (a pleasant fantasy this). Clare reveals himself to be witty and a little obtuse, upsetting Thomas à Becket by telling him how he died. At one point, Samuel Beckett gets impatient with Clare for claiming to have had sex with Lucia Joyce – James Joyce's daughter, who was resident in the Northampton Asylum long after Clare, and whom Beckett visited. Beckett uses history to explain:

BECKETT: No, I'm afraid that's just your lunacy talking. Though it's true that you were both settled at the same asylum you weren't congruent in the chronology of things. You hail from two entirely different periods.

JOHN CLARE: Why, you could say the same of you and me, yet here we are.[37]

The fiction puts Beckett in the wrong, and makes of Clare a prophet of eternity. As he has done in many other works, Moore revels in fusing historical horizons into one awkward, comedic creative plane, freeing himself of the temporal limits with which historicist literary criticism always seems to delimit inquiry: Lucia Joyce and Mary Joyce effectively become sisters, haunting these ghosts of literary men, and this place. Place remains the primary rationaliser for Moore, however: all four men had real associations with Northampton and spent time in the town.

Similarly, the temporal horizon metaphor set up by Gadamer to consider historical situation is founded upon a visual impression, and metaphorical use, of topographical horizons. These are generated uniquely for a subject by its unique location in a particular place. As with historical understanding, the scope of a topographical horizon depends entirely upon the situated viewpoint of the subject in a particular place. For Moore in *Jerusalem*, time is folded into this singular place of Northampton: temporal horizons are fused, but the topographical horizon is one and the same, and forms permanent ground.

John Clare was drawn to the thought of horizons fusing and expanding, expressing his own interest with poignant self-doubt. Writing autobiographically in the 1820s (about his youth in either the late 1790s or early 1800s), he provides the greatest account of an expansion of a personal horizon in Romantic literature:

> I lovd this solitary disposition from a boy and felt a curiosity to wander about the spots were I had never been before   I remember one incident of this feeling when I was very young   it cost my parents some anxiety   it was in summer and I started off in the morning to get rotten sticks from the woods but I had a feeling to wander about the fields and I indulged it   I had often seen the large heath calld Emmonsales stretching its yellow furze from my eye into unknown solitudes when I went with the mere openers and my curosity urgd me to steal an oppertunity to explore it that morning   I had imagind that the worlds end was at the edge of the orison and that a days journey was able to find it   so I went on with my heart full of hopes pleasures and discoverys expecting when I got to the brink of the world that I coud look down like looking into a large pit and see into its secrets the same as I believd I coud see heaven by looking into the water   so I eagerly wanderd on and rambled among the furze the whole day till I got out of my knowledge when the very wild flowers and birds seemd to forget me and I imagind they were the inhabitants of new countrys   the very sun seemd to be a new one and shining in a different quarter of the sky   still I felt no fear   my wonder seeking happiness had no room for it   I was finding new wonders every minute and was walking in a new world often wondering to my self that I had not found the end of the old one   the sky still touchd the ground in the distance as usual and my childish wisdoms was puzzld in perplexitys   night crept on before I had time to fancy the morning was bye when the white moth had begun to flutter beneath the bushes the black snail was out upon the grass and the frog was leaping across the rabbit tracks on his evening journeys and the little mice was nimbling about and twittering their little earpiercing song with the hedge cricket whispering the hour of waking spirits was at hand which made me hasten to seek home   I knew not which way to turn but chance put me in the right track and when I got into my own fields I did not know them   every thing seemd so different[38]

Tom Paulin has called this 'the most profound experience of Clare's childhood',[39] and from a poetic or visionary point of view it is hard to disagree. The lack of fear as this little boy expands and changes his horizons, denaturing and alienating himself from his usual fellow travellers; the plurality and sheer dynamism of the community of newness which he uncovers; the reliance not on knowledge or instinct, but on chance, to rediscover his accustomed haunts; and the anticipation of heaven in a reflecting pool that drives him on and which – in fertile terms – he finds at the ever-receding 'edge of the orison': all these amount to an opening up, geographically speaking, of Clare's original circumscription to a horizon of another shape, another imagination even. He returns home transformed by the expansion of his horizon, by the challenging of his tightly localised prejudices, by their fusing with wider horizons. The world is bigger and he is merged with it: he has become a poet and a visionary by losing his sense of place.

In the way that it is foundational to Jonathan Bate's biography[40] (and in no small measure because of Bate's biography), this moment at the 'edge of the orison' has been key to some contemporary creative responses to Clare. Adam Foulds's novel *The Quickening Maze* opens with a rewriting of it:

> He thought that the edge of the world was a day's walk away, there where the cloud-breeding sky touched the earth at the horizon. He thought that when he got there he would find a deep pit and he would be able to look down into it and see the world's secrets. Same as he knew he could see heaven in water, a boy on his knees staring into the heavy, flexing surface of the gravel-pit ponds or at a shallow stream flashing over stones... He walked quite out of his knowledge, into a world where the birds and flowers did not know him, where his shadow had never been.[41]

The novel ends with a similar walking away, to get beyond confines. In *Edge of the Orison: In the Traces of John Clare's Journey out of Essex*, Iain Sinclair writes a sociable walk in pursuit of the line of flight Clare took in solitude, from his asylum at High Beech in Essex all the way to Helpston in Northamptonshire, tracking the pursuits of his own family history as he does so. As made clear by its title, the dominant motif of Sinclair's book is also the 'orison' passage: 'Helpston is all horizon', he writes.[42] If any contemporary writer could be said to fuse horizons of time and of place, or to 'grapple with the coevalness and connectedness of past and present' in Felski's words, it is Sinclair: a palimpsest-mapping, multiply referential flâneur-with-purpose, who does in various psychogeographical forms what Alan Moore does in novel and comic form. History, place, buildings, personalities, roads and lines of pursuit – all are layered synchronically, resonate and interlock as dialogic, interweaving memories constructing contemporary cultures through the specifics, the oral and textual stories, the artefacts and the histories, of a locality. For Sinclair, the reason so many writers have recourse to Clare is down to freedom from time, and from knowledge horizons:

> Contemporary poets reiterate Clare's experience: and in doing so discover themselves. Myth becomes truth. Modernist 'open field poetics'...defy the system of enclosures imposed upon language by formalist reactionaries. Rip out hedges, fences, prohibitions, for a method of reading the world from horizon to horizon. No ceilings in time. No knowledge that may not be accessed and inserted. Such metaphors are wasted on Peterborough, a town without irony. How else could they boast of a John Clare pub, library and – theatre?[43]

For Sinclair, situating Clare in a property, making his name identify and display a brick-and-mortar building, can only militate against the land freedoms Clare voiced; such delimitations of the poet's presence codify and regulate Clare's horizon-collapsing 'sense of place' into meaningless municipal functionalism (as indicated in the opening chapter). For Sinclair, Clare is a poet of boundless space, not circumscribed place. We can read the same distinction between place and space in Michel de Certeau, where place maintains a rule-bound stability and a moment in time; whereas 'space exists when one takes into consideration vectors of direction, velocities, and time variables'.[44] In any Sinclair book, time is never as significant as the space that allows a consideration of variable times; Sinclair purposefully collapses horizons of history into one another. Clare is as 'alive' in *Edge of the Orison* as Sinclair's wife or anyone else accompanying him on his rambles. In Sinclair, history collapses into space, into the present of his narrative situation. Therefore, alongside Gadamer, Sinclair provokes the final move of this essay: a trans-historical comparison of two bifurcating case studies covering historical, scholarly and creative texts. I have selected these instances in order to expose the 'tension between the text and the present',[45] in Gadamer's terms. This book now concludes with an experiment, to test out what happens when criticism aims towards Gadamer's dictum that the 'hermeneutic task consists in not covering up this tension by attempting a naïve assimilation of the two but in consciously bringing it out'.[46] Tensions, versions of historical truth, and versions of who, when and where Clare was, need to be teased out.

We will now consider two stories about Clare: one starts in 1816, the other in 1822.

The first sees Clare watching his friends violently engage with the Littleport and Ely riots of 1816. Clare is detached from the action a little ways, unless it comes to speaking about the changes to the land both enclosure and 'improvement' more generally are threatening to bring to his version of a working, sensual arcadia. Distracted by the impulsiveness of lust throughout, it is his love for Mary in the end that means he misses his friends' most dangerous acts against the local parson. Clare then visits his friends in prison. He hears about the execution of some and the deportation of others to Australia, and he is damagingly impacted by the extreme punishments meted out by a violently repressive state. This Clare is generated by a specific historical context, and his politics are formed out of the horror of hunger, violence and the hierarchy's suppression of the riotous poor. Out of his 1816 experience, Clare writes poems such as 'On Entering Paradise':

> If tomorrow the gates of paradise flew open
> When you touched them
> It would still have cost much blood
>   To open them
>
> Look behind you down the long sluice
> Of blood and debris of war past time
> And remember this when a voice calls
>   How shall we open the gates of paradise?
>
> Blood of itself is not enough
> Even in the veins to keep men alive
> And spilt it will not make history
>   *That* is the work of reason
>
> But whenever the tongue of reason is cut out
> Then violence rises like a madwoman over her toys
> Reason is not reborn from her own ashes
> Prometheus has been saved a thousand times
>   By the vulture that tears his liver

> Remember this when you stand at the gates of paradise
> And a voice calls from the sluice

The second story has another Clare observing the East Anglian riots of 1822, again from afar. He writes to no one about the riots and nobody writes to him about them. But Clare reads all about them in newspapers – regional and national – across nearly the whole of 1822. Here is an extract from one of those national papers, the *Morning Chronicle*:

> Letters received from Suffolk and Norfolk this morning, represent these two fine Counties still labouring under severe distress. The examples already made, have had the effect of putting an end to the riots among that formerly quiet peasantry, but on the night of Thursday last a barley stock-yard was set on fire at Harlingfield and consumed, and on the night of Monday last, one stackyard was consumed at Stonham and another at Earl Soham. In the neighbourhood of Diss and also of Thetford, additional burnings are reported to have taken place. This is one way to get rid of excess of production. The supplies now coming into the Suffolk markets are small, from the use of threshing machines not being allowed, and also from the crop getting out of the farmers hands. The want of consumption however renders this circumstance of no benefit to agriculturists, and there is not the least improvement in the value of their grain.[47]

For the *Chronicle*, it is squarely the 'peasantry' who are damaging the interests of 'agriculturists' – the latter being the newspaper's implied readership. *The Bury and Norwich Post*, reporting on similar incidences a few weeks earlier, said it was 'a body of the labouring class' which was responsible for the violence against property.[48] The poem Clare writes in response to this 1822 context is 'The Labourers Hymn': ten stanzas of four iambic heptameter couplets. The first verse paragraph of this manuscript variant reads:

> Ye Peasantry of England support your hardy name
> Nor leagued with ~~midnight treachery~~ ʌ [cunning knaves] grow infamous in fame
> Dishonour not the soil where our fathers they were born
> Nor let them boast of honesty be lost in utter scorn
> Stand up & join the honest both in courage & in mind
> Nor let the day light blush at deeds that darkness leaves behind

> For ʌ [your] symbol is the Lion whose courage is the true
> Then never shame your colours with the deeds that ʌ [pirates] do[49]

Above the first two words of the first line is written 'Reforming men'. 'Ye Peasantry' is not crossed out and replaced, as other words are in this variant text. The editorial, revising implication (rightly taken by the Oxford editors[50]) is that 'Ye Peasantry' has been replaced by 'Reforming men'. But the phrases are set out one above the other: they run in parallel; neither is deleted or usurped. One implication may be that 'Reforming men' and 'Ye Peasantry' are mutually interchangeable for Clare; and in this manuscript, they remain equally prominent as they are simultaneously articulated. 'Peasantry' does not appear again in any version of this poem, and it is not a word Clare uses frequently – even if 'Northamptonshire Peasant' appears as his occupational branding on the title pages of his publications from *Poems Descriptive* onwards. Occasionally he does use the term, especially when discussing folk culture and the manner in which it is distinct from the culture of other classes; for example, in this prose account of chapbooks:

> I was fond of books before I began to write poetry   these were such that chance came at – 6py Pamphlets that are in the possession of every door calling hawker and found on every book stall at fairs and markets whose titles are as familiar with every one as his own name... these have memorys as common as Prayer books and Psalters with the peasantry   such were the books that delighted me and I savd all the pence I got to buy them for they were the whole world of literature to me and I knew of no other[51]

I quote this passage to suggest that Clare does not use 'peasantry' idly: he uses it when he considers a class differential needs to be established. Here it is in reading, in divergent forms of cultured literacy beyond literature; in 'The Labourers Hymn', the differential is to specify a social source of political hope. By contrast, derivatives of 'reform' do appear with some regularity in Clare's work, if never making it into print much during his lifetime – perhaps a learned precaution against censorship in his poetic efforts towards book publication. Its appearance here is made more interesting by the closing flourish of the autobiographical 'Sketches in the Life', as follows:

> but I believe the reading a small pamphlet on the Murder of the french King many years ago with other inhuman butcheries cured me very early from thinking favourably of radicalism   the words 'revolution and reform' so much in fashion with sneering arch infidels thrills me with terror when ever I see them – there was a Robspiere, or somthing like that name, a most indefatigable butcher in the cause of the french levellers, and if the account of him be true, hell has never reeked juster revenge on a villain since it was first opened for their torture – may the foes of my country ever find their hopes blasted by dissappointments and the silent prayers of the honest man to a power that governs with justice for their destruction meet always with success.[52]

This is an account – for John Taylor and a polite readership (if only ever in prospect) – of Clare's schooling in the chiaroscuro of Napoleonic war-time propagandist chapbook politics, yet it is still of a piece with the designs of this poem. By the time he was writing 'The Labourers Hymn', Clare's political awareness was developing sufficiently to accommodate 'reform' in the national interests and to claim the labouring classes as the moderate reforming belly of the English body politic, against the threat of radicalism and even revolution (as he read it) under the new King George IV. Clare wants transformation and mobility – but through slow-paced, permanent and peaceful reform. The fact that there is another variant of Clare's poem – probably a fairer copy – entitled 'The Reformers Hymn'[53] is further indication that 'labourer' equates directly with 'reformer', and that Clare's hope for reform rests with the labouring classes. In the sixth stanza of 'The Labourers Hymn' version of the poem appears a model of localist, communal political activism:

> Our courage shall correct foes mistakes in the end
> & honesty erase all suspicions in a friend
> For freedom is our birthright & ere the sneakey knave
> Our fireside shall grow parliments our cottages be towers
> For wrong shall never claim the right that all acknowledge ours
> For our symbol is the lion & his courage is the true
> & well never join or side with deeds that knaves or cowards do[54]

The question, as always with Clare, is whether this commitment to King ('a sailor...our helm' in this post-Napoleonic wars poem[55]) and country make him a nationalistic conservative, as some have proposed.[56] Clare claims full emancipation for all people by bringing the sizeable power and size of parliament within the domestic space of the cottage; by claiming 'freedom' as a 'birthright'. These are straightforward enough symbols (and even the word 'symbol' is used, as if to ensure no reader misses the intended purport) and they are deployed purposefully as the poem seeks to calm with a clarity of vision and rhetoric. This is poetry for all – because it hopes for political power for all. The eighth stanza of this same manuscript variant of 'The Labourers Hymn' does not obviously clarify the matter of the poet's political affiliation:

> Well do no wrong to any one to make ourselves amends
> & all whose hearts are honest shall be first among our friends
> & well assist & join them tho few the number be
> For brooks will run to rivers & the rivers grow a sea
> & so our ʌ [reform] honest cause shall flourish into oceans at the end
> When our griefs shall be with enemys & our pleasures with a friend
> For our symbol is the lion & his followers the true
> & well scorn to cause the sun to blush on deeds that cowards do[57]

And, as it turns out, Clare was right to think of his intended audience as being 'labourers', right to qualify and replace his opening use of the term 'peasantry', and right to assume the violence was not radicalised or structured around an explicit political end.[58]

So: two stories. In the first, of 1816, Clare's friends are localised revolutionaries, furious about social disparities of wealth, power and their own lack of independence. Clare himself is a strange character – stand-offish – always at a remove from the action, though always threatening to take things in an odd direction. He is uncontrollably libidinous, yet recalcitrant and introverted. Eventually, many years after the trauma of 1816, his mind is shown to have been broken both by the loss of his friends and by his exploitation at the hands of the literary bourgeoisie, and by their subsequent rejection of his work. Inevitably Clare goes completely insane. He ends this story in a catatonic state, medicalised and wheeled about by the same codifying forces of institutionalised capitalism against which his friends of 1816 were shown to be rebelling. In the second story of 1822, by contrast, Clare is a reformer, but also a 'king and country' peasant version of John Bull. He wants to conserve and maintain peace at all costs. He believes in reform. He believes in the power of poetry both to mollify and to marshal the masses. In the masses, specifically the labouring peasantry, Clare maintains hope not for revolution, but for reform and change – beneath the directing figurehead of the king, cast as a manly captain, in battling contradistinction to the lawless pirates and brigands who threaten the fabric of the nation and, worse still, the promise of reform.

Now, in fact the first story is a fiction. It is my summary of Edward Bond's 1975 play *The Fool*, and the poem 'On Entering Paradise' is by Bond's Clare, appearing in print after the play.[59] Bond transports Clare to a place and time of genuinely violent revolutionary fervour, in order to dramatise and intensify Clare's class-bound understanding of social and economic unfairness. The place and time Bond chooses are not so far away from Clare's own village, and 1816 was the poet's twenty-third year. As far as we know, Clare never visited Littleport – though it is only forty miles south-east of his village of Helpston. As far as we know, he did not write about the notorious riots of 1816 either. He did not witness the stripping, mauling and humiliation of a local parson or the shooting of a friend by a gamekeeper. He probably never knew anyone who was executed or deported, or punished in any way for riotous acts against farm equipment. The Marxist Bond has always been adept at staging physical violence to drive home a moral agenda, especially when energised by intensities of class stratification and economic injustice.

The second story is my own historicised reading of an 1822 poem by Clare, 'Ye reforming men'. This poem, unpublished in his lifetime, is a corrective to those cultural materialists who want Clare to be aligned with radicalism – as Edward Bond certainly does. Romantic-period labouring-class poets are rarely as directly or coherently politically radical as 1970s versions of working-class history would have them be. Academics who presume that radical politics suffused labouring-class life of the eighteenth and nineteenth centuries are often surprised by the actual poetic evidence they find.[60] However, Clare's poem can also serve as a corrective to critics of a different political persuasion, who sometimes portray Clare as a holy fool who, if he ever did act politically, only did so 'almost without realising it', in Jonathan Bate's words.[61] Finally, the poem puts right those who think Clare was always preternaturally sympathetic and naively angry in his responses to the depravations of the rural poor. He was at times, but not at all costs. This is how this 'slice of time' might help us read him.

Edward Bond's prejudiced horizon of 1975 fuses with Clare's in a series of events of 1816, with which, as the historical record suggests, Clare was not directly involved at all. The creative and politicised 'record' of the 1970s says something quite distinct about its own times when it reaches out to the late 1810s. To a great extent, Bond's version of Clare is eminently plausible. *The Fool* is an important play, signalling a radical playwright's Thompsonian version of working-class consciousness, brought to the stage at a time of severe economic decline in the United Kingdom. But there are many historical horizons fusing here, many in 'dialogue' – the term used by Gadamer to describe such interplays. Such a dialogic mindset not only allows our own contexts to fuse with those of Clare; we can use another creative set of prejudices to fuse into a broader literary horizon than would be available to us through a narrow focus on what happened in 1822.

More problematic than Bond's placing and timing of Clare in 1816 is my historicising response to the poem of 1822. This poem never indicates what violence, what 'pirates', 'sneaky knaves' and 'cowards' are being lambasted; the poem never reveals in which specific context it is written. I have forced Clare's stock villainous types to mean the violent machine-breakers and arsonists, those hungry, miserable farm workers of East Anglia of 1822, in villages across Norfolk and Suffolk, between sixty-five and one hundred miles distant from Clare's Helpston. Other than the happy convenience of a matching 'slice of time', I have no more legitimacy in applying this context of 1822 to the poem than Edward Bond does when he places Clare forty miles south-east to fields around Littleport in Cambridgeshire in 1816. In fact, Littleport is geographically closer to the geographical horizon of Helpston than were any of the villages which burst into flames and violence across the whole of 1822.[62] The historical fusions offered by Bond are more energising as a provocation to literary analysis than my historicist, supposedly 'fact'-based plodding through possible relevancies in East Anglia of 1822.

Modest though this experiment might seem, it suggests to me that critics should sometimes allow their historical prejudices, their critical horizons, to be openly assessed alongside the creative present, as a way of complicating their recourse to the historical past. Assessing Marxist literary criticism in 1983, Jerome McGann claimed that it 'fails to take account of its own investment in the Ideological State Apparatuses which we operate within... critics do not recognize, or take account of, the specific ideological determinants of their work'.[63] In a parallel fashion, Gadamer asserts that ideally '[h]istorical consciousness is aware of its own otherness and hence foregrounds the horizon of the past from its own'[64] – and this, I contend, is specifically relevant to recent historicist criticism that has developed since McGann's critique. Historicism will only be relevant if it continually refreshes its original provocation to be open about the necessarily historicised prejudices and contingencies; not just of literary artefacts but of all literary criticism, and of all politicised approaches too. In this same way, contemporary ecocritical approaches to the literary past – as we explored in the opening chapter – have to confront their own utilisation of the literary text and the historical past to their own contemporary ends. Furthermore, rather than pushing aside creative responses to the past as being historically and critically irrelevant, literary criticism should draw on the literary present. Criticism would be more aware of its own historical contingency if it paid closer attention to rewritings of the literary past in contemporary imaginative work.

Notes

1. Iain Sinclair, *Edge of the Orison: in the Traces of John Clare's 'Journey out of Essex'* (London: Penguin Books, 2005), p. 343.
2. For accounts of John Ashbery's engagements with Clare, see Ben Hickman, *John Ashbery and English Poetry* (Edinburgh: Edinburgh University Press, 2012) and Stephanie Kuduk Weiner, *Clare's Lyric: John Clare and Three Modern Poets* (Oxford: Oxford University Press, 2014), pp. 161–78; Ken Babstock, 'As Marginalia in John Clare's *The Rural Muse*', in *Methodist Hatchet* (Toronto: House of Anansi Press, 2011), p. 5; David Baker, 'Fives Odes on Absence', in *Scavenger Loop: Poems* (New York: W.W. Norton, 2015), pp. 27–33, and note, pp. 107–8; William Bedford, 'The Flitting, i.m. John Clare', *JCSJ*, 35 (2016), 53–8; Alison Brackenbury, 'Visit', 'Still young', 'On the boards', 'Divided', 'Enclosure', 'Breaking', in *Breaking Ground and Other Poems* (Manchester: Carcanet Press, 1984), pp. 99–132; Wendy Cope, 'John Clare', in *If I Don't Know* (London: Faber and Faber, 2001), p. 29; Sarah Corbett, 'Pictures of Power: Sonnets and Variations after John Clare', *JCSJ*, 33 (2014), 41–7; Patrick James Dunagan, *Drops of Rain/Drops of Wine* (New York City: Spuyten Duyvil, 2016), p. 5 [untitled]; Paul Farley and Michael Symmons Roberts, *Edgelands: Journeys into England's True Wilderness* (London: Jonathan Cape, 2011), pp. 32, 65, 67, 74 and 89; Paul Farley (ed.), *John Clare: Poet to Poet* (London: Faber and Faber, 2007); Anthony Hecht, 'Coming Home' (From the journals of John Clare), *Millions of Strange Shadows* (Oxford: Oxford University Press, 1977), pp. 25–7; Edward Hirsch, 'Three Journeys', in *Wild Gratitude: Poems* (New York: Knopf, 2010; first edn, 1986), p. 64–6; Michael Longley, 'Journey out of Essex or, John Clare's Escape from the Madhouse', *Poems 1963–1983* (Harmondsworth: Penguin, 1986; poem first published 1969), p. 56 – see Bate, *Biography*, p. 557; Jeanette Lynes, *Bedlam Cowslip: The John Clare Poems* (Hamilton,

Ontario: Buckrider Books, 2016); Glyn Maxwell, *Drinks with Dead Poets: The Autumn Term* (London: Oberon Books, 2016); David Morley, *The Gypsy and the Poet* (Manchester: Carcanet, 2013) and Simon Kövesi, 'Interview with David Morley: *The Gypsy and the Poet*', *JCSJ*, 32 (2013), 49–72; Wendy Mulford, 'John Clare's Mountain', in Denise Riley (ed.), *Poets on Writing: Britain, 1970–1991* (Basingstoke: Macmillan, 1992), pp. 114–20; Alice Oswald (ed.) includes Clare's poetry in – and uses a Clare quotation for the title of – her environmental anthology, *The Thunder Mutters: 101 Poems for the Planet* (London: Faber and Faber, 2005); Tom Paulin's various responses to Clare are covered in Bate, *Biography*, p. 557–8; Derek Walcott, 'The Bounty' in *The Bounty* (London: Faber and Faber, 1997), pp. 3–16; Sam Willetts, 'Honest John', in *New Light for the Old Dark* (London: Jonathan Cape, 2010), p. 15; David Wojahn, 'Napping on my Fifty-Third Birthday', in *World Tree* (Pittsburgh: University of Pittsburgh Press, 2011), pp. 22–4.
3. *London Magazine*, August 1824, 143–5 (144, 143).
4. For an extensive account of the ways poets have responded to Clare, see Bate, *Biography*, pp. 545–59. See also John Lucas (ed.), *For John Clare: an Anthology of Verse* (Helpston: John Clare Society, 1997), pp. ix–x.
5. James Dacres Devlin, *Go to Epping!* (London: Effingham Wilson, 1841). See my discussion of Devlin's poem, in 'John Clare's deaths: poverty, education and poetry', in *New Essays on John Clare*, pp. 146–66 (pp. 154–8).
6. The most comprehensive collection of such poems appears in John Lucas (ed.), *For John Clare: an Anthology of Verse*.
7. Bate, *Biography*, p. 558; see also Mary Jacobus, *Romantic Things: A Tree, a Rock, a Cloud* (Chicago and London: The University of Chicago Press, 2012), p. 15.
8. Edward Bond, *The Fool and We Come to the River* (London: Methuen, 1976). First produced in 1975; revived in 2010 in Kilburn, London.
9. Simon Rae, *Grass* (Bampton: Top Edge Press, 2003).
10. D. C. Moore, *Town and Honest* (London: Methuen Drama, 2010).
11. Alan Moore, *Voice of the Fire: A Novel* (Atlanta and Portland: Top Shelf Productions, 2003; first published 1996), pp. 223–36.
12. Alan Moore, *Jerusalem: A Novel* (London: Knockabout, 2016).
13. Hugh Lupton, *The Ballad of John Clare* (Sawtry, Cambs.: Dedalus, 2010): 'There is nowhere a body can cast its eye but there is activity upon the face of the land... With the setting of fences comes a new order', pp. 217–18.
14. John MacKenna, *Clare: A Novel* (Belfast: Blackstaff Press, 1993).
15. Adam Foulds, *The Quickening Maze* (London: Jonathan Cape, 2009).
16. Judith Allnatt, *The Poet's Wife* (London: Doubleday, 2010).
17. Richard Mabey, *Nature Cure* (London: Chatto and Windus, 2005). Among the many engagements with Clare of which Mabey writes, see especially *Whistling in the Dark: in Pursuit of the Nightingale* (London:

Sinclair-Stevenson, 1993), *Flora Britannica* (London: Sinclair-Stevenson, 1996), *Weeds: The Story of Outlaw Plants* (London: Profile Books, 2012), and *The Perfumier and the Stinkhorn* (London: Profile Books, 2011). For an excellent account of Mabey and Clare, see Theresa M. Kelley, *Clandestine Marriage: Botany and Romantic Culture* (Baltimore: Johns Hopkins University Press, 2012), pp. 126–58 and 246–7.
18. Iain Sinclair, *Edge of the Orison: in the Traces of John Clare's 'Journey out of Essex'* (London: Penguin Books, 2005).
19. Christopher Innes, 'Elemental, My Dear Clare: The Case of the Missing Poet', in Martin Middeke and Werner Huber (eds), *Biofictions: The Rewriting of Romantic Lives in Contemporary Fiction and Drama* (London: Camden House, 1999), pp. 187–200 (p. 199).
20. Rita Felski, '"Context Stinks!"', *New Literary History*, 42 (2011), 573–91 (576 and 577–8).
21. Allen Dunn and Thomas F. Haddox (eds), *The Limits of Literary Historicism* (Knoxville, TN: University of Tennessee Press, 2011), p. xvi.
22. Eric Hayot, 'Against Periodization; or, On Institutional Time', *New Literary History*, 42 (2011), 739–56 (742).
23. James Chandler, 'Introduction' to his *Cambridge History of Romantic Literature* (Cambridge: Cambridge University Press, 2009), pp. 1–18 (p. 3).
24. Jerome McGann, 'Is Romanticism Finished?', in James Chandler (ed.), *Cambridge History of Romantic Literature* (Cambridge: Cambridge University Press, 2009), pp. 648–64 (pp. 651 and 650).
25. McGann, 'Is Romanticism Finished?', pp. 656–7.
26. McGann, 'Is Romanticism Finished?', p. 663.
27. McGann, 'Is Romanticism Finished?', p. 662.
28. McGann, 'Is Romanticism Finished?', p. 657.
29. Alan Liu, 'Review of David Simpson, *Wordsworth's Historical Imagination*' in *Wordsworth Circle*, 19.4 (1988), 172–81 (179). Quoted in introduction to Damian Walford Davies (ed.), *Romanticism, History, Historicism: Essays on an Orthodoxy* (London and New York: Routledge, 2009), p. 5.
30. See, for example, Jerome McGann, 'Keats and the Historical Method in Literary Criticism', *Modern Language Notes*, 94.5 (December 1979), 988–1032 and *The Romantic Ideology: A Critical Investigation* (University of Chicago Press, 1983).
31. Jeffrey Insko, 'The Prehistory of Posthistoricism', in Allen Dunn and Thomas F. Haddox (eds), *The Limits of Literary Historicism* (Knoxville, TN: University of Tennessee Press, 2011), pp. 105–23 (p. 106).
32. Rita Felski, '"Context Stinks!"', 579.
33. Hans-Georg Gadamer, *Truth and Method*, 2nd rev. edn., trans. Joel Weinsheimer and Donald G. Marshall (London and New York: Continuum, 2004), p. 305. First published in German, 1960.

34. Gadamer, *Truth and Method*, pp. 304–5.
35. Gadamer, *Truth and Method*, p. 305.
36. Robert Piercey, *The Crisis in Continental Philosophy* (London: Continuum, 2009), pp. 146–7.
37. Alan Moore, *Jerusalem: A Novel* (London: Knockabout, 2016), pp. 923–68 (p. 940).
38. *By Himself*, pp. 40–41.
39. Tom Paulin, 'Gentlemen and Ladies Came to See the Poet's Cottage', *London Review of Books* 26.4 (19 February 2004), 17–20 (17) [review of Bate's *Biography*, his Farrar, Straus and Giroux selection, MPV and Alan Vardy's *John Clare, Politics and Poetry*].
40. Bate, *Biography*, pp. 41–4 (start of chapter 3, 'Horizons').
41. Foulds, *The Quickening Maze*, p. 3.
42. Sinclair, *Edge of the Orison*, p. 148.
43. Sinclair, *Edge of the Orison*, p. 278.
44. Michel de Certeau, *The Practice of Everyday Life*, trans. Steven Rendall (Berkeley and Los Angeles: University of California Press, 1984), p. 117.
45. Gadamer, *Truth and Method*, p. 305.
46. Ibid., p. 305.
47. *Morning Chronicle*, 15 March 1822, [column 1, p. 4].
48. *Bury and Norwich Post: Or Suffolk, Essex, Cambridge, Ely, and Norfolk Telegraph*, 27 February 1822, p. 634.
49. Nor. 7, p. 3A.
50. EPII, pp. 590–3. See also the editors' note to a separate publication of 'The reformers hymn': 'Not published in Clare's lifetime. An earlier draft was entitled "The Labourers Hymn"... The fact that "The reformers hymn" was copied into his fair copy book Pet. A40 suggests that it is the later and definitive version.' P. M. S. Dawson, Eric Robinson and David Powell (eds), *John Clare, A Champion for the Poor* (Ashington and Manchester: MidNAG/Carcanet, 2000), p. 261.
51. *By Himself*, p. 68. This is also a key passage in George Deacon's account of the significance of song to Clare's life and contexts. See Deacon, p. 38.
52. *By Himself*, p. 30.
53. EPII, pp. 593–7.
54. Nor. 7, pp. 3A–B.
55. Nor. 7, p. 3A. See also EPII, p. 591, ll. 11 and 22.
56. See, for example, my discussion above of Richard Heath's 1893 claim that Clare was 'capable of being developed into the intensest patriotism, with a love of old customs and old institutions – in fact, a Conservative by nature'.
57. Nor. 7, p. 3B.
58. Paul Muskett summarises the sorts of people involved: 'One hundred and twenty-three men appeared before the courts in connection with the

agrarian disturbances of 1822. *The Bury Gazette* suggested that "great spouting radicals" had fomented discontent, but of all those whose occupations were given only 5 were designated as other than labourers; a yeoman, a farmer, an innkeeper, a carpenter and, almost predictably, a shoemaker. The rioters were usually active in their own villages and no evidence was produced of any general conspiracy or "organized system"... in 1822 the labourers were singleminded in their determination to put a stop to machinery.' Paul Muskett, 'The East Anglian Riots of 1822', *Agricultural History Review*, 32.1 (1984), 1–13 (9).
59. Edward Bond, *The Fool* and *We Come to the River* (London: Methuen, 1976). 'On Entering Paradise' appears on p. 75.
60. A summary of the contents and political predispositions of labouring-class poetry in the first decades of the nineteenth century is offered by Scott McEathron (ed.), *Nineteenth-Century Labouring-Class Poets*, 3 vols (Pickering and Chatto, 2006), 1, pp. xvii–xxiv.
61. Bate, *Biography*, p. 351.
62. See Muskett, 'The East Anglian Riots of 1822', 9.
63. Jerome McGann, *The Romantic Ideology*, p. 158.
64. Gadamer, *Truth and Method*, p. 305.

BIBLIOGRAPHY

WORKS BY JOHN CLARE

A Champion for the Poor: Political Verse and Prose, ed. P. M. S. Dawson, Eric Robinson and David Powell (Ashington and Manchester: MidNAG/Carcanet, 2000).

The Early Poems of John Clare 1804–1822, ed. Eric Robinson and David Powell, assoc. ed. Margaret Grainger, 2 vols (Oxford: Clarendon Press, 1989).

"I Am": The Selected Poetry of John Clare, ed. Jonathan Bate (New York: Farrar, Straus and Giroux, 2003).

John Clare By Himself, ed. Eric Robinson and David Powell (Ashington and Manchester: MidNAG/Carcanet, 1996).

John Clare: *Major Works*, ed. Eric Robinson and David Powell with an Introduction by Tom Paulin (Oxford: Oxford World's Classics, 2004).

John Clare: Selected Poems, ed. Jonathan Bate (London: Faber and Faber, 2004).

John Clare: *Selected Poetry and Prose*, ed. Merryn and Raymond Williams (London and New York: Methuen, 1986).

John Clare: The Living Year 1841, ed. Tim Chilcott (Nottingham: Trent Editions, 1999).

The Later Poems of John Clare, ed. Eric Robinson and Geoffrey Summerfield (Manchester: Manchester University Press, 1964).

The Later Poems of John Clare 1837–1864, ed. Eric Robinson and David Powell, assoc. ed. Margaret Grainger, 2 vols (Oxford: Clarendon Press, 1984).

The Letters of John Clare, ed. Mark Storey (Oxford: Clarendon Press, 1985).

The Midsummer Cushion, ed. Anne Tibble and R. K. R. Thornton (Ashington and Manchester: MidNAG/Carcanet, 1979; paperback reissue 1990).

The Natural History Prose Writings of John Clare, ed. Margaret Grainger (Oxford: Clarendon Press, 1983).
Northborough Sonnets, ed. Eric Robinson, David Powell and P. M. S. Dawson (Ashington and Manchester: MidNAG/Carcanet, 1995).
The Parish: A Satire, ed. Eric Robinson and David Powell (London: Penguin Books, 1986).
Poems Descriptive of Rural Life and Scenery (London: Taylor and Hessey, 1820).
Poems of the Middle Period 1822–1837, ed. Eric Robinson, David Powell and P. M. S. Dawson (Oxford: Clarendon Press. Vols. I–II: 1996; vols III–IV: 1998; vol. V: 2003).
The Rural Muse (London: Whittaker & Co., 1835).
The Rural Muse, ed. R. K. R. Thornton (Ashington and Manchester: MidNAG/ Carcanet, 1982).
The Shepherd's Calendar (London: John Taylor, 1827).
The Shepherd's Calendar, ed. Eric Robinson, Geoffrey Summerfield and David Powell (Oxford: Oxford University Press, 1993).
The Shepherd's Calendar: Manuscript and Published Version, ed. Tim Chilcott (Manchester: Carcanet, 2006).
The Village Minstrel and Other Poems, 2 vols (London: Taylor and Hessey, 1821).

Select Critical Bibliography

Abrams, M. H., *The Mirror and the Lamp: Romantic Theory and the Critical Tradition* (Oxford: Oxford University Press, 1953).
Allnatt, Judith, *The Poet's Wife* (London: Doubleday, 2010).
Ashbery, John, 'John Clare: "Grey Openings Where the Light Looks Through"', in *Other Traditions* (Cambridge, MA: Harvard University Press, 2000), pp. 1–22.
Babstock, Ken, 'As Marginalia in John Clare's The Rural Muse', in *Methodist Hatchet* (Toronto: House of Anansi Press, 2011), p. 5.
Bachelard, Gaston, *The Poetics of Space*, trans. Maria Jolas (London: Penguin Books, 2014).
Baker, David, 'Fives Odes on Absence', in *Scavenger Loop: Poems* (New York: W. W. Norton, 2015), pp. 27–33.
Barrell, John, *The Idea of Landscape and the Sense of Place, 1730–1840: An Approach to the Poetry of John Clare* (Cambridge: Cambridge University Press, 1972).
Barton, Anne, 'John Clare Reads Lord Byron', *Romanticism*, 2.2 (1996), 127–48.
Batchelor, Thomas, *General View of the Agriculture of the County of Bedford* (Board of Agriculture) (London: Richard Phillips, 1808).
Bate, Jonathan, *John Clare: A Biography* (London: Picador, 2003).

―――― 'John Clare's Copyright, 1854–1893', *John Clare Society Journal*, 19 (2000), 19–32.
―――― *Romantic Ecology: Wordsworth and the Environmental Tradition* (London and New York: Routledge, 1991).
―――― *The Song of the Earth* (London: Picador, 2000).
Baugh, Albert C., and Thomas Cable, *A History of the English Language*, 3rd edn (London and New York: Routledge, 1978).
Bedford, William, 'The Flitting, i.m. John Clare', *John Clare Society Journal*, 35 (2016), 53–8.
Birns, Nicholas, '"The riddle nature could not prove": Hidden Landscapes in Clare's poetry', in Hugh Haughton, Adam Phillips, and Geoffrey Summerfield (eds), *John Clare in Context* (Cambridge: Cambridge University Press, 1994), pp. 189–220.
Bloom, Harold, *The Visionary Company: A Reading of English Romantic Poetry*, rev. edn (Ithaca, NY: Cornell University Press 1971).
Blythe, Ronald, 'A Message from the President', *John Clare Society Journal*, 1 (1982), 5.
―――― *Talking About John Clare* (Nottingham: Trent Books, 1999).
Boden, Helen, 'Clare, gender and art', in John Goodridge (ed.), *The Independent Spirit: John Clare and the Self-Taught Tradition* (Helpston: The John Clare Society and The Margaret Grainger Memorial Trust, 1994), pp. 198–208.
Bond, Edward, *The Fool and We Come to the River* (London: Methuen, 1976).
Boos, Florence S., 'The Poetics of the Working Classes', *Victorian Poetry*, 39.2 (Summer 2001), 103–10.
Brackenbury, Alison, 'Visit', 'Still young', 'On the boards', 'Divided', 'Enclosure', 'Breaking', in *Breaking Ground and Other Poems* (Manchester: Carcanet Press, 1984), pp. 99–132.
Branch, Michael P., 'Saving All the Pieces: The Place of Textual Editing in Ecocriticism', in Steven Rossendale (ed.), *The Greening of Literary Scholarship: Literature, Theory, and the Environment* (Iowa City: University of Iowa Press, 2002), pp. 3–25.
Brewer, William D., 'John Clare and Lord Byron', *John Clare Society Journal*, 11 (1992), 43–56.
Bygrave, Stephen, *Coleridge and the Self: Romantic Egotism* (New York: St. Martin's Press, 1986).
Casey, Edward S., *The Fate of Place: A Philosophical History* (Berkeley: University of California Press, 1997).
Canton, James, *Out of Essex: Re-imagining a Literary Landscape* (Oxford: Signal Books, 2013).
Certeau, Michel de, *The Practice of Everyday Life*, trans. Steven Rendall (Berkeley and Los Angeles: University of California Press, 1984).

Chandler, James, (ed.), *Cambridge History of Romantic Literature* (Cambridge: Cambridge University Press, 2009).
Cheeke, Stephen, *Byron and Place: History, Translation, Nostalgia* (Basingstoke: Palgrave Macmillan, 2003).
Cherry, J. L., *The Life and Remains of John Clare* (London: F. Warne, 1873).
Chilcott, Tim, 'Child Harold or Child Harolds: The Editing of Clare's Texts', *John Clare Society Journal*, 19 (2000), 5–17.
Chirico, Paul, *John Clare and the Imagination of the Reader* (Basingstoke: Palgrave, 2007).
Clare, Johanne, *John Clare and the Bounds of Circumstance* (Kingston: McGill-Queen's University Press, 1987).
Clarke, John James, *Oriental Enlightenment: The Encounter Between Asian and Western Thought* (London and New York: Routledge, 1997).
Colman, Felicity J., 'Rhizome', in Adrian Parr (ed.), *The Deleuze Dictionary* (Edinburgh: Edinburgh University Press, 2005), pp. 231–3.
Cook, Eliza 'John Clare, The Northamptonshire Poet', *Eliza Cook's Journal*, 94 (15 February 1851), 241–3.
Cope, Wendy, 'John Clare', in *If I Don't Know* (London: Faber and Faber, 2001), p. 29.
Corbett, Sarah, 'Pictures of Power: Sonnets and Variations after John Clare', *John Clare Society Journal*, 33 (2014), 41–7.
Coupe, Laurence, (ed.), *The Green Studies Reader: From Romanticism to Ecocriticism* (London: Routledge, 2000).
Cronin, Richard, 'In Place and Out of Place: Clare in the Midsummer Cushion', in John Goodridge and Simon Kövesi (eds), *John Clare: New Approaches* (Helpston: John Clare Society, 2000), pp. 133–48.
—— 'John Clare and the *London Magazine*', in Simon Kövesi and Scott McEathron (eds), *New Essays on John Clare: Poetry, Culture and Community* (Cambridge: Cambridge University Press, 2015), pp. 209–27.
Crossan, Greg, 'Thirty Years of the John Clare Society Journal: A Retrospective Survey', *John Clare Society Journal*, 31 (2012), 5–22.
Crowley, Tony, *The Politics of Discourse: The Standard Language Question in British Cultural Debates* (Basingstoke: MacMillan, 1989).
Curzan, Anne, *Fixing English: Prescriptivism and Language History* (Cambridge: Cambridge University press, 2014).
Dawson, P. M. S., 'Common Sense or Radicalism? Some Reflections on Clare's Politics', *Romanticism*, 2.1 (1996), 81–97.
—— 'John Clare—Radical?', *John Clare Society Journal*, 11 (1992), 17–27.
—— 'The Making of Clare's "Poems Descriptive of Rural Life and Scenery" (1820)', *Review of English Studies*, n.s., 56.224 (April 2005), 276–312.
Deacon, George, *John Clare and the Folk Tradition* (London: Francis Boutle, 2002. First pub. 1983).

Deleuze, Gilles, and Claire Parnet, *Dialogues II*, trans. Hugh Tomlinson and Barbara Habberjam (London and New York: Continuum, 2002).

Deleuze, Gilles, and Félix Guattari, *A Thousand Plateaus: Capitalism and Schizophrenia*, trans. Brian Massumi (London and New York: Continuum, 2004).

—— *Kafka: Toward a Minor Literature*, trans. Dana Polan (Minneapolis: University of Minnesota Press, 1986). Original French publication 1975.

Dentith, Simon, *Society and Cultural Forms in Nineteenth-Century England* (Basingstoke: Macmillan Press, 1998).

Devlin, James Dacres, *Go to Epping!* (London: Effingham Wilson, 1841).

Dijkstra, Bram, *Idols of Perversity; Fantasies of Feminine Evil in Fin-de-Siècle Culture* (Oxford: Oxford University Press, 1986).

Dobson, Andrew, *Green Political Thought*, 4th edn (London and New York: Routledge, 2007).

Dunagan, Patrick James, *Drops of Rain/Drops of Wine* (New York City: Spuyten Duyvil, 2016).

Dunn, Allen, and Thomas F. Haddox, (eds), *The Limits of Literary Historicism* (Knoxville, TN: University of Tennessee Press, 2011).

Farley, Paul, (ed.), *John Clare: Poet to Poet* (Faber and Faber, 2007).

Farley, Paul, and Michael Symmons Roberts, *Edgelands: Journeys into England's True Wilderness* (London: Jonathan Cape, 2011).

Feder, Helen, 'Ecocriticism, New Historicism, and Romantic Apostrophe', in Steven Rossendale (ed.), *The Greening of Literary Scholarship: Literature, Theory, and the Environment* (Iowa City: University of Iowa Press, 2002), pp. 42–58.

Felski, Rita, '"Context Stinks!"', *New Literary History*, 42 (2011), 573–91.

Felstiner, John, *Can Poetry Save the Earth? A Field Guide to Nature Poems* (New Haven: Yale University Press, 2009).

Ferrer, Daniel, 'Production, Invention, and Reproduction: Genetic vs. Textual Criticism', in Elizabeth Bergmann Loizeaux and Neil Fraistat (eds), *Reimagining Textuality: Textual Studies in the Late Age of Print* (Madison: University of Wisconsin Press, 2002), pp. 48–59.

Ferrer, Daniel and Michael Groden, 'Introduction: A Genesis of French Genetic Criticism', in Jed Deppman, Daniel Ferrer and Michael Groden (eds and trans), *Genetic Criticism: Texts and Avant-textes* (Philadelphia, 2004), pp. 1–16.

Fletcher, Angus, *A New Theory for American Poetry: Democracy, the Environment and the Future of the Imagination* (Cambridge, MA: Harvard University Press, 2004).

Foss, Arthur and Kerith Trick, *St Andrew's Hospital Northampton: The First One Hundred and Fifty Years (1838–1988)* (Cambridge: Granta Editions, 1989).

Foucault, Michel, 'Different Spaces', in James D. Faubon (ed.), *Aesthetics, Method, and Epistemology*, trans. Robert Hurley et al. (New York: New Press, 1998), pp. 175–85.

Foulds, Adam, *The Quickening Maze* (London: Jonathan Cape, 2009).
Freeman, Mark, 'The agricultural labourer and the "Hodge" stereotype, c. 1850–1914', *Agricultural History Review*, 49 (2001), 172–86.
Fulford, Tim, 'Personating Poets on the Page: John Clare in his Asylum Notebooks', *John Clare Society Journal*, 32 (2013), 27–48.
—— *Romantic Poetry and Literary Coteries* (New York: Palgrave Macmillan, 2015).
Gadamer, Hans-Georg, *Truth and Method*, 2nd rev. edn., trans. Joel Weinsheimer and Donald G. Marshall (London and New York: Continuum, 2004).
Gardner, H. W., and H. V. Garner, *The Use of Lime in British Agriculture* (London: Farmer & Stock-Breeder Publications Ltd., 1953).
Garrard, Greg, *Ecocriticism* (London: Routledge, 2004).
—— 'Wordsworth and Thoreau: Two Versions of Pastoral', in Lawrence Buell and Richard J. Schneider (eds), *Thoreau's Sense of Place: Essays in American Environmental Writing* (Iowa City: University of Iowa Press, 2000), pp. 194–206.
Goatly, Andrew, 'Green Grammar and Grammatical Metaphor, or Language and Myth of Power, or Metaphors We Die By', in Alwin Fill and Peter Mühlhäusler (eds), *The Ecolinguistics Reader: Language, Ecology and Environment* (London and New York: Continuum, 2001), pp. 203–25.
Goldsmith, Jason N., 'The Promiscuity of Print: John Clare's "Don Juan" and the Culture of Romantic Celebrity', *Studies in English Literature, 1500–1900*, 46.4 (Autumn, 2006), 803–32.
Goldsmith, Oliver, *A History of the Earth and Animated Nature*, 6 vols (London: Wingrave and Collingwood et al., 1816).
Goodridge, John, *John Clare and Community* (Cambridge: Cambridge University Press, 2013).
—— '"Now wenches, listen, and let lovers lie": Women's storytelling in Bloomfield and Clare', *John Clare Society Journal*, 22 (2003), 77–92.
—— 'Review of John Clare, *Poems of the Middle Period V*, *Romanticism*, 9.2 (2003), 215–19.
Goodridge, John and Kelsey Thornton, 'John Clare: The trespasser', in Hugh Haughton, Adam Phillips, and Geoffrey Summerfield (eds), *John Clare in Context* (Cambridge: Cambridge University Press, 1994), pp. 87–129.
—— *John Clare: The Trespasser* (Nottingham: Five Leaves Publications, 2016).
Goodridge, John, William Christmas, Bridget Keegan, Tim Burke and Simon Kövesi, (eds), *Eighteenth-Century English Labouring-Class Poets, 1700–1800*, 3 vols (London: Pickering and Chatto, 2003).
Goodridge, John, Kaye Kossick and Scott McEathron, (eds), *Nineteenth-Century English Labouring-Class Poets, 1800–1990*, 3 vols (London: Pickering and Chatto, 2006).

Goody, Jack, *The Culture of Flowers* (Cambridge: Cambridge University Press, 1993).
Gorji, Mina, *John Clare and the Place of Poetry* (Liverpool: Liverpool University Press, 2008).
—— 'John Clare's Weeds', in John Rignall, H. Gustav Klaus and Valentine Cunningham (eds), *Ecology and the Literature of the British Left: The Red and the Green* (Farnham, Surrey: Ashgate, 2012), pp. 61–74.
Grainger, Margaret, *A Descriptive Catalogue of the John Clare Collection in Peterborough Museum and Art Gallery* ([Peterborough]: [Peterborough Museum Society], 1973).
Greetham, D. C., *Textual Scholarship: An Introduction* (New York and London: Garland Publishing, 1994).
Guattari, Félix, *The Three Ecologies*, trans. Ian Pindar and Paul Sutton (London and New York: Continuum, 2000).
Guyer, Sara, *Reading With John Clare: Biopoetics, Sovereignty, Romanticism* (New York: Fordham University Press, 2015).
Harrison, Gary, 'Hybridity, Mimicry and John Clare's "Child Harold"', *Wordsworth Circle*, 34.3 (Summer 2003), 149–55.
—— 'John Clare's Poetics of Acknowledgement', *Romanticism*, 18.1 (2012), 41–54.
Haughton, Hugh, 'Revision and Romantic Authorship: The Case of Clare', *John Clare Society Journal*, 17 (1998), 65–73.
Havinden, Michael, 'Lime as a means of agricultural improvement: The Devon example', in C. W. Chalklin and M. A. Havinden (eds), *Rural Change and Urban Growth 1500–1800* (London and New York: Longman, 1974), pp. 104–34.
Hay, Louis, 'Genetic Editing, Past and Future: A Few Reflections by a User', trans. J. M. Luccioni and Hans Walter Gabler, *Text: Transactions of the Society for Textual Scholarship*, 3 (1987), 117–33.
Hayot, Eric, 'Against Periodization; or, On Institutional Time', *New Literary History*, 42 (2011), 739–6.
Hazlitt, William, *The Plain Speaker: Opinions on Books, Men, and Things*, 2 vols (London: Henry Colburn, 1826).
—— *The Round Table: A Collection of Essays on Literature, Men, and Manners*, 2 vols (Edinburgh: Archibald Constable; London: Longman et al., 1817).
—— *The Spirit of the Age: Or Contemporary Portraits* (London: Henry Colburn, 1825).
Hecht, Anthony, 'Coming Home', in *Millions of Strange Shadows* (Oxford: Oxford University Press, 1977), pp. 25–7.
Heidegger, Martin, *Off the Beaten Track*, trans. Julian Young and Kenneth Haynes (Cambridge: Cambridge University Press, 2002).

Heise, Ursula K., *Sense of Place and Sense of Planet: The Environmental Imagination of the Global* (Oxford: Oxford University Press, 2008).

Helsinger, Elizabeth, 'Clare and the Place of the Peasant Poet', *Critical Inquiry*, 13.3 (Spring, 1987), 509-31.

Herzogenarth, Bernd, (ed.), *An [Un]Likely Alliance: Thinking Environment[s] with Deleuze|Guattari* (Cambridge: Cambridge Scholars Publishing, 2008).

―― (ed.), *Deleuze|Guattari & Ecology* (Basingstoke: Palgrave, 2009).

Hess, Scott, *William Wordsworth and the Ecology of Authorship: The Roots of Environmentalism in Nineteenth-Century Culture* (Charlottesville and London: University of Virginia Press, 2012).

Hickman, Ben, *John Ashbery and English Poetry* (Edinburgh: Edinburgh University Press, 2012).

Hirsch, Edward, 'Three Journeys', in *Wild Gratitude: Poems* (New York: Knopf, 2010; first edn., 1986), pp. 64-6.

Hobsbawm, E. J., and George Rudé, *Captain Swing* (Old Woking: Lawrence and Wishart, 1969).

Hold, Trevor, 'The Composer's Debt to John Clare', *John Clare Society Journal*, 1 (1982), 25-30.

Honey, John, *Language is Power: The Story of Standard English and its Enemies* (London: Faber and Faber, 1997).

Hood, Edwin Paxton, *The Literature of Labour: Illustrious Instances of the Education of Poetry in Poverty*, 2nd edn (London: Partridge and Oakey, 1852).

Houghton, Sarah, '"Some little thing of other days/Saved from the wreck of time": John Clare and Festivity', *John Clare Society Journal*, 23 (2004), 21-43.

Houghton-Walker, Sarah, *John Clare's Religion* (Farnham: Ashgate, 2009).

―― *Representations of the Gypsy in the Romantic Period* (Oxford: Oxford University Press, 2014).

Houston, Keith, *Shady Characters: The Secret Life of Punctuation, Symbols & Other Typographical Marks* (New York and London: W. W. Norton, 2013).

Innes, Christopher, 'Elemental, My Dear Clare: The Case of the Missing Poet', in Martin Middeke and Werner Huber (eds), *Biofictions: The Rewriting of Romantic Lives in Contemporary Fiction and Drama* (London: Camden House, 1999), pp. 187-200.

Insko, Jeffrey, 'The Prehistory of Posthistoricism', in Allen Dunn and Thomas F. Haddox (eds), *The Limits of Literary Historicism* (Knoxville, TN: University of Tennessee Press, 2011), pp. 105-23.

Jacobus, Mary, *Romantic Things: A tree, a rock, a cloud* (Chicago and London: University of Chicago Press, 2012).

Jameson, Frederic, *Postmodernism, or, The Cultural Logic of Late Capitalism* (London and New York: Verso, 1991).

Kahn, Mary, 'The Passive Voice of Science: Language Abuse in the Wildlife Profession', in Alwin Fill and Peter Mühlhäusler (eds), *The Ecolinguistics*

Reader: Language, Ecology and Environment (London and New York: Continuum, 2001), pp. 241–4.

Keegan, Bridget, 'Boys, Marvellous Boys: John Clare's "Natural Genius"', in John Goodridge and Simon Kövesi (eds), *John Clare: New Approaches* (Helpston: John Clare Society, 2000), pp. 65–76.

—— *British Labouring-Class Nature Poetry, 1730–1837* (Basingstoke: Palgrave Macmillan, 2008).

Kelemen, Erick, *Textual Editing and Criticism: An Introduction* (New York and London: W. W. Norton, 2009).

Kelley, Theresa M., *Clandestine Marriage: Botany and Romantic Culture* (Baltimore: Johns Hopkins University Press, 2012).

—— 'Postmodernism, Romanticism, and John Clare', in Thomas Pfau and Robert F. Gleckner (eds), *Lessons of Romanticism: A Critical Companion* (Durham, NC: Duke University Press, 1998), pp. 157–70.

Kinnaird, John, *William Hazlitt: Critic of Power* (New York: Columbia University Press, 1978).

Kroeber, Karl, *Ecological Literary Criticism: Romantic Imagining and the Biology of Mind* (New York: Columbia University Press, 1994).

Lafford, Erin, 'Clare's Mutterings, Murmurings, and Ramblings: The Sounds of Health', *John Clare Society Journal*, 33 (2014), 24–40.

Landow, George P., *Hypertext 3.0* (Baltimore: Johns Hopkins University Press, 2006).

Leader, Zachary, *Revision and Romantic Authorship* (Oxford: Oxford University Press, 1996).

Lefebvre, Henri, *The Production of Space*, trans. Donald Nicholson-Smith (Malden, MA, and Oxford: Blackwell, 1991).

Leonard, Tom, 'Honest', in *Three Glasgow Writers: A collection of writing by Alex. Hamilton, James Kelman, Tom Leonard* (Glasgow: Molendinar Press, 1976).

Lewis, C. Day, *The Lyric Impulse* (London: Chatto & Windus, 1965).

Loney, Alan, *& The Ampersand* (Wellington: Black Light, 1990).

Longley, Michael, 'Journey out of Essex or, John Clare's Escape from the Madhouse', *Poems 1963–1983* (Harmondsworth: Penguin, 1986), p. 56.

Lucas, John, 'Clare's Politics', in Hugh Haughton, Adam Phillips and Geoffrey Summerfield (eds), *John Clare in Context* (Cambridge: Cambridge University Press, 1994), pp. 148–77.

—— *England and Englishness: Ideas of Nationhood in English Poetry, 1688–1900* (London: Hogarth Press, 1990).

—— (ed.), *For John Clare: An Anthology of Verse* (Helpston: John Clare Society, 1997).

—— *John Clare* (Plymouth: Northcote House, 1994).

Lupton, Hugh, *The Ballad of John Clare* (Sawtry, Cambs.: Dedalus, 2010).

Lynch, Tom, Cheryll Glotfelty and Karla Armbruster, (eds), *The Bioregional Imagination: Literature, Ecology, and Place* (Athens, GA: University of Georgia Press, 2012).
Lynes, Jeanette, *Bedlam Cowslip: The John Clare Poems* (Hamilton, Ontario: Buckrider Books, 2016).
Mabey, Richard, *Flora Britannica* (London: Sinclair-Stevenson, 1996).
—— *Nature Cure* (London: Chatto and Windus, 2005).
—— *Weeds: The Story of Outlaw Plants* (London: Profile Books, 2012).
MacKenna, John, *Clare: A Novel* (Belfast: Blackstaff Press, 1993).
Mahood, M. M., *The Poet as Botanist* (Cambridge: Cambridge University Press, 2008).
Maidment, Brian, 'Popular Exemplary Biography in the Nineteenth Century: Edwin Paxton Hood and His Books', *Prose Studies*, 7.2 (September 1984), 148–67.
Malpas, J. E., *Place and Experience: A Philosophical Topography* (Cambridge: Cambridge University Press, 1999).
Martin, Frederick, *The Life of John Clare* (London and Cambridge: Macmillan, 1865).
Martin, Philip W., 'Authorial Identity and the Critical Act: John Clare and Lord Byron', in John Beer (ed.), *Questioning Romanticism* (Baltimore, MD: Johns Hopkins University Press, 1995), pp. 71–91.
Maskit, Jonathan, 'Subjectivity, Desire, and the Problem of Consumption', in Bernd Herzogenrath (ed.), *Deleuze | Guattari & Ecology* (Basingstoke: Palgrave, 2009), pp. 129–44.
Mason, Emma, 'Ecology with religion: Kinship in John Clare', in Simon Kövesi and Scott McEathron (eds), *New Essays on John Clare: Poetry, Culture and Community* (Cambridge: Cambridge University Press, 2015), pp. 97–117.
Maxwell, Glyn, *Drinks with Dead Poets: The Autumn Term* (London: Oberon Books, 2016).
McCue, Kirsteen, (ed.), *James Hogg: Contributions to Musical Collections and Miscellaneous Songs* (Edinburgh: Edinburgh University Press, 2014).
McEathron, Scott, 'John Clare and Charles Lamb: Friends in the Past', *Charles Lamb Bulletin*, 95 (July 1996), 98–109.
McGann, Jerome, 'Is Romanticism Finished?', in James Chandler (ed.), *Cambridge History of Romantic Literature* (Cambridge: Cambridge University Press, 2009), pp. 648–64.
—— 'Keats and the Historical Method in Literary Criticism', *Modern Language Notes*, 94.5 (December 1979), 988–1032.
—— *The Romantic Ideology: A Critical Investigation* (Chicago and London: University of Chicago Press, 1983).
McKusick, James C., '"A language that is ever green": The Ecological Vision of John Clare', *University of Toronto Quarterly*, 61 (Winter 1991–2), 30–52.

——— 'Beyond the Visionary Company: John Clare's Resistance to Romanticism', in Hugh Haughton, Adam Phillips and Geoffrey Summerfield (eds), *John Clare in Context* (Cambridge, Cambridge University Press, 1994), pp. 221–37.
——— *Green Writing: Romanticism and Ecology* (New York: St. Martin's Press. 2000).
Mellor, Anne K., *Romanticism and Gender* (New York and London: Routledge, 1993).
Moore, Alan, *Jerusalem: A Novel* (London: Knockabout, 2016).
——— *Voice of the Fire: A Novel* (Atlanta and Portland: Top Shelf Productions, 2003).
Moore, Bryan L., *Ecology and Literature: Ecocentric Personification from Antiquity to the Twenty-first Century* (New York: Palgrave Macmillan, 2008).
Moore, DC, *Town and Honest* (London: Methuen Drama, 2010).
Moretti, Franco, *Graphs, Maps, Trees: Abstract Models for Literary History* (London and New York: Verso, 2007).
Morley, David, *The Gypsy and the Poet* (Manchester: Carcanet, 2013).
Morton, Timothy, *Ecology Without Nature: Rethinking Environmental Aesthetics* (Cambridge, MA: Harvard University Press, 2007).
——— 'John Clare's Dark Ecology', *Studies in Romanticism*, 47.2 (2008), 179–93.
Moulthrop, Stuart, 'Rhizome and Resistance: Hypertext and the Dreams of a New Culture', in George P. Landow (ed.), *Hyper/Text/Theory* (Baltimore: Johns Hopkins University Press, 1994), pp. 299–319.
Moyse, Mary, 'John Clare's family Tree', *John Clare Society Journal*, 8 (1989), 24–30.
Mulford, Wendy, 'John Clare's Mountain', in Denise Riley (ed.), *Poets on Writing: Britain, 1970–1991*, (Basingstoke: Macmillan, 1992), pp. 114–20.
Murray, Alexander, (ed.), *Sir William Jones, 1746–94: A Commemoration* (Oxford: Oxford University Press, 1998).
Muskett, Paul, 'The East Anglian Riots of 1822', *Agricultural History Review*, 32.1 (1984), 1–13.
Noble, Shalon, '"Homeless at Home": John Clare's Uncommon Ecology', *Romanticism*, 21:2 (July 2015), 171–81.
O'Neill, Michael, 'The Romantic Sonnet', in A. D. Cousins and Peter Howarth (eds), *The Cambridge Companion to the Sonnet* (Cambridge: Cambridge University Press, 2011), pp. 185–203.
Oswald, Alice, (ed.), *The Thunder Mutters: 101 Poems for the Planet* (London: Faber and Faber, 2005).
Paulin, Tom 'John Clare: A Bicentennial Celebration', in Richard Foulkes (ed.), *John Clare: A Bicentenary Celebration* (Northampton: University of Leicester, Department of Adult Education, 1994), pp. 69–78.

Pearce, Lynne, 'John Clare's "Child Harold": A Polyphonic Reading', *Criticism*, 31.2 (1991), 139–57.

—— 'John Clare's *Child Harold*: The Road Not Taken', in Susan Sellers (ed.), *Feminist Criticism: Theory and Practice* (Hemel Hempstead: Harvester Wheatsheaf, 1991), pp. 143–56.

—— *John Clare and Mikhail Bakhtin: The Dialogic Principle. Readings from John Clare's Manuscripts 1832–1845* (University of Birmingham: PhD thesis, 1987).

Pedlar, Valerie, 'John Clare's Child Harold', *John Clare Society Journal*, 8 (1989), 11–16.

—— 'John Clare's Recollections of Home: The Poetics of Nostalgia', *John Clare Society Journal*, 33 (2014), 5–19.

—— '"Written by Himself"—Edited by Others: The Autobiographical Writings of John Clare', in John Goodridge and Simon Kövesi (eds), *John Clare: New Approaches* (Helpston: John Clare Society, 2000), pp. 17–31.

Pepper, David, *Eco-Socialism: From Deep Ecology to Social Justice* (London: Routledge, 1993).

Phelan, Joseph, *The Nineteenth-Century Sonnet* (Basingstoke: Palgrave Macmillan, 2005).

Piercey, Robert, *The Crisis in Continental Philosophy* (London and New York: Continuum, 2009).

Powell, David, *Catalogue of the John Clare Collection in the Northampton Public Library* (Northampton: County Borough of Northampton Public Libraries, Museums and Art Gallery Committee, 1964).

Powell, Margaret A., 'Clare and his Patrons in 1820: Some Unpublished Papers' *John Clare Society Journal*, 6 (1987) 4–9.

Pownall, Helen, 'Syntax and World-view in John Clare's Fen poems', *John Clare Society Journal*, 34 (2015), 37–50.

Rae, Simon, *Grass* (Bampton: Top Edge Press, 2003).

Redding, Cyrus, *Past Celebrities Whom I Have Known* (London, 1866).

Reeves, James, 'The Savage Moon: A Meditation on John Clare', *Selected Poems* (London: Allison and Busby, 1967), pp. 31–8.

Reno, Seth T., 'John Clare and Ecological Love', *John Clare Society Journal*, 35 (2016), 59–76.

Rigby, Kate, *Topographies of the Sacred: The Poetics of Place in European Romanticism* (Charlottesville and London: University of Virginia Press, 2004).

Robinson, Eric, 'John Clare's Learning', *John Clare Society Journal*, 7 (1988), 10–25.

Robinson, Eric and Geoffrey Summerfield, 'John Clare: An Interpretation of Certain Asylum Letters', *The Review of English Studies*, n.s., 13.50 (May 1962), 135–46.

Robinson, Solveig C., 'Of "Haymakers" and "City Artisans": The Chartist Poetics of Eliza Cook's "Songs of Labor"', *Victorian Poetry*, 39.2 (Summer 2001), 229–54.

Rounce, Adam, 'John Clare, William Cowper and the eighteenth century', in Simon Kövesi and Scott McEathron (eds), *New Essays on John Clare: Poetry, Culture and Community* (Cambridge: Cambridge University Press, 2015), pp. 38–56.

Russett, Margaret, 'Like "Wedding Gowns or Money from the Mint": Clare's Borrowed Inheritance', *Romantic Circles* (February 1999), https://www.rc.umd.edu/praxis/law/russett/mruss.htm.

Sadie, Stanley, et al., (eds), *The New Grove Dictionary of Music and Musicians*, 2nd edn., 29 vols (London: Grove, 2001).

Sales, Roger, *John Clare: A Literary Life* (Basingstoke: Palgrave, 2002).

Schyrava, Juliet, *Schiller to Derrida: Idealism in Aesthetics* (Cambridge: Cambridge University Press, 1989).

Scrimgeour, Cecil, 'John Clare and the Price of Experience', *John Clare Society Journal*, 2 (1983), 28–39.

Simpson, Jacqueline, and Steve Roud, *Oxford Dictionary of English Folklore* (Oxford: Oxford University Press, 2000).

Sinclair, Iain, *Edge of the Orison: In the Traces of John Clare's 'Journey out of Essex'* (London: Penguin Books, 2005).

Smith, Mark J., *Ecologism: Towards Ecological Citizenship* (Buckingham: Open University Press, 1998).

Soper, Kate, *What is Nature? Culture, Politics and the non-Human* (Oxford: Blackwell, 1995).

Spedding, Patrick, Paul Watt, Ed Cray, David Gregory and Derek B. Scott, (eds), *Bawdy Songbooks of the Romantic Period*, 4 vols (London: Pickering and Chatto, 2011).

Stafford, Fiona, 'Wordsworth's Poetry of Place', in Richard Gravil and Daniel Robinson (eds), *The Oxford Handbook of William Wordsworth* (Oxford: Oxford University Press, 2015), pp. 309–24.

Stillinger, Jack, 'Textual Primitivism and the Editing of Wordsworth', *Studies in Romanticism*, 28.1 (Spring 1989), 3–28.

Storey, Mark, (ed.), *Clare: The Critical Heritage* (London: Routledge & Kegan Paul, 1973).

—— 'Clare and the Critics', in Hugh Haughton, Adam Phillips and Geoffrey Summerfield (eds), *John Clare in Context* (Cambridge, Cambridge University Press, 1994), pp. 28–50.

—— 'Edward Drury's "Memoir" of Clare', *John Clare Society Journal*, 11 (1992), 14–16.

—— 'Edwin Paxton Hood (Not the Reverend Romeo Elton) and John Clare', *Notes and Queries*, 18.10 (October 1971), 386–7.

Strang, Barbara M. H., 'John Clare's Language', in R. K. R. Thornton (ed.), *The Rural Muse: Poems by John Clare* (Ashington: MidNAG and Carcanet, 1982), pp. 159–73.
Strickland, Edward, 'Boxer Byron: A Clare Obsession', *Byron Journal*, 17 (1989), 57–76.
Tally Jr., Robert T., *Spatiality* (London and New York: Routledge, 2013).
Taplin, Kim, *Tongues in Trees: Studies in Literature and Ecology* (Bideford: Green Books, 1989).
Thomas, Edward, *Feminine Influence on the English Poets* (London, 1910).
Thompson, E. P., *Customs in Common* (London: Penguin, 1993).
Thornton, R. K. R., 'The Raw and the Cooked', *John Clare Society Journal*, 24 (2005), pp. 78–86.
——— 'What John Clare Do We Read?', *PN Review*, 31.4 (March-April 2005), pp. 54–6.
Tibble, J. W., and Anne Tibble, *John Clare: A Life* (London: Cobden-Sanderson, 1932; revised edn., London: Michael Joseph, 1972).
Trehane, Emma, '"Emma and Johnny": The Friendship between Eliza Emmerson and John Clare', *John Clare Society Journal*, 24 (2005), 69–77.
Trower, Shelley, 'Nerves, Vibration and the Aeolian Harp', *Romanticism and Victorianism on the Net*, 54 (2009), http://www.erudit.org/revue/ravon/2009/v/n54/038761ar.html.
Tschichold, Jan, *The Ampersand: Its Origin and Development*, trans. Frederick Plaat (London: Woudhuysen, 1957).
Tuaillon, David, (ed.), *Edward Bond: The Playwright Speaks* (London: Bloomsbury Academic, 2015).
Tuan, Yi-Fu, *Space and Place: The Perspective of Experience* (London: Edward Arnold, 1977).
Vardy, Alan, *John Clare, Politics and Poetry* (Basingstoke: Palgrave Macmillan, 2003).
Vincent, Andrew, *Modern Political Ideologies*, 3rd edn (Chichester: Wiley-Blackwell, 2010).
Walcott, Derek, 'The Bounty', in *The Bounty* (London: Faber and Faber, 1997), pp. 3–16.
Walford Davies, Damian, (ed.), *Romanticism, History, Historicism: Essays on an Orthodoxy* (London and New York: Routledge, 2009).
Waller, Robert, 'Enclosures: The Ecological Significance of a Poem by John Clare', in *Mother Earth: The Journal of the Soil Association*, 13 (1964), 231–7.
Ward, Sam, '"This is radical slang": John Clare, Admiral Lord Radstock and the Queen Caroline Affair', in Simon Kövesi and Scott McEathron (eds), *New Essays on John Clare: Poetry, Culture and Community* (Cambridge: Cambridge University Press, 2015), pp. 189–208.

Weiner, Stephanie Kuduk, *Clare's Lyric: John Clare and Three Modern Poets* (Oxford: Oxford University Press, 2014).
White, Adam, 'Identity in Place: Lord Byron, John Clare and Lyric Poetry', *Byron Journal*, 40.2 (2012), 115–27.
—— 'John Clare: "The Man of Taste"', *John Clare Society Journal*, 28 (2009), 38–54.
—— 'The Love Songs and Love Lyrics of Robert Burns and John Clare', *Scottish Literary Review*, 5.2 (2013), 61–80.
White, Simon J., 'John Clare's Sonnets and the Northborough Fens', *John Clare Society Journal*, 28 (2009), 55–70.
—— 'Otaheite, Natural Genius and Robert Bloomfield's The Farmer's Boy', *Romanticism*, 17.2 (July 2011), 160–74.
Whyte, Ian D., *Landscape and History since 1500* (London: Reaktion Books, 2002).
Willetts, Sam, 'Honest John', in *New Light for the Old Dark* (London: Jonathan Cape, 2010), p. 15.
Williams, Frederick S., *The Midland Railway: Its Rise and Progress. A Narrative of Modern Enterprise* (London: Strahan, 1876).
Williams, Richard, *Limekilns and Limeburning* (Princes Risborough, Bucks.: Shire, 2004).
Wojahn, David, 'Napping on my Fifty-Third Birthday', in *World Tree* (Pittsburgh: University of Pittsburgh Press, 2011), pp. 22–4.
Wu, Duncan, *30 Great Myths About the Romantics* (Chichester: Wiley Blackwell, 2015).
Young, Linda, 'Literature, Museums, and National Identity; or, Why are there So Many Writers' House Museums in Britain?', *Museum History Journal*, 8.2 (July 2015), 229–46.

INDEX

A
Abrams, M. H., 64n26
academia, 191–192, 220
Adelaide, queen consort of the United Kingdom, 200, 213n99
Aeolian harp, 8, 63–64n26
agency (authorial), 8, 81, 109, 132, 138, 146, 155
agricultural improvement, 10, 18–21, 47–48, 66n55, 73n140, 226–227
agricultural labour, 2–3, 15–17, 19–23, 27–28, 39, 44–48, 62–63n10, 79, 90, 102–103, 110, 122n66, 144–145, 167–168, 227–230, 236–237n58
Allen, Matthew, 49, 143, 190, 200
Allnatt, Judith, 217
anthropomorphism, 22, 88, 94, 115, 120n45, 147
April fools' day, 167–170
Argosy, The, 60
Ashbery, John, 142, 157n33, 215
asylum, 10, 31, 49, 59, 143, 163, 164, 184, 190, 193, 194, 196–199, 216, 224
audience, *see* readership
Austen, Jane, 42

Australia, 226
authorship, 18, 146, 147, 152–154

B
Babstock, Ken, 215
Bachelard, Gaston, 11, 26, 42
Baker, David, 215
Bakhtin, Mikhail, 193
Barrell, John, 10, 13, 17, 100, 102
Bate, Jonathan, 6, 15, 30, 55, 66n53, 93, 97, 121n56, 132, 136, 138, 196, 199, 216, 224, 231
Becket, Thomas á, 222
Beckett, Samuel, 222
Bedford, William, 215
Behnes, Henry, 69n94, 85
Belle Assemblée, La, 56
Bible, 86, 87, 174
bigamy, 87, 201
biography, 7, 61, 97, 132, 134, 144, 224
Birns, Nicholas, 5
Blackwood's Edinburgh Magazine, 79
Blake, William, 51, 172
Bloom, Harold, 141
Bloomfield, Robert, 2, 139, 171
Blunden, Edmund, 97
Blythe, Ronald, 1, 203

Boden, Helen, 192
Bond, Edward, 44, 216, 231, 232
books, 35, 37, 101, 132, 135, 137, 144, 200, 203
boxing, 198, 199
Brackenbury, Alison, 215
Branch, Michael P., 149
Broadhurst, Mr, 56, 75n160
Bryan, Mary, 139
Bunyan, John, 222
Burghley Park, 66n53
Burke, Tim, 62n4
Burns, Robert, 109, 174
Bushell, Sally, 61n2
Bygrave, Stephen, 81
Byron, 3, 32–39, 42, 49, 59, 69n101, 82, 89, 91, 96, 198, 199, 200, 219, 220

C
Caledonian Mercury, 59
Campbell, F., 57
canon, 49, 51, 97, 219
Canton, James, 64n34
Captain Swing riots, *see* Swing riots
Carew, Thomas, 174, 180
Casey, Edward S., 11, 65n46
Catnach, James, 57, 76n170
censorship, 5, 23, 99, 135, 190, 228
Certeau, Michel de, 11, 16, 18, 19–20, 21, 36, 225
Chandler, James, 218
chapbooks, 56, 200, 228
Chartism, 11, 82, 165, 199, 216, 217
Chatterton, Thomas, 124n84, 171
Cheeke, Stephen, 37–38
Cherry, J. L., 7, 45
Chilcott, Tim, 132, 140, 156n19
childhood, 13, 21–27, 44–47, 102, 171–172

Chirico, Paul, 8, 41, 62n3, 141
Christ, 86, 87, 148
Clare, Johanne, 6
Clare, John
books, titled manuscripts; *By Himself*, 92; *Poems Descriptive of Rural Life and Scenery*, 4, 52–53, 57, 67n72, 73n146, 162, 164, 228; *The Midsummer Cushion*, 131; *The Parish*, 22, 25, 90–92, 186; *The Rural Muse*, 34, 79, 84, 182; *The Shepherd's Calendar*, 46, 128, 140; *The Village Minstrel*, 25, 40, 41, 44, 99
poems; 'A Character', 205n8; 'A Maiden-Haid', 205n8; 'A Scene', 207n21; '& every morning passing gives a call', 123n68; 'Among the orchard weeds from every search', 123n68; 'Angels of earth', 186; 'Child Harold', 70n105, 167, 192, 201, 213n102; 'Close by the road the traveller set his cart', 123n68; 'Come come my love the bush is growing', 181, 182; 'Dolly's Mistake', 23, 67n72; 'Don Juan', 7, 87, 167, 192, 197, 201, 202, 210n61; 'Familiar Epistle to a Friend', 121n55; 'First Love', 165, 180; 'From place to place they go afar they roam', 122n67; 'Genius', 32, 34, 35; 'Going to the Fair', 207n21; 'Good e'enin to ye lassie', 210n59; 'He eats a moments stoppage to his song', 123n68; 'He fights with all the whasps nests in his

way', 123n68; 'He finds his old knife where the gipseys lay', 123n68; 'He never knew a book & never bought', 103, 123n68; 'He smokes his pipe & drinks his pint of ale', 123n68; 'He waits all day beside his little flock', 123n68; 'Helpstone', 29; 'Helpstone Green', 68n75; 'Hodges Confession', 207n21; 'Home', 68n75; 'Honey words make charms of blisses', 187, 188; 'Hue & Cry', 110; 'I Am', 67n74, 79, 95; 'If I was bonny Mary Lee', 67n71; 'I love to hear the evening crows go bye', 101, 104, 105, 107, 122n68; 'In beauty there is joy', 186; 'Lapt up in sacks to shun the rain & wind', 123n68; 'Lord Byron', 35; 'Love Epistles Between Richard and Kate', 206n8; 'Love lives beyond', 162; 'Maids set their buckets down & run the while', 123n68; 'Maids shout to breakfast in a merry strife', 207n21; 'Mary Lee', 67n71; 'Morning Walk', 181, 209n38; 'My Mary', 163, 205n7; 'My spirit lives in silent sighs', 180; 'Nelson & the Nile', 120n48; 'Of thee I keep dreaming still thee', 187; 'Oh whither fair maiden', 186; 'On Seeing the Bust of Princess Victoria by Behnes', 120n48; 'O sweet is the sound', 187; 'Robin and Suke; or The Midnight Quarrel. A Ballad', 205n8;

'Rural Morning', 125n85, 207n21; 'St Martins Eve', 207n21; 'Sighing for Retirement', 142, 145, 146, 148; 'She is a sweet and bonny thing', 210n57; 'Song' 'Fast by a Brook beneath a bending willow', 205n8; 'Song' 'If Kittys rosy presence now', 206n8; 'Song: O beautifull Sorrow', 197; 'Song' 'She is a sweet and bonny thing', 210n57; 'Song' 'Since Flora disdains me—her once loving swain', 205n8; 'Song: Sweet Susan', 200; 'Song' 'We'll walk my love at eve unseen', 181, 184, 209n38; 'Sonnet After the Manner of X X X X X', 124n83; 'Sonnet' 'England with pride I name thee', 120n48; 'Summer Evening', 110, 124n85; 'The cloudy morning brought a pleasant day', 123n68; 'The corn craiks rispy song', 210n56, 210n58; 'The cowboy shuns the shower & seeks the mat', 123n68; 'The cowboys hut of straw neglected lies', 123n68; 'The crows drive onward through the storm of snow', 123n68; 'The Enthusiast: A day-dream in summer', 170; 'The f[l]aggy forrest beat the willows breast', 125n85; 'The Flitting', 30, 125n85; 'The horses are took out the cows are fed', 123n68; 'The Invocation', 205n8; 'The Labourers Hymn', 227–230,

236n50; 'The Lament of Swordy Well', 22, 109; 'The Lodge House: A Gossips Tale', 207n21; 'The maiden ran away to fetch the cloaths', 123n68, 124n75, 124n76; 'The maiden shout to breakfast round the yard', 122n66, 123n68; 'The Meeting', 53–57, 60, 162, 165, 166; 'The merry childern shout the herd is come', 207n21; 'The Mouse's Nest', 6; 'The Nightingales Nest', 178; 'The noisy blathering calves are fed & all', 123n68; 'The old hens cackle & begin the day', 207n21; 'The ploughman are out before the cock crows', 207n21; 'The Powerful Smile', 206n8; 'The reeking supper waits the labourer home', 124n76; 'The reformers hymn', 229, 236n50; 'The school boy sets his basket down to play', 123n68; 'The shepherds almost wonder where they dwell', 96, 100, 123n68; 'The Village Minstrel', 25, 40, 41, 44, 99; 'The wild duck startles like a sudden thought', 122n65, 123n68; 'The Woodman', 125n85; 'The Workhouse Orphan, A Tale', 21; 'There is a place scarce known that well may claim', 102, 123n68; 'They pelt about the snow the birds to scare', 123n68; 'Tis late the labouring men come dropping in', 123n68, 124n75, 124n76; 'To My Cottage', 25, 28; 'Up crows the cock with bouncing brawl', 167; 'Waterloo', 120n48; 'When milking comes then home the maiden wends', 123n68, 124n75; 'With boots of monstrous leg & massy strength', 123n68; 'With careful step to keep his balance up', 123n68; 'With hand in waistcoat thrust the thresher goes', 72n133; 'With hands in pocket hid & buttoned up', 123n68; 'With hook tucked neath his arm that now & then', 123n68; 'Wonder!! If a Woman Keeps a Secret', 205n8

prose; 'Journey out of Essex', 6, 31, 64n34, 213n102, 224; 'Sketches in the Life', 228

Clare, John, children of, 201, 214n104

Clare, John, family of, 18, 21, 41, 43, 45, 55, 57, 84, 100, 190

Clare, Martha ('Patty'), 86, 191, 214n104

Clarke, John James, 91

class, 1, 3, 5–9, 14, 16–17, 25, 28, 31–32, 36, 41, 60, 80, 82, 87–88, 90, 92, 98, 117, 139, 145–146, 168, 199, 200, 216–217, 227–228, 231–232

cockneyism, 40–41, 188

Coetzee, J.M., 219–220

Coleridge, Samuel Taylor, 81, 158n40

Colman, Felicity J., 111

community, 27, 41–42, 47, 102, 104, 116, 166–168, 170, 204, 224

conservatism, 14, 96–97, 130, 137–148, 229, 236n56

Constable, John, 142
Cook, Eliza, 199, 212n95
Cope, Wendy, 215
copyright, 136–137, 156n18, 156n19
Corbett, Sarah, 215
Corri, Haydn, 55, 74n155
Cowper, William, 49, 80
creativity, 1, 9–10, 19, 58, 61, 83, 86, 91, 95, 102, 134, 136, 138, 146, 154, 193, 203, 216–217, 219–220, 222, 224–225, 231–233
Cronin, Richard, 4, 41, 48, 63n12, 156n22
Crossan, Greg, 65n42
Crowley, Tony, 155n4
cultural materialism, 231
Cummings, Bob, 119n33
Cunningham, Allan, 2, 139
Curzan, Anne, 207n24

D
Dante, 181
Darley, George, 85
Darling, George, 118n19
Darwin, Erasmus, 181, 209n39
Davies, Damian Walford, 235n29
Dawson, P. M. S., 73n146, 97
Day Lewis, Cecil, 141
Deacon, George, 55, 213n97, 236n51
de Certeau, Michel, *see* Certeau
Deleuze, Gilles, 18, 66n59, 125n89, 125n93
Dentith, Simon, 167, 168, 207n20
deportation, 226
Descartes, René, 142
Devlin, James Dacres, 216, 234n5
DeWint, Peter, 85
dialect, 6, 48, 52, 129, 138, 139, 148, 219

Dibdin, Charles, 55, 74n151
Dijkstra, Bram, 210n47
displacement, 3, 11, 21, 28, 30, 35–36, 52, 62n8, 68n85, 166
Dobson, Andrew, 120n42
Donne, John, 180, 208n36
dream, 48, 73n147, 146, 170–173, 176, 178–180, 182–184, 187–188
Drury, Edward, 44
Dunagan, Patrick James, 215
Dundee Courier, 59, 77n180
Dunn, Allen, 218

E
Early Modern poetry, 62n8, 157n33, 208n36
East Anglian riots of 1822, 227, 236–237n58
ecocentrism, 10, 79–126, 166
ecocriticism, 3, 12, 15, 29, 68n83, 97, 100, 157n25
ecology, ecologism, 25, 79–80, 93–95, 97, 114, 140
ecopoetics, 177
ecopolitics, 127, 162, 176
editing, 4, 10, 106–107, 127–140, 144, 149–153, 164, 193
See also genetic editing
editorial methodology, 131, 134, 140, 149–150, 153–154
education, 4, 8, 13, 42, 57, 61, 71n119, 129–130, 144, 213n95
egocentrism, 153
egoism, 80–81
egotism, 79–85, 88, 93–95, 146
elitism, 96
Elton, Charles, 215–216
Ely riots of 1816, *see* Littleport
Emmerson, Eliza, 84–86, 92, 196

enclosure, 10, 14–28, 30, 51, 66n51, 66n53, 72n129, 100, 216, 225
English Journal, The, 142, 143
enjambment, 108
environmentalism, 12, 14, 43, 65n47, 93, 157n25, 217
Epping Forest, *see* asylum

F
Farley, Paul, 156n19, 215
Feder, Helen, 68n83
Felski, Rita, 217, 218, 220, 225
Felstiner, John, 141, 146
femininity, 164, 172, 177, 197
  See also sexuality
feminism, 191–192, 197, 217
Fenland, 101, 121n62, 126n98, 142
Ferrer, Daniel, 151, 152
fiddle playing, 55, 139, 216
Fitzwilliam, Earl, *see* Milton, Lord
Fletcher, Angus, 8, 63n25, 157n33
flowers, 28, 48, 52, 76n167, 94, 162, 164, 172, 174–175, 186–188, 206n11, 208n31, 223
folk culture, 23, 42, 58, 139, 149, 189, 203, 216, 228
Foucault, Michel, 11, 65n35, 65n36
Foulds, Adam, 216, 224
Fowles, John, 203
France, 39, 81, 102–103, 190, 228–229
freedom, 36, 39, 69n101, 91, 92, 164, 172, 217, 225, 229
Freeman, Mark, 207n20
Fulford, Tim, 193, 195

G
Gadamer, Hans-Georg, 220–226, 232
games, 92, 98, 168, 172, 198
Garrard, Greg, 61n2, 157n25

gender, 87, 88, 93
genetic editing, 151–154
genius, 2, 28, 31–36, 61, 62n10, 64n30, 96, 131
genre, 35, 87, 152, 162, 164, 193, 216
George IV, king of the United Kingdom, 229
Gilchrist, Octavius, 2, 7, 37, 61, 73–74n148
Goatly, Andrew, 125n87
God, 9, 34, 46, 51, 86, 95, 146, 148, 166, 186, 186
Goldsmith, Edward, 15
Goldsmith, Oliver, 69n98
Goodridge, John, 19, 27, 66n55, 102, 204
Goody, Jack, 175
Gorji, Mina, 4, 206n11
Gosse, Edmund, 63n25, 113
Gossett, Philip, 55
Grainger, Margaret, 5, 130, 131, 194, 203, 209n40, 214n112
grammar, 116, 131–133
Greetham, D. C., 155n8
Grigson, Geoffrey, 97
Guattari, Félix, 18, 66n59, 110, 111, 113, 115, 125n89, 125n91, 145, 148, 149, 150
Guyer, Sara, 30, 62n8

H
Haddox, Thomas F., 218
Harrison, Gary, 177
Haughton, Hugh, 132, 156n18
Hay, Louis, 149, 152
Hayot, Eric, 218
Hazlitt, William, 32, 81–94, 88, 92, 213n97
health, 6, 93, 157n23
Heath, Richard, 96, 97, 99, 236n56

Hecht, Anthony, 215
Heidegger, Martin, 11, 71n127
Heise, Ursula K., 12
Helpston, 2, 13, 14, 17, 20, 22,
    29–30, 38, 39, 41, 46, 49, 54,
    68n85, 72n129, 90, 92, 100,
    123n70, 141, 224, 231, 232
Helsinger, Elizabeth, 2, 3
Henson, J. B., 2
Herrick, Robert, 180–181, 208n36
Herring, Jon, 207n24
Herzogenarth, Bernd, 125n91
Hess, Scott, 66n47
Hessey, James, 40, 55, 83, 85,
    115, 128
Hewlett, S. M., 58
Heyes, Robert, 20, 66n55, 98,
    121n56
Hickman, Ben, 157n33, 233n2
High Beech, Epping Forest, Essex, *see*
    asylum
Hirsch, Edward, 215
Historicism and New Historicism, 97,
    215–237
history, 5, 10, 11, 13, 14, 29, 34, 35,
    38, 46, 49, 97, 112, 127, 129,
    130, 131, 141, 168, 176, 177,
    181, 192, 194, 203, 215–237
Hobsbawm, E. J., 73n141, 90
Hogg, James, 2, 56, 139
Hold, Trevor, 55
home, 10, 24–28, 30–31, 34, 39–44,
    46, 51, 85, 102, 143, 149,
    165, 175, 189, 195, 201, 223,
    224, 231
Honey, John, 155n4
Hood, Edwin Paxton, 144–145
horizons (geographical and
    temporal), 37, 49, 164, 203,
    220–233
Houghton, Sarah, *see* Houghton-
    Walker, Sarah

Houghton-Walker, Sarah, 103,
    119n35, 167–168, 170
Humboldt, Alexander von, 69n99
Hunt, Leigh, 80, 188
Hunt, Richard, 123n69
hypertextual theory, 150–155

I

I (first person singular pronoun), 80,
    81, 84, 88, 89, 95, 118n21, 183
Innes, Christopher, 217
insanity, *see* madness
Insko, Jeffrey, 220
interpretation, 3, 6, 105, 106, 133,
    151, 218, 219
isolation, 21, 25, 34, 100, 165, 167,
    194, 202

J

Jacobus, Mary, 216
Jameson, Frederic, 11, 28
John Clare Cottage, 3, 25–28, 40–49,
    70n117, 71n126, 72n129
Johnson, B. S., 137
Jones, Leonidas M., 70n107
Jones, William, 91, 119n33
Joyce, James, 222
Joyce, Lucia, 222
Joyce, Mary, 6–7, 87, 173, 176,
    179–181, 184–185, 188, 201,
    213n100, 213n102, 222, 226

K

Kafka, Franz, 66n59
Kahn, Mary, 125n87
Keats, John, 39, 42, 49, 80, 83, 84,
    87, 88, 92, 174, 235n30
Keegan, Bridget, 64n30, 114, 121n62

Kelemen, Erick, 155n8
Kelley, Theresa M., 6, 30, 235n17
Kent, Elizabeth, 5
king, 96, 98, 229, 230, 231
Kinnaird, John, 82
Kirke White, Henry, 171
Knight, William F., 136, 184, 190, 199
Kroeber, Karl, 97

L

labour, 3, 16, 17, 22, 27, 41, 44–46, 48, 59, 77n179, 102, 103, 110, 144–145, 166
labouring class, 1, 36, 62n4, 80, 139, 227, 229, 231, 237n60
Lafford, Erin, 74n153, 157n23
Lake District, 66n47
Lamb, Charles, 40, 70n113, 124n84
Landon, Laetitia, 196
Landow, George P., 150
language, 6–7, 9, 30, 80, 84, 88, 89, 91, 93, 110, 115, 125n87, 129–131, 133, 136–140, 150, 154, 158n42, 165, 166, 174, 177, 188, 189
Leader, Zachary, 97, 113, 115, 132
Lefebvre, Henri, 11
Leonard, Tom, 139
lime burning, 17–19
linguistic reappropriation, 168, 207n24
lists, listing, 10, 57, 59, 84, 115, 161–205, 220, 231
Literary Souvenir, 128
Littleport and Ely riots of 1816, 226
Liu, Alan, 219
locality, 3, 4, 9, 13, 29, 42, 100, 109, 116, 148, 225
Lofft, Capel, 171
London, 36, 40, 51, 58, 59, 84, 85, 189, 198, 199, 215, 216

London Magazine, 2, 40, 62n7, 70n107, 70n113, 85, 215
Loney, Alan, 113
Longley, Michael, 215
love, 10, 25, 26, 53, 54, 58, 61, 82, 96, 161–167, 169, 170, 172–178, 180–183, 186, 191, 203, 226
  See also sexuality
Lucas, John, 90, 97, 120n50, 234n4, 234n6
lunacy, *see* madness
Lupton, Hugh, 216
lust, *see* sexuality; love
Lynd, Robert, 113
Lynes, Jeanette, 215

M

Mabey, Richard, 175, 206n11, 208n31, 217, 234n17
MacKenna, John, 216–217
madness, 21, 22, 217
Mahood, M. M., 132, 158n41, 206n11, 207n22
Maidment, Brian, 157n36
male gaze, 178, 185, 188
Malpas, J. E., 11–12
manuscripts, 10, 107, 123n69, 124n82, 131, 132, 134–136, 139, 149, 152, 153, 156n19, 163, 190, 193, 194, 200
Market Deeping, 2
Marlowe, Christopher, 208n36
Martin, Frederick, 45, 55
Martin, Philip W., 206n17
Marvell, Andrew, 180, 208n36
Marxist criticism, 44, 130, 231, 232
masculinity, 17, 160–214
Maskit, Jonathan, 152
Mason, Emma, 68n74, 71n127
Maxwell, Glyn, 215

McCue, Kirsteen, 56
McEathron, Scott, 36, 62n4, 69n104, 70n113, 237n60
McGann, Jerome, 219–220, 232, 235n30
McKusick, James C., 29, 30
Mellor, Anne K., 185
Merrick, James, 57
Milton, John, 81, 144
Milton, Lord Wentworth Fitzwilliam, 3–4, 62n10, 213n99
misogyny, 167, 192–193, 201–203
Mitford, Mary, 64n33
monarchy, 45, 96, 99, 200–201, 228–230
Moore, Alan, 216, 222, 225
Moore, Bryan L., 120n45
Moore, D.C., 216
Moretti, Franco, 10, 64n33
Morley, David, 215
Morning Chronicle, 38, 59, 77n179, 227
Morton, Timothy, 67n74, 147, 149, 158n42
Moulthrop, Stuart, 150, 158n48
Moyse, Mary, 214n104
Mulford, Wendy, 8, 215
music, 54–61, 64n26, 74n154, 74n155, 75n158, 75n160, 139
Muskett, Paul, 236n58

N
Napoleon, 81
Napoleonic wars, 32, 39, 229
National Lottery, 70n118
natural history, 34, 168, 181, 203, 209n40
nature, 2–13, 24, 25, 29, 34, 42–43, 52–53, 61, 80, 82, 91, 93–95, 97, 99, 100, 109, 110, 113–117, 139, 140, 143, 145–150, 152, 158n42, 161–166, 170–177, 181–182, 188–189, 217
New Historicism, *see* Historicism
New Monthly Magazine, 143
newspapers, 90, 227
Noble, Shalon, 30
Norfolk, 119n30, 232
Northampton, 49, 196, 216, 222, 223
Northampton General Lunatic Asylum, *see* asylum
Northampton, Marquis of, 213n99
Northamptonshire, 2, 13, 16, 56, 59, 119n30, 141, 194, 211n77, 224, 228
Northborough, 8, 27, 30, 68n85, 96, 100–103, 107, 114, 122n68, 123n70, 167, 182, 195, 204

O
O'Neill, Michael, 6
oral culture, 138–139, 225
organicism, 8–9, 63n26, 88, 116, 131, 140, 145–146, 164, 171
orthography, *see* spelling
Oswald, Alice, 215
Oxford edition of Clare's poetry, 101–102, 106–107, 122n66, 122n67, 130–139, 156n18, 156n19, 163, 180, 194, 228

P
parable, 85–87
paratext, 149, 163, 193, 197
parliament, 13, 42, 230
Parnet, Claire, 112
Parry, John, 57, 76n167
Pasta, Giuditta, 58
patronage, 84, 96, 98, 99

Paulin, Tom, 3, 95, 215, 224
Paul Pry, 89
Pearce, Lynne, 191–196, 198–200, 202
peasant poet, 2, 41, 62n10, 199, 216
peasantry, 227–230
Pedlar, Valerie, 26, 156n16
Pepper, David, 157n25
Peterborough, 13, 49, 50, 73n143, 141, 225
Petrarch, 181
Phelan, Joseph, 102, 123n70
Phipps, T. B., 57
Piepenbring, Dan, 118n21
Piercey, Robert, 221
place, 1–61, 80, 87, 88, 92, 96, 100, 106, 110, 116, 139, 140, 143, 146, 148, 171, 173, 179, 181, 184, 189, 190, 193, 195, 216, 217, 222–225, 231, 232
poetry as a profession, 55, 96
politics, 32, 40, 84, 95, 96, 98, 99, 138, 140, 150, 154, 199, 226, 229, 231
polysyndeton, 113, 116
poverty, 19, 23, 29, 43, 44, 52, 98, 216
Powell, David, 5, 130
Pownall, Helen, 121n62
primitivism, *see* textual primitivism
print culture, 128, 137, 138
prison, 47, 190, 226
prosopopoeia, 22, 109
punctuation, 57, 89, 90, 131, 134, 135, 137, 155n8
puns, 198

Q
Queen Caroline affair, 99, 121n58

R
radical politics, 133, 231
Radstock, Admiral Lord, 23, 98–99, 121n58
Rae, Simon, 216
Raleigh, Walter, 208n36
Ray, John, 181, 209n40
readership, 2, 227, 229
Redding, Cyrus, 142–143
Rees, James, 58, 73n148
Reeves, James, 30
reform, 228–231
Reid, Thomas, 81
religion, 91, 92
Reno, Seth T., 176
revision (textual), 144, 179
revolution, 116, 229, 230
Reynolds, John Hamilton, 70n107
rhizome, 107–117, 150, 154, 178
Rigby, Kate, 13–16, 29
riots, 48, 119n30, 227, 231
Roberts, Michael Symmons, 215
Robespierre, Maximilien, 229
Robinson, Eric, 5, 62n10, 107, 130, 155n3, 156n19, 193, 194, 202, 213n100
Robinson, Solveig C., 212n95
Romanticism, 37, 97, 219, 220
Rossetti, Christina, 74n147
Rossini, Gioachino, 55–57, 59
Rounce, Adam, 117n3
Rudé, George, 73n141, 90, 119n30

S
St Botolph's Church, Helpston, 49, 92
Sales, Roger, 97–99, 132
school, 13, 45, 49, 89, 123, 129, 172, 200, 203, 204, 218, 229
Schyrava, Juliet, 64n27
Scott, Derek B., 58
Scott, Walter, 32, 35, 36, 38, 59

Scrimgeour, Cecil, 30
sense of place, *see* place
sexuality, 6, 7, 111, 164, 167, 170,
    180, 185–205, 222
Shakespeare, William, 49, 57, 59, 87
Sheerman, Barry, 42, 71n119,
    71n120, 71n126
Shelley, Percy Bysshe, 89, 91, 94,
    146, 166
Sinclair, Iain, 64n34, 217, 224–225
Sinclair, John, 47, 73n140
Smith, Mark J., 95
solitude, 91, 217, 223–224
song, *see* music
sonnet, 6, 8, 25–27, 80, 96, 98,
    100–110, 113, 114, 116, 122n66,
    122n67, 122n68, 123n70,
    124n76, 125n85, 142, 167
Soper, Kate, 43, 93
space, *see* place
spelling, 87, 110, 116, 131, 135, 138
Stafford, Fiona, 61n2
Stamford, 2, 3
Stamford Champion, 35
standard English, 129
standardisation, 128–131, 137, 154
steam trains, 48, 141
Stephens, Catherine, 55, 58
stereotypes, 6, 62n10, 122n66, 167
Stillinger, Jack, 155n6
Storey, Edward, 30
Storey, Mark, 63n25, 131, 144, 194
Strang, Barbara M. H., 89
subjectivity, 29, 32, 37–38, 52, 94, 96,
    114–116, 142, 146–149,
    152–154
Suckling, John, 180
Suffolk, 2, 232
Summerfield, Geoffrey, 130, 193,
    202, 213n100
Swing riots, 48, 73n141
Symons, Arthur, 97

T
Tally, Robert T., 65n36
Taplin, Kim, 9
Taylor, James Ely, 57, 75n162
Taylor, John, 4, 5, 6, 41, 44, 52, 53,
    57, 83, 84, 85, 92, 98, 99, 113,
    116, 128, 161, 229
Tennyson Lord, Alfred, 49, 80,
    73n147
text, 8, 10, 22, 37–39, 46, 48, 58, 61,
    105–107, 127–155, 165, 194,
    197–198, 202–203, 225, 228, 233
textuality, *see* text
textual primitivism, 106, 124n82,
    130–137, 150, 155n6
Thomas, Edward, 162
Thompson, E. P., 66n51, 97, 232
Thoreau, Henry David, 1
Thornton, Kelsey, 19, 130, 131, 132,
    140, 155n5
Thornton, R. K. R, *see* Thornton,
    Kelsey
threshing, 44–48, 73n140, 73n141,
    90, 227
Tibble, Anne, 131
time, 2, 6, 11, 15–20, 28, 29, 34–37,
    39, 42, 44, 46–49, 55, 57, 59, 90,
    94, 96, 100, 101, 108, 117,
    138–141, 161, 173, 174, 180,
    182, 190, 192, 198, 199, 204,
    222–225, 229, 231
Todd, Janet, 192
tourism, 10, 28, 29, 37, 41, 44, 46
trains, *see* steam trains
travel, 12, 13, 34, 37–40, 44, 102, 195
Trehane, Emma, 84
Trower, Shelley, 64n26
truth, 1, 44, 134, 164, 187, 190, 191,
    221, 226
Tschichold, Jan, 113
Tuan, Yi-Fu, 11, 12, 27
Tyndale, William, 174

V

Vardy, Alan, 90, 97
Vestris, Lucia ('Madame Vestris'), 55, 58
Vincent, Andrew, 120n42
violence, 34, 204, 226, 227, 230, 231, 232

W

Walcott, Derek, 215
walking, 7, 39, 44, 49, 173, 181, 182, 184, 186, 198, 223, 224
Waller, Robert, 15
Ward, Sam, 99, 121n58
Waring, John, 56
Watts, Alaric, 144
Weiner, Stephanie Kuduk, 62n8, 157n33
White, Adam, 166
White, Simon J., 101
Whyte, Ian D., 6
Willetts, Sam, 215
William IV, king of the United Kingdom, 200
Williams, Frederick, 141
Williams, Merryn, 48, 156n19
Williams, Raymond, 48, 61, 97, 156n19
Wilson, John, 79–81, 94
Wojahn, David, 215
Wood, Ellen (Mrs Henry Wood), 60
Woolf, Virginia, 118n21
Wordsworth, Peter, 72n129
Wordsworth, William, 1, 73–74n148
working class, 5, 6, 7, 42, 98, 200, 231
working-class poets, poetry, 2, 144, 199, 216, 237n60
writing, 5–7, 9, 16–18, 35, 37, 42, 55, 79, 80, 82–84, 86–88, 90–93, 95, 101, 105, 106, 115, 129, 138, 141, 145, 146, 148, 152–154, 163, 164, 171, 181, 190, 199, 200, 203, 204, 217–219, 223, 229
Wu, Duncan, 35, 69n101

Y

Yearsley, Ann, 2
Young, Edward, 84
Young, Linda, 42

The manufacturer's authorised representative in the EU is Springer Nature Customer Service Centre GmbH, Europaplatz 3, 69115 Heidelberg, Germany. If you have any concerns regarding our products, please contact ProductSafety@springernature.com

Printed and bound by CPI Group (UK) Ltd, Croydon, CR0 4YY

25/03/2026

02078224-0001